ARTIFICIAL INTELLIGENCE:
The Heuristic Programming Approach

McGraw-Hill Series in Systems Science

Berlekamp Algebraic Coding Theory

Canon, Cullum, and Polak Theory of Optimal Control and Mathematical Programming

Gill Linear Sequential Circuits

Harrison Introduction to Switching and Automata Theory

Jelinek Probabilistic Information Theory: Discrete and Memoryless Models

Mangasarian Nonlinear Programming

Nilsson Learning Machines: Foundations of Trainable Pattern-classifying Systems

Papoulis Probability, Random Variables, and Stochastic Processes

Papoulis Systems and Transforms with Applications in Optics

Sage and Melsa Estimation Theory with Applications to Communications and Control

Slagle Artificial Intelligence: The Heuristic Programming Approach

Viterbi Principles of Coherent Communication

Weber Elements of Detection and Signal Design

Zadeh and Desoer Linear System Theory: The State Space Approach

Artificial Intelligence: The Heuristic Programming Approach

JAMES R. SLAGLE, Ph.D.
Johns Hopkins University

McGraw-Hill Book Company
NEW YORK ST. LOUIS SAN FRANCISCO
DÜSSELDORF LONDON MEXICO
PANAMA SYDNEY TORONTO

Artificial Intelligence:
The Heuristic Programming Approach

Library of Congress Catalog Card Number 76–121667

58005

1 2 3 4 5 6 7 8 9 0 MAMM 7 9 8 7 6 5 4 3 2 1 0

This book was set in Times New Roman, and was printed on permanent paper and bound by The Maple Press Company. The designer was Edward Zytko; the drawings were done by Philip Cohen. The editors were Richard F. Dojny and Sally Mobley. Matt Martino supervised production.

Preface

This book consists of an organized description of "intelligent" machines. It shows that machines are doing things often called intelligent when done by humans. Among the machines to be described are some that deduce answers to questions from given facts, play games, prove theorems, and balance assembly lines. Almost all of the projects discussed have reached the stage of experimenting with correctly operating machines. Each machine or at least some component of the machine seems extendable to solve more difficult problems.

Although the book is primarily intended for students of computer science, it should also be of value to computer scientists, to other scientists including the psychologist and mathematician, and even to the philosopher and general reader. For the philosopher and general reader, the examples of heuristic programs collected in this volume may throw some light on the important, hotly argued questions arising from the widely misunderstood "intelligent" machines. I give my own opinions on these questions, especially in the final chapter. The scientist needs to know about artificial intelligence to see what present and future applications might be made in his field. The psychologist needs to know how and to what extent machines are thinking so that he might get more insight into how people think. The mathematician needs to know how computers are already acting as mathematical assistants, manipulating mathematical expressions, proving theorems, and verifying proofs of theorems. For the artificial intelligence researcher, the book organizes much of the work in the field of heuristic programming and contains something that will be new to him. Some of the material in this book has been taken from nearly inaccessible sources, and other material appears in print for the first time.

The book is primarily a textbook for undergraduate and graduate students of computer science in general, and artificial intelligence in particular. Exercises and a bibliography are given at the end of each chapter. I hope that the book will lead more students to enter the fascinating, important, and rapidly growing field of artificial intelligence. The book furnishes a textbook for already existing courses and will, I hope, lead to the creation of more courses in artificial intelligence. The book is based largely on lecture notes for courses I have taught at the Massachusetts Institute of Technology, the University of California at Berkeley, and Johns Hopkins University. I wish to thank my students for suggestions which have improved the book. I also wish to thank John K. Dixon for proofreading the manuscript and preparing the index.

JAMES R. SLAGLE

Contents

1
The Heuristic Programming Approach to Artificial Intelligence

The beginning of this chapter describes the general nature and purposes of heuristic programming. The chapter then defines and discusses game trees and concludes with an introduction to the heuristic programs that play games.

1.1 ARTIFICIAL INTELLIGENCE

Research scientists in Artificial Intelligence try to get machines to exhibit behavior that we call intelligent behavior when we observe it in human beings. Since the machine is almost always a computer, Artificial Intelligence is a branch of computer science. Dictionaries now define three kinds of intelligence—human, animal, and military. Although we all have a good subjective notion of what is meant by human intelligence, it may be of some interest to present the following definitions from "Webster's New Collegiate Dictionary" (1956):

A. The power of meeting any situation, especially a novel situation, successfully by proper behavior adjustments.

B. The ability to apprehend interrelationships of presented facts in such a way as to guide action toward a desired goal.[1]

These definitions can just as well be applied to the behavior of a machine as to that of a human. Intelligence is multipurpose and involves the ability to learn, and we shall have much to say about the desirability of incorporating these aspects of intelligence into heuristic programs.

1.2 DIGITAL COMPUTERS

Almost all the machines to be discussed in this book are computers. By a computer is here meant a high-speed general-purpose stored-program electronic digital computer. A computer consists of input units (for example, a punched-card reader), output units (for example, a card punch), a storage unit (for example, magnetic cores), an arithmetic unit, and a control unit. For a particular problem, such a general-purpose computer receives a program and data through the input units. A program is a list of detailed instructions which tells how to solve problems of a certain type. The data given to the computer are the data associated with a particular problem of that type that the program can handle. The computer puts the program and data into the storage unit. The control unit examines the instructions one by one and uses the arithmetic units when appropriate. Temporary results are put into the storage unit. An output unit is used to communicate final results.

Computers are extremely fast and accurate. They can, for example, multiply about a million 12-digit numbers in 1 sec and perform billions of operations without making a single mistake. They manipulate the given data by obeying their instructions to the letter. More will be said about this last point in the final chapter. In some applications, computers simulate (behave like) other systems. For example, they have been used to simulate the United States economy, the operation of a particular firm, various networks, and even other computers. The behavior of the computer may be anything from a crude approximation to a near replica of the system being simulated. The behavior of the computer may be faster or slower than the system being simulated. Here and elsewhere in these chapters, when we say that a computer or program *does something*, we mean that the combination of computer and program does that thing.

1.3 APPROACHES TO ARTIFICIAL INTELLIGENCE

The three approaches that researchers have taken to Artificial Intelligence are *artificial networks*, *artificial evolution*, and *heuristic programming*. Since

[1] By permission from "Webster's New Collegiate Dictionary," copyright 1916, 1925, 1931, 1936, 1941, 1949, 1951, 1953, and 1956, G. and C. Merriam Co., Springfield, Mass.

this book is about heuristic programming (the approach preferred by the author), only a few words will be said about the other approaches.

A network consists of a large number of simple elements and their interconnections. An artificial network is either simulated on a computer or is real. Often each element is an artificial neuron (nerve cell). One advantage of this approach is that the network is usually adaptive; that is, it can "learn" from experience. The researchers who take the artificial-network approach point out that many people think that natural intelligence is based on (natural) neural networks alone. About the best the artificial networks have done is to "learn" to recognize simple visual and aural patterns. Thus the performance of the networks is far short of intelligent behavior. One difficulty with this approach is that there is little prospect of making an artificial network as large as the network in the human brain, which consists of approximately 10^{10} neurons. In addition, neural physiologists are far from completely understanding how neurons operate and are interconnected.

In the artificial-evolution approach to Artificial Intelligence, computer-simulated systems are made to evolve by mutation and selection. Artificial systems have been made to evolve into systems which can solve very simple equations. Researchers who take this approach point out that many people think that human intelligence evolved through a process involving mutations and natural selection. One difficulty with this approach is that natural evolution is not completely understood. Another is that this approach is practical only if artificial evolution can be made to proceed enormously faster than natural evolution.

Heuristic programming is the only approach described in the following chapters. A heuristic is a rule of thumb, strategy, method, or trick used to improve the efficiency of a system which tries to discover the solutions of complex problems. A heuristic program is a computer program that uses heuristics. According to "Webster's New Collegiate Dictionary" (1956), the adjective "heuristic" means "serving to discover."[1] It is related to the word "eureka" (I have found it, from the Greek *heuriskein*, to discover, find). Some of the heuristic programs to be discussed can play checkers, chess, and several card games. Others can deduce answers to questions from given facts. Still others solve calculus and chess problems. Others prove theorems in mathematical logic and geometry. For example, the geometry program can prove the following rather difficult theorem. If the segment joining the midpoints of the diagonals of a trapezoid is extended to intersect a side of the trapezoid, it bisects that side. Some of the heuristic programs to be discussed can learn from their experience. A few are multipurpose in the sense that they can solve several kinds of problems. Some heuristics are specific; that is, they are limited to one problem-solving domain, such as proving theorems in

[1] Ibid.

geometry. Other heuristics are general; that is, applicable to several domains. For example, the heuristic "working backward" is useful in many theorem-proving and problem-solving domains.

1.4 PURPOSES OF HEURISTIC PROGRAMMING

The main purposes of Artificial Intelligence and therefore heuristic programming are (1) to understand natural (human) intelligence and (2) to use machine intelligence to acquire knowledge and solve intellectually difficult problems. A researcher having the first purpose is a psychologist. He constructs, in the form of a computer program, a model of some behavior regarded as human intelligence. To do this, he reads the psychological literature, ponders experimental data, and sometimes uses what is known as the *protocol method.* In the protocol method he observes subjects thinking aloud while trying to solve complex problems. He constructs a model of such problem solving in the form of a computer program. He notes how the performance of his program deviates from the performances of his subjects. He observes the subjects some more and constructs an improved model. The cycle is repeated over and over. There are two important advantages in embodying a model in a computer program. The psychologist is forced to specify his model in complete detail, and consequences of the model may be obtained by simply running the program on a computer.

A researcher having the second purpose is interested in getting intelligent behavior and does not care whether or not the computer uses methods that people use. He hopes that the computer will eventually solve important complex problems, including problems in economics and the social sciences. This book emphasizes the second purpose of Artificial Intelligence.

Those purposes that the heuristic programmer emphasizes cannot be easily deduced from the heuristic program itself. This is largely a result of the fact that a researcher with the purpose of obtaining successful machine performance necessarily tends to furnish his machine with methods used by people, since people are more intelligent than present-day machines. The future work of researchers will probably diverge according to the purposes of the individual researcher, unless the problem domain under study largely determines the methods needed to solve problems in that domain.

1.5 GAME TREES

An important part of most heuristic programs is a procedure for searching a "tree" of logical possibilities. Two kinds of trees are *game trees* and *goal trees.* The branches in a game tree are moves, replies, counterreplies, etc. In a goal tree, some original goal is shown to be achievable if certain

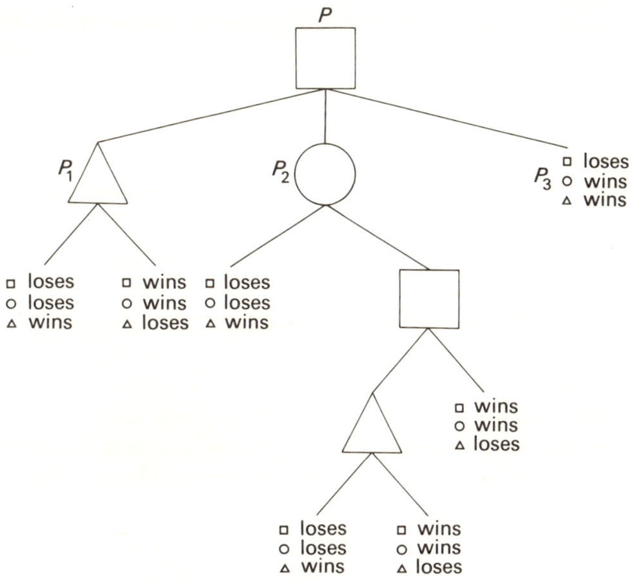

Figure 1-1 An explicit game tree.

subgoals are achievable. A subgoal may be shown to be achievable if certain of its subgoals are achievable, etc. Since trees have a tendency to become very large, an important part of most heuristic programs is concerned with how to search efficiently for relevant parts of the tree. Since we shall first study heuristic programs that play games, we shall first discuss game trees. However, many of the concepts concerning game trees carry over to other kinds of trees. In fact, we show in Chapter 4 that a certain kind of game tree is in a sense equivalent to a certain kind of goal tree. A game tree is either explicit or implicit. An explicit game tree is given explicitly, as in Figure 1-1. An implicit game tree is given only by means of an initial position and rules for generating the tree, as in checkers, chess, etc.

Explicit Trees In these trees, nodes (squares, circles, triangles) represent game positions, and line segments represent moves. The top node represents the starting position. The shape of the node represents the player whose turn it is to move. We shall refer to square-positions, circle-positions, and triangle-positions. In the game represented by the explicit tree of Figure 1-1, player square makes the first move from position P. If square moves to position P_3, then square loses, circle wins, and triangle wins. We shall say that the successors of position P are P_1, P_2, P_3. Position P is said to be at level 0. The successors of P are said to be at level 1. The successors of the successors of P are said to be at level 2, etc. In Figure 1-1, assuming good play on the part

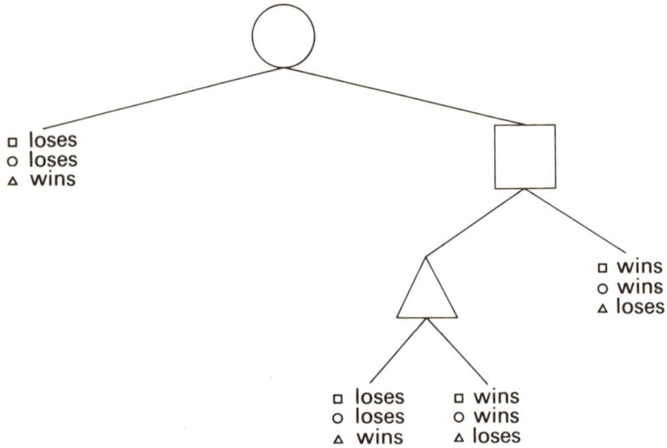

Figure 1-2 Moving to position P_2 transforms the tree in Figure 1-1 into the tree in Figure 1-2.

of the other players, square can force a win by choosing to move to position P_2. The only good move for circle is to move to the square-position, from which square will immediately cause himself (and circle) to win. An actual move transforms a game tree into another game tree. For example, moving to position P_2 transforms the tree in Figure 1-1 into the tree in Figure 1-2.

Implicit Trees An implicit tree is a top position together with rules which can be used to generate an explicit tree. The rules give *termination criteria* and tell how to generate successors of any position. In the tree, no successors occur for a position which meets the termination criteria. Various termination criteria will be discussed later. One termination criterion is met by positions in which the game is over. The rules of checkers furnish an example of an implicit tree. A procedure which makes an implicit tree explicit is called a *generation procedure.* Generation procedures vary in the order in which they generate positions of the tree. Breadth-first and depth-first are two of the many kinds of generation procedures. Roughly speaking, a breadth-first procedure generates from the top, whereas a depth-first procedure generates from the left.

A breadth-first procedure generates all the positions at level 1, then all the positions at level 2, and then all those at level 3, etc. For example, suppose that the top position of a given implicit tree is the square-position P. A breadth-first procedure would use the rule (defined by the implicit tree) to generate in order the explicit trees shown in Figure 1-3. As a second example, suppose that a breadth-first procedure is to generate the top two levels of the checker tree starting with the original position. The procedure generates the

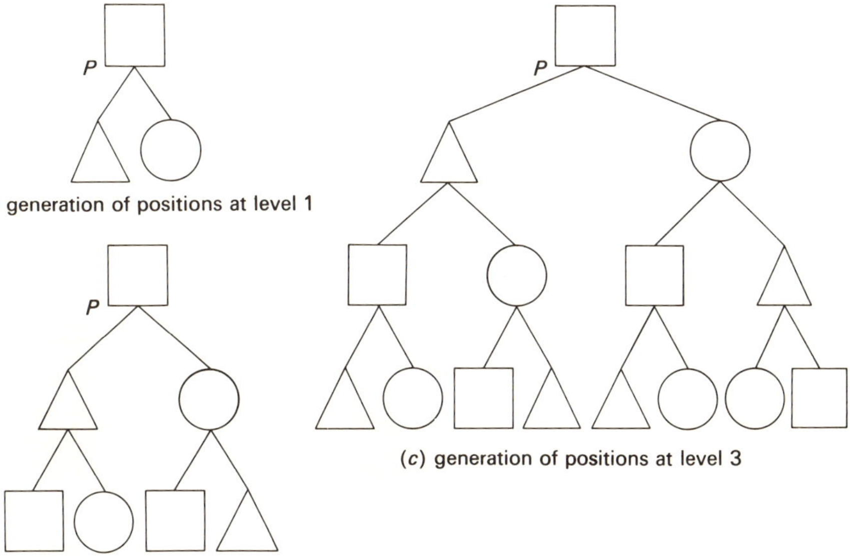

(*a*) generation of positions at level 1

(*b*) generation of positions at level 2

(*c*) generation of positions at level 3

Figure 1-3 Breadth-first generation procedure.

seven successors of the original position and then the seven successors of each successor. Forty-nine positions occur at level 2.

A depth-first procedure generates a tree from the left in the following sense. The procedure starts by generating the top position's first successor, and then, in turn, its first successor, etc. For example, suppose a depth-first procedure is to generate the top three levels of a tree whose top position is *A*. As in Figure 1-4(*b*), the procedure starts with position *A* and generates in order positions *B*, *C*, *D*, . . . , *O*. Figure 1-4(*a*) shows the explicit tree generated up to position *F*. In this example, we say that the termination criterion is a maximum depth of 3. In any depth-first generation procedure, termination criteria must be given.

As a second example, suppose a depth-first procedure is to generate the top two levels of the checker tree starting with the original position. The procedure generates the first successor of the original position, and then the seven replies to that successor. It then generates the second successor of the original position, and then the seven successors of that successor, etc.

1.6 PROGRAMS THAT PLAY GAMES

The next two chapters describe programs that play checkers, chess, kalah, five-in-a-row, qubic, and several card games. The rules of kalah, five-in-a-row, and qubic are given later.

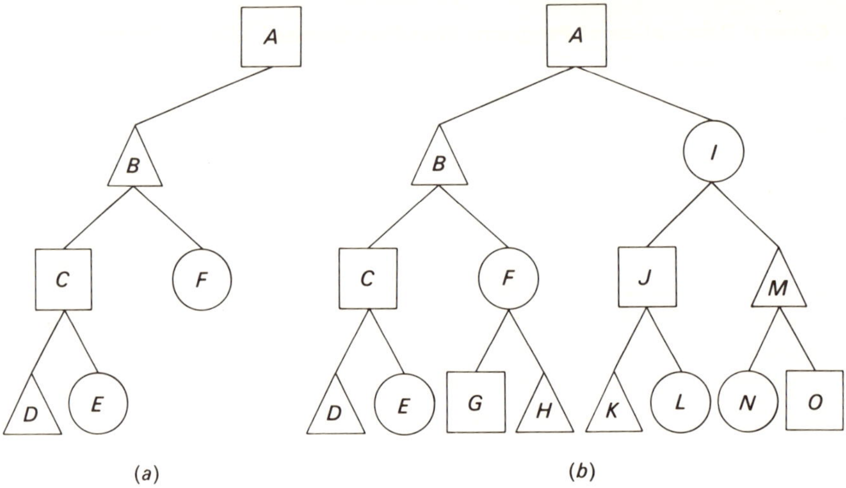

Figure 1-4 Depth-first generation procedure. The positions are generated in alphabetical order.

Purposes of Programming a Computer to Play a Game The general purposes of programming a computer to play a game are the same as for other heuristic programs, as discussed in Section 1.4. In addition, people program computers to play games because it is fun and because games are far simpler than and yet resemble many important real problems. The researcher does not know how to make a direct attack on many difficult, real problems, and he hopes that the methods he develops to handle simple problems will extend to difficult problems. Games resemble real problems. The intelligent participant chooses his actions based on his search of the tree of future possibilities, on his rough evaluations of possible future situations, and on expectations about what others will do. Business games and war games are intended as models for real problems.

Games are simple because their rules are well defined and relatively simple. Most of the other heuristic programs work on well-formulated problems, and it is important to understand why so many heuristic programmers choose well-defined problem areas. It is because such a problem domain has a kind of simplicity and certainly not because they think that only well-defined problems are important. Many important problems in economics and the social sciences are ill defined. The rules of a game are simpler than those for even well-defined real problems. Most researchers decide that the advantages of simplicity outweigh the advantages of more realistic problems. However, we shall see that some heuristic programs do work on well-defined "real" problems, for example, the heuristic programs that manipulate mathematical expressions, prove theorems, and balance assembly lines.

General Description of Programs That Play Games Most of the games played by the programs described in the next two chapters are two-person, strictly competitive games. *Two-person* means that there are two players, for example, square and circle. *Strictly competitive* (also called *zero sum*) means that whatever one player wins, the other player may be considered to lose, so that cooperation is never worthwhile. Thus, the outcome of such a game may be described by telling what happens to one player, say square.

An essential part of each program to be described evaluates (makes numerical estimates of) how good a position is for the machine. (In practice, a machine will often play against a machine, but to make the discussion simpler and more interesting, we shall assume that a machine is playing against a human.) The program evaluates well to the extent that it assigns high (positive) values to good positions and low (negative) values to bad positions. Since ordinarily the game is strictly competitive, the negation of this value estimates how good the position is for the human player.

Each program consists of the following steps, to be taken consecutively except where otherwise indicated. Each step carried out by the computer consists of hundreds of program instructions.

A. The human puts in an arbitrary position in the game. Go to step B or step E according to whether it is the human's or the computer's turn to move.
B. The human puts in his move.
C. Generate the new position.
D. If the game is over, print the result and stop. Otherwise, go to step E.
E. Generate some or all successors of the (top) computer position.
F. Evaluate each successor. For some of the programs, each evaluation involves elaborate searching of future possibilities.
G. Move to the successor with the highest value.
H. Print the computer's move.
I. If the game is over, print the result and stop. Otherwise, go to step B.

EXERCISES

1. Name the three approaches to Artificial Intelligence. Which do you believe is the best? Why?

2. Define in your own words

  a. Heuristic.

  b. Heuristic program.

3. What are the purposes of heuristic programming?

4. Into what tree will moving to position P_1 transform the tree in Figure 1-1? Assuming correct play, will triangle then win?

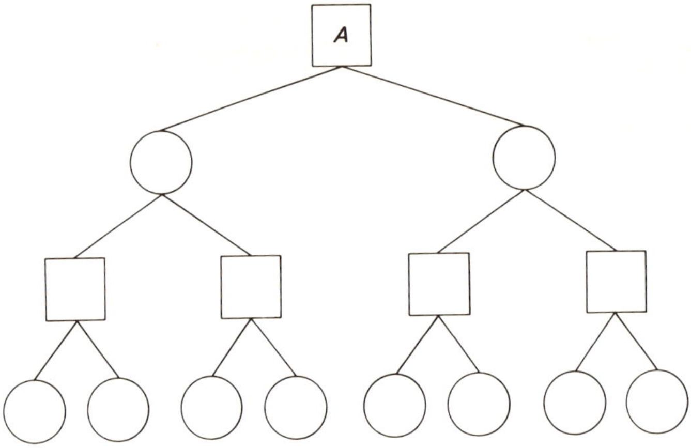

Figure 1-5 The tree for Exercise 6.

5. Neglecting the possibility that the game ends during the search, how many nodes does a breadth-first procedure generate at

- **a.** Level 5 if every node has two successors?
- **b.** Level *d* if every node has *b* successors?

6. In the tree in Figure 1-5, label alphabetically the positions in the order in which they would be generated by a depth-first generation procedure.

BIBLIOGRAPHY

Booth, A. D.: "Digital Computers in Action," Pergamon Press, New York, 1966.

Feigenbaum, Edward, and Julian Feldman (eds.): "Computers and Thought," McGraw-Hill Book Company, New York, 1963.

Fogel, L., A. Owens, and M. Walsh: in Maxfield, Callahan, and Fogel (eds.), Artificial Intelligence Through a Simulation of Evolution, "Biophysics and Cybernetic Systems," Spartan Books, Washington, D.C., 1965.

———: "Artificial Intelligence Through Simulated Evolution," John Wiley & Sons, Inc., New York, 1966.

2
Programs That Play Checkers, Kalah, and Chess

The beginning of this chapter describes the common characteristics of programs that play checkers, kalah, and chess. After describing the general purposes for writing such programs, the chapter defines and discusses various procedures for searching for good moves on implicit game trees. A search procedure consists of a generation procedure, a (static) evaluation function, and a backing-up procedure. By definition, a (static) evaluation function assigns a value to a position without generating any of its successors. By definition, a backing-up procedure assigns to a position a value based on the values of the successors of that position. Before giving conclusions, the chapter describes the nature and performance of each of the programs.

The general purposes of writing programs to play checkers, kalah, and chess are the same as for other games. As discussed in Section 1.6, people program computers to play games because it is fun and because games provide a rather simple environment for studying many similar and important real problems. In addition, the programmers of checkers, kalah, and chess wish to study search procedures. The search procedures needed for these games resemble procedures needed to solve many important real problems. The primary purpose of Arthur Samuel, who wrote the checker program, was to study machine "learning."

2.1 EVALUATING A POSITION IN CHECKERS, KALAH, AND CHESS

We now give a procedure needed for step F in Section 1.6, which includes a general description of all the programs that play games. The procedure for

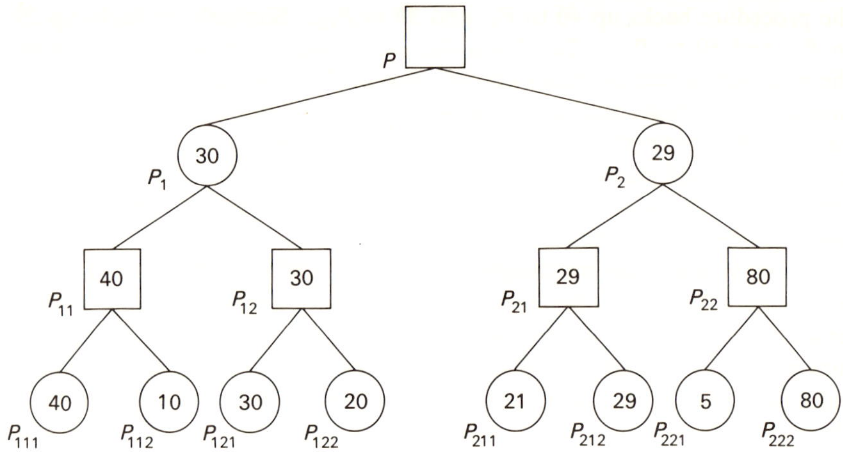

Figure 2-1 The minimax backing-up procedure.

evaluating a position has two steps, to be taken in order except where otherwise indicated.

A. If the termination criteria are met, use the (static) evaluation function to evaluate the position. Otherwise go to step B.
B. Evaluate some or all the successors of the position.

To evaluate each successor, use this same two-step procedure. Thus the procedure uses itself as a subprocedure and is, by definition, a recursive procedure. The value of the position is backed up from the values of its successors.

By far the most commonly used backing-up procedure is the minimax backing-up procedure, which is described below. Assume that the program has a function, called the (static) evaluation function, which assigns a numerical value to each game position. For definiteness, assume that the greater the value of the function, the better the position tends to be for the program. For this reason the machine is called the *maximizing player* or simply *Max*. Its opponent is called the *minimizing player* or *Min*. A position in which it is Max's turn to move is called a max-position. A position in which it is Min's turn to move is called a min-position. For example, in Figure 2-1, square (the maximizing player, the computer) uses its given termination criteria to determine not to generate (make explicit) below level 3. Using its evaluation function, the computer obtains the value $v_{111} = 40$ for P_{111}. Similarly, $v_{112} = 10$; $v_{121} = 30$; $v_{122} = 20$; $v_{211} = 21$; $v_{212} = 29$; $v_{221} = 5$; $v_{222} = 80$. To obtain the backed-up value of a max-position, the minimax procedure backs up the value of the best successor of the max-position. The best successor of a max-position is the one that has the maximum value. Hence the procedure backs up 40 to P_{11} and 30 to P_{12}. Similarly, it backs up 29 to P_{21} and 80 to P_{22}. To obtain the backed-up value of a min-position, the minimax procedure backs up the value of the best successor of the min-position. The best successor of a min-position is the one that has the minimum value. Hence the procedure backs up 30 to P_1 and 29 to P_2. Hence the procedure would choose the move leading to position P_1. In summary, to obtain the backed-up value of a position, the minimax backing-up procedure backs up the value of the best successor of that position.

The *m* & *n* procedure (Slagle and Dixon, 1969)[1] is a different backing-up procedure. To obtain the backed-up value of a max-position, the *m* & *n* procedure backs up a value which depends on the *m* best successors of the max-position. The idea is to add a relatively large bonus to the (minimax) value of the best successor if other successors are as good or almost as good as the best and to add little or no bonus if all other successors are much worse than the best successor. In other words, for a given value of the best successor, the procedure deems it better to have several good successors than it is to have just one. To obtain the backed-up value of a min-position, the procedure backs up a value which depends on the *n* best successors of the min-position. Experiments with the 2 & 2 backing-up procedure indicate that it is better than the minimax backing-up procedure.

2.2 SEARCH PROCEDURES

A search procedure is a combination of a (static) evaluation function, a backing-up procedure, and a generation procedure. The two kinds of search procedures discussed below are the depth-first minimax procedure and the alpha-beta procedure.

Depth-first Minimax Procedure A search procedure is obtained if the minimax backing-up procedure is combined with a generation procedure. As one might expect, the depth-first minimax procedure is a search procedure that combines an evaluation function, the depth-first generation procedure, and the minimax backing-up procedure. A discussion of the depth-first minimax procedure is given here for two reasons. First, it prepares the way for a discussion of the alpha-beta search procedure used in present-day checker, kalah, and chess programs. Second, the depth-first minimax procedure has been used in programs that played these games.

Suppose the tree of Figure 2-1 had been given implicitly. The depth-first minimax procedure (just as a depth-first generation procedure) starts with position *A* (which is labeled *P* in Figure 2-1) and generates positions *B*, *C*, and *D* [see Figure 2-2(*a*)]. The depth-first minimax procedure then uses its

[1] Names and dates in parentheses refer to bibliographic entries at the end of the chapter.

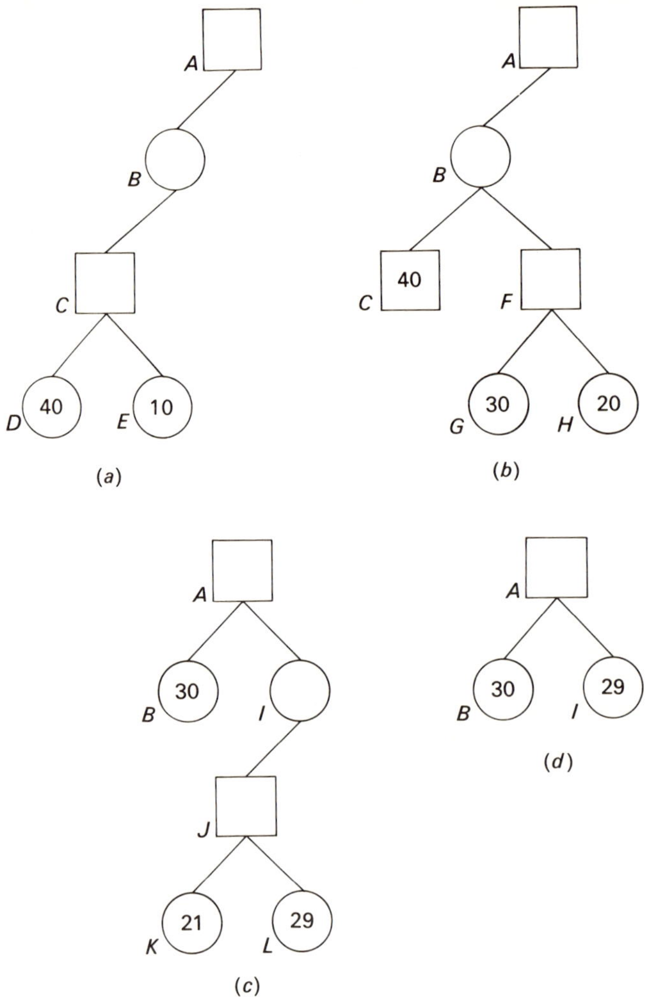

Figure 2-2 Depth-first minimax procedure.

evaluation function to evaluate position *D*, which has a value of 40. It then generates *E* and gets the value 10. The better value of *D* and *E*, namely, 40, is backed up to *C*. The procedure generates *F*. It generates and evaluates *G* and likewise *H* [see Figure 2-2(*b*)]. To *F* it backs up the better value of *G* and *H*, namely, 30. It then backs up to *B* the better value of *C* and *F*, which is also 30. It generates *I* and *J*. It generates and evaluates *K* and *L* [see Figure 2-2(*c*)]. It continues until it obtains the result shown in Figure 2-2(*d*). It chooses to move to position *B*, which has a higher value than that of position *I*.

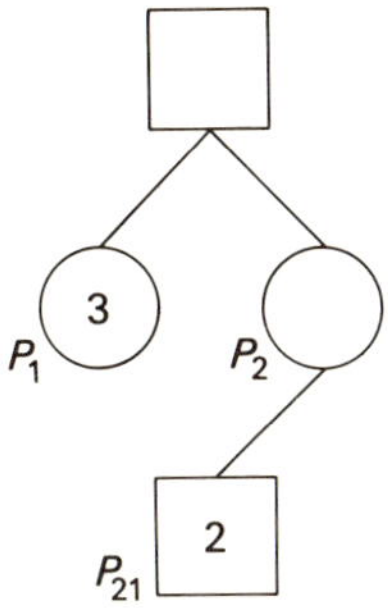

Figure 2-3 The alpha-beta procedure finds an alpha cutoff.

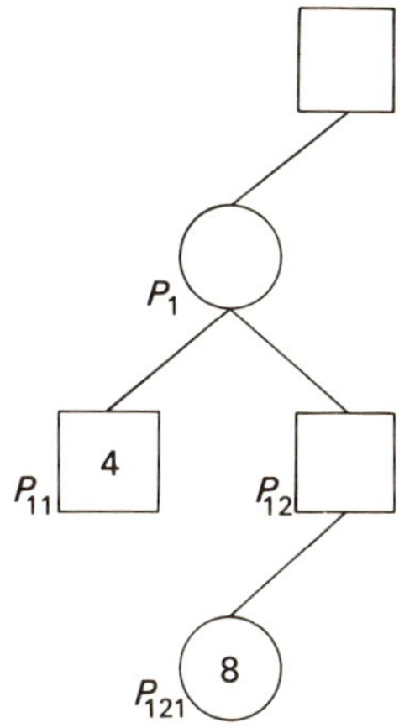

Figure 2-4 The alpha-beta procedure finds a beta cutoff.

Alpha-Beta Procedure The "alpha-beta procedure" (sometimes called the backward pruning procedure) is like the depth-first minimax procedure but has a modified depth-first generation procedure. The two procedures are equivalent in the sense that each will always choose the same move as the other, when given the same top position, termination criteria, and evaluation function. However, the alpha-beta procedure will almost always choose its move after it has generated only a very small fraction of the tree which would be generated by the equivalent depth-first minimax procedure when choosing the identical move. The two very simple examples given below show why the alpha-beta procedure chooses the same move as, although generating fewer positions than, the equivalent depth-first minimax procedure. The alpha-beta procedure is used in the tree at levels deeper than 2 or 3. The reader is urged to think about such extensions. In Figure 2-3, the alpha-beta procedure has already obtained the (possibly backed-up) value $v_1 = 3$. The alpha-beta procedure sets $\alpha = 3$ at P_2. In general, alpha is the least that Max (square) can be held to; beta is the most that Min can be held to. When the procedure finds that the (possibly backed-up) value of a max-position does not exceed alpha, it finds an *alpha cutoff*; that is, the procedure does not bother to generate more successors of the predecessor of the max-position, but generates the next successor of the predecessor of the predecessor of the max-position. Thus, after obtaining $v_{21} = 2$, the procedure finds an alpha cutoff; that is, the procedure does not bother to generate positions P_{22}, P_{23}, P_{24}, . . . (and their successors), but generates next P_3. Since the minimax *backing-up* procedure is being used and $v_{21} = 2$, the depth-first minimax procedure would obtain a backed-up value of v_2 which did not exceed 2, which is worse than $v_1 = 3$.

Hence, we know without generating any more positions below P_2 that square will not choose to move to P_2. This shows that the further generation below P_2 performed by the depth-first minimax procedure is a waste of time. Similarly, in Figure 2-4, after obtaining $v_{11} = 4$, the alpha-beta procedure sets $\beta = 4$ at P_{12}. In general, when the procedure finds that the (possibly backed-up) value of a min-position is greater than or equal to beta, it finds a *beta cutoff*; that is, the procedure does not bother to generate more successors of the predecessor of the min-position, but generates the next successor of the predecessor of the predecessor of the min-position. Thus, after obtaining v_{121}, the procedure finds a beta cutoff; that is, the procedure does not bother to generate $P_{122}, P_{123}, P_{124}, \ldots$ but generates next P_{13}.

Shallow Search Procedure Within the (deep) alpha-beta search, many shallow searches may occur. For example, the deep search might look 10 levels, whereas the shallow search might look 3 levels, from each position which occurs in the top 6 levels in the deep search. The shallow search procedure may be either a depth-first minimax procedure or an alpha-beta procedure. Shallow search may be used for "*n*-best forward pruning" or for arranging moves in order of plausibility, as explained in the next two sections.

Plausibility Ordering of Moves When the alpha-beta procedure searches first the moves that turn out to be good, many alpha-beta cutoffs tend to occur. The effort thereby saved can be very large, especially when a cutoff occurs near the top of the tree. Hence an alpha-beta procedure can profitably spend some effort in arranging moves in order of plausibility. The profit in arranging moves from a position near the top of the tree tends to be greater than that obtained in arranging those from a position near the bottom of the tree. For example, in a search that looks 10 levels, the moves may be ordered from a position lying at or above level 6 and not ordered from a position lying below level 6. As explained below, the ordering can be done by a move generator, by a shallow search, or by dynamic-ordering. As an example of ordering by a move generator, checking and capturing moves in chess can be generated and considered (searched) first.

If the successors of a position are ordered once and for all by means of a shallow search, the alpha-beta search procedure is called a *fixed-ordering* procedure. Fixed-ordering means that the ordering of the successors is not revised. For example, given a position, a shallow search might look ahead 3 levels to evaluate the successors of the position; the successors are then ordered according to their back-up values, from best to worst. We shall now illustrate an important special case in which the shallow search looks ahead no levels to evaluate the successors of the position; that is, the succesors are ordered according to their static values. Suppose that such a fixed-ordering

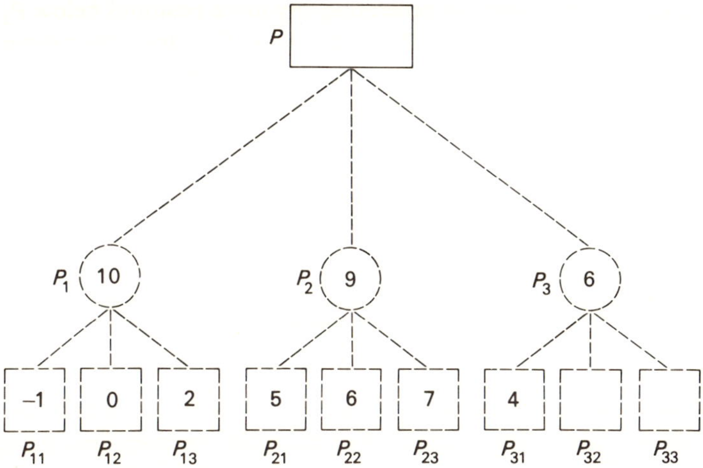

Figure 2-5 The top two levels of the implicit tree searched by the fixed-ordering and *A-B* alpha-beta procedures. The values given with the positions are static, not backed-up, values.

procedure is to search the tree in Figure 2-5 to a maximum depth of 2. Note that the values given with the positions in the figure are static and not backed-up values. The procedure generates and evaluates positions P_1, P_2, and P_3, with static values of 10, 9, and 6, respectively. It then orders these positions according to their static values, from highest to lowest. For the reader's convenience, these positions "happen" to be in the correct order from left to right. Since the procedure is going to look only to level 2, no ordering at level 2 is done. Hence from now on, the procedure acts like an ordinary alpha-beta procedure. After evaluating the three successors of P_1, the procedure gets a backed-up value for P_1 of -1, which becomes alpha. It evaluates all three successors of P_2 and gets a backed-up value of 5, which becomes alpha. Finally, it evaluates P_{31} as 4 and gets an alpha cutoff. Its final choice, therefore, is to move to P_2.

A dynamic-ordering procedure orders the successors once, but, as it gains more knowledge about the successors, it may decide to reorder them one or more times. As it searches below a given successor, its state of knowledge about that successor gradually improves. It becomes possible to make more and more accurate estimates of the true value of the successor. Suppose, for definiteness, that the procedure estimates that a certain successor of a max-position is the best. The procedure may discover that this original estimate is quite wrong and that the successor will probably have a very low backed-up value. Intuition suggests that if not too much work has been done on the successor, it might be wise to assign the low value as the new estimate for the value of the successor, to reorder the successors, and to make another choice for the first successor to search. This process is continued until some successor receives a deep backed-up value. Because of the nature of the procedure, this value will tend to be high and therefore gives a high alpha. Hence many alpha cutoffs are likely to occur.

The *A-B* alpha-beta procedure (Slagle and Dixon, 1969) is one kind of dynamic-ordering procedure. Again consider the tree in Figure 2-5. The *A-B* alpha-beta procedure starts by ordering the positions at level 1 on the basis of their static values. The static values are $v_1 = 10$, $v_2 = 9$, and $v_3 = 6$. The static value of P_2 is called A. This value is important because P_2 is the next choice in case the decision is made to reorder. Next the procedure begins to search below P_1. P_{11} is evaluated, and the result, -1, is compared with A, which is 9. Since -1 is much less than 9, the procedure decides to suspend work on P_1 and to reorder. The new order is $v_2 = 9$, $v_3 = 6$, and $v_1 = -1$. Now A is set to 6, and P_2 is searched. P_{21} has the value 5, which is only slightly less than A. The procedure decides to continue with P_2. P_{22} and P_{23} are evaluated, and the minimum value 5 is backed up to P_2. Alpha is now assigned the value 5, and the rest of the successors are evaluated by the alpha-beta procedure. The alpha cutoff occurring at P_{31} saves two level-2 evaluations. The alpha cutoff occurring at P_{11} saves another two evaluations. The reader should verify that a total of six level-2 positions are evaluated. This compares with seven evaluations made by the fixed-ordering procedure. B is the variable used to decide about reordering successors of a min-position. Note that A and B are always shallow or estimated values, whereas alpha and beta are always deep values which have been backed up from the bottom of the tree.

An important parameter R, called the reluctance, determines how reluctant the *A-B* alpha-beta procedure is to reorder. More exactly, reordering of the successors of a max-position takes place if the current estimated value of the first choice is less than $A - R$; reordering of the successors of a min-position takes place if the current estimated value of the first choice is greater than $B + R$. With a large enough R the procedure never reorders and so acts like the fixed-ordering procedure. If R is too small, the procedure reorders excessively. Hence, the reluctance should be chosen carefully.

Forward Pruning In forward pruning, not all successors of a given position are searched (considered). The time saved by not searching unpromising branches of the tree may be used in searching more promising branches to a deeper level. This advantage must be balanced against the risk of failing to search relevant branches. In one method of forward pruning called *n-best forward pruning*, the search procedure searches below only the n seemingly best successors of a position as determined either by a move generator or by values obtained from shallow searches. In *tapered n*-best forward pruning, the parameter n is decreased as the level (depth) of the search is increased.

In another method, called *convergence forward pruning*, pruning occurs in case the difference between alpha and beta becomes sufficiently small, in which case very little further information could be gained by further searching.

In the method called *optimistic-pessimistic* forward pruning, the search procedure does not search below a position whose optimistic (from Max's point of view) value is less than or equal to alpha. In other words, it does not search below a position whose backed-up value will almost certainly be too small to be relevant. Similarly, it does not search below a position whose pessimistic (again from Max's point of view) value is greater than or equal to beta. One way to get an optimistic (pessimistic) value for a position is to add (subtract) some fixed number to the static value of that position. This kind of optimistic-pessimistic forward pruning is called *marginal* forward pruning. Optimistic-pessimistic forward pruning may also be tapered. In tapered marginal pruning, for example, the quantity used to modify the (static) value may be decreased as the level is increased.

Evaluation Functions A (static) evaluation function is a function which evaluates a game position without generating any of its successors. The more frequently that a real-valued evaluation function assigns relatively high values to positions good for the computer, the better that function is considered to be. For the sake of simplicity the evaluation function is often chosen to be linear; that is, it is of the form $c_1 y_1 + c_2 y_2 + \cdots + c_n y_n$. This may be represented as the scalar product of two vectors $C \cdot Y$. Each y_j is some real-valued function called a feature of the position, for example, a number representing the piece advantage, relative mobility, etc. Each coefficient c_j is the weight of the corresponding y_j. A miniature evaluation function in checkers is, for example, $6k + 4m + u$ where k is the king advantage, m is the (plain) man advantage, and u is the undenied mobility advantage. (Undenied mobility will be defined in Section 2.3.) The coefficients for these features are 6, 4, and 1, respectively. Suppose that in a position to be evaluated, the computer has two more kings, two fewer men, and one more unit of undenied mobility than its opponent has. The evaluation function assigns a value of $6(2) + 4(-2) + 1 = 5$ to the position.

Termination Criteria Termination criteria tell a search procedure when to stop searching. Termination criteria are often used in combination with one another. Three termination criteria that have already been discussed are "game over," maximum depth, and forward pruning. Another termination criterion says to stop searching when the position is "dead." A position whose static value is not apt to differ much from its value backed up from a little more searching is called a *dead position*. For example, a chess position in which no immediate captures or checks are possible may be considered a dead position. A checker position in which jumps are available is not a dead position. Searching below a dead position is a relatively unprofitable use of time. Probably even more important, the application of the dead-position criterion avoids getting (static) values for live positions. Such a value is usually not a realistic value and is very uncertain. With another termination criterion, called *minimum depth*, successors of a position at or above some specified minimum depth are always searched except when the game is over in that position. This guarantees a complete search of the crucial top levels of the tree.

A typical example of how termination criteria are used in combination will further clarify the above discussion. Suppose that an alpha-beta search procedure is going to decide whether to terminate its search at some position, P. The search terminates if the game ends at P. Otherwise, if P is at or above some minimum depth, say 4, successors of P are searched. If P lies at the maximum depth, say 10, the search ends. But if P is at level 5, 6, 7, 8, or 9, then the search is terminated if and only if the position is either thrown out by forward pruning or a dead position.

2.3 A DETAILED EXAMPLE OF A MYTHICAL MINIATURE CHECKER PROGRAM

The discussion of search procedures given above will be further clarified by an example. The example uses a mythical program, rather than the real program discussed in Section 2.4, because an example using the latter would be excessively lengthy. Suppose that the evaluation function is $6k + 4m + u$, where k is king advantage, m is (plain) man advantage, and u is undenied mobility advantage. The undenied mobility of a player, say "white," in a position is the number of moves he has such that black can make no jumps in the successor positions. In the top position in Figure 2-6, for example, white has an undenied mobility of 4, since without getting jumped, he can move his king from square 15 to three other squares or his king from square 32 to one other square. Black has an undenied mobility of 2, since without getting jumped he can move his king to one square or his man to one square. Hence the undenied mobility advantage of white is $4 - 2 = 2$. Suppose that the termination criteria say to stop searching if some level (1 in shallow and 3 in deep) has been reached and if the position is dead; that is, no immediate jumps are available. These criteria are a combination of minimum depth and dead position. The shallow search is performed at only the top level in this example. Suppose that the machine (white) is to make a move in the position which is the top position in Figure 2-6. The shallow search is depicted in Figure 2-6. The first move to be considered is A (15–10); that is, white moves his king on square 15 to square 10. The position obtained from the move is dead and is therefore

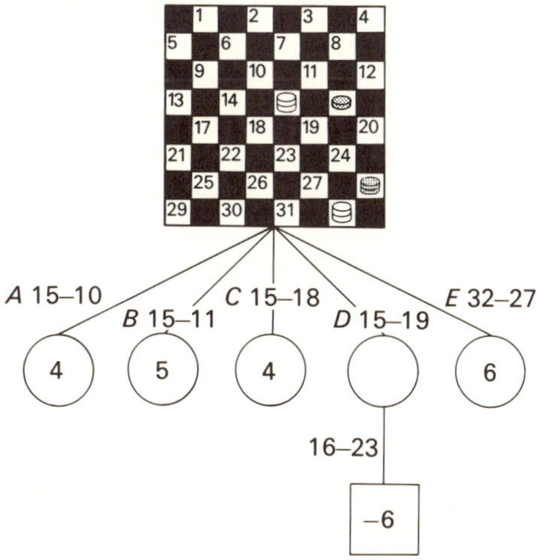

Figure 2-6 Shallow-search procedure. Black's plain man is moving from top to bottom of the page.

evaluated. Since in this position white has one more king, one fewer man, and two units more of undenied mobility, the value of this position is $6(1) + 4(-1) + 2 = 4$. Similarly, the value of the position obtained from *B* (15–11) is 5. White has an undenied mobility of 5. Black has an undenied mobility of 2, since, if the king moves, the plain man will be jumped. The value of the position obtained from *C* (15–18) is 4. The position obtained from *D* (15–19) is not dead, since an immediate jump exists. Therefore this jump is made before obtaining the value of –6. The value of the position obtained from *E* (32–27) is 6. Thus the moves are tried in the (plausible) order *E*, *B*, *A*, *C*, *D*.

Figure 2-7 depicts the alpha-beta search. It is left as an exercise to the reader to verify that the alpha and beta cutoffs are performed correctly and that the machine would make the move *B* (15–11). It is left as another exercise to the reader to construct an analysis similar to the above for white's next move under the assumption that black replied 16–19.

2.4 A REAL PROGRAM THAT PLAYS CHECKERS

The 1967 version of a checker program written by Arthur Samuel is described below. The program is an alpha-beta procedure which uses convergence forward pruning and tapered marginal forward pruning, and which uses shallow search for tapered n-best forward pruning and for plausibility ordering of moves. The termination criteria used are game over, minimum depth, maximum depth, forward pruning, and dead position. Some of the

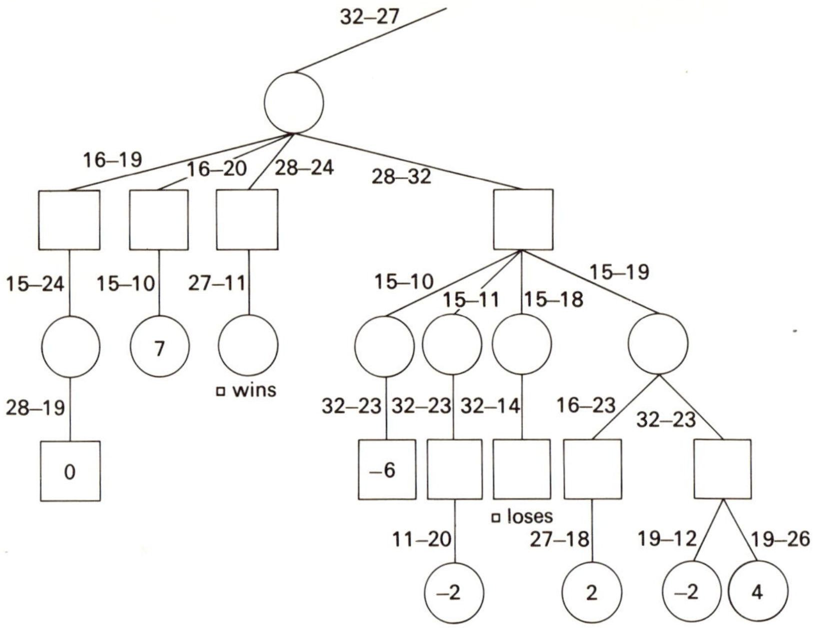

(*a*)

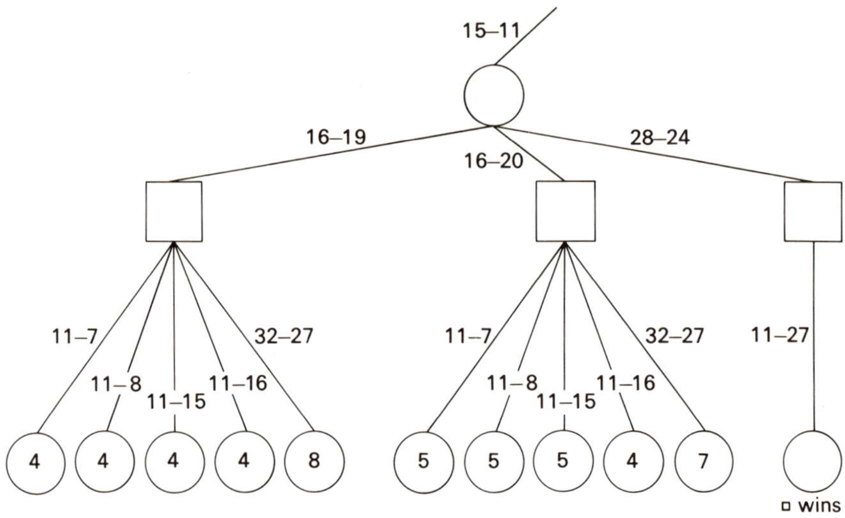

(*b*)

Figure 2-7 Alpha-beta search procedure.

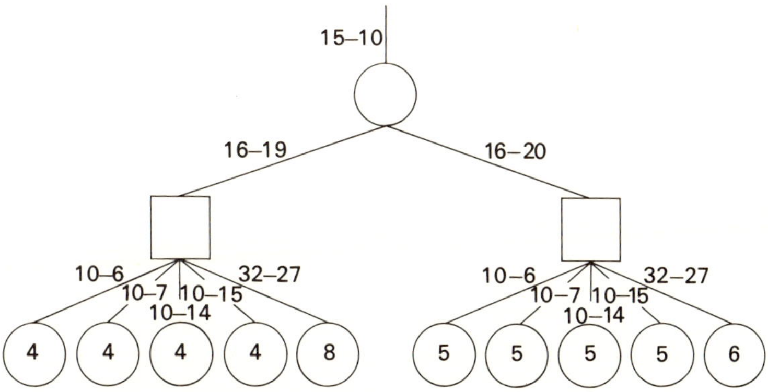
15–10
16–19
16–20
10–6
10–7
10–14
10–15
32–27
10–6
10–7
10–14
10–15
32–27
4
4
4
4
8
5
5
5
5
6

(*c*)

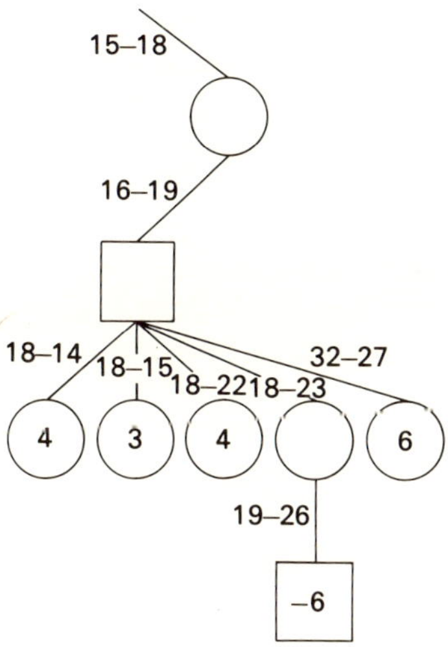
15–18
16–19
18–14
18–15
18–22
18–23
32–27
4
3
4
6
19–26
–6

(*d*)

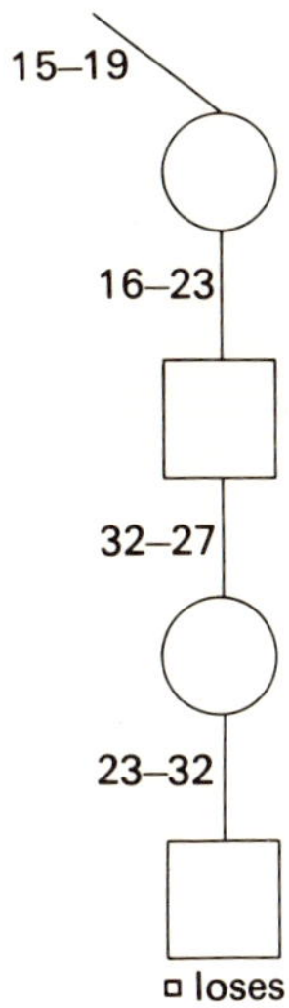
15–19
16–23
32–27
23–32
□ loses

(*e*)

other heuristics (including a kind of dynamic-ordering) used by the program can be found in Samuel's 1967 article. The features consist of man advantage, king advantage, mobility advantage, and about 24 others. All these features have been given to and not learned by the computer. Starting with the often vague descriptions of features given by experts, Samuel specified these features as programs.

Performance of the Program Samuel wrote his first checker program at the University of Illinois in 1947. Since then, the program has gone through many improvements as a result of changes made by Samuel in the search procedure and as a result of machine "learning." The program has improved itself in various ways from experience. This experience took much computer time. At one time, newly manufactured IBM computers were being tested during the day but not during the night. Samuel, who worked for IBM, tells how he used to have four or five computers madly playing checkers all night. As explained below, the checker program does a kind of "generalization learning" and "rote learning." Actually, the rote learning was done by an earlier version of the program (Samuel, 1959).

In generalization learning, the program improves its own evaluation function. Toward this end, Samuel has specified practical procedures for the computer to learn a good evaluation function by doing a statistical analysis of the "checker book." (Actually there are many such books.) The book contains many *book games*, each ending in a draw. Each move in a book game is recommended by experts. Given a search procedure (with an evaluation function restricted to be of a certain form) and such a book, there is an evaluation function of the given form which will select the book moves at least as often as would any other such evaluation function. Such an evaluation function is called optimal. In his earlier efforts, Samuel restricted the evaluation function to linear functions. (See Chapter 11 for a discussion of linear evaluation functions.) A more recent (and more successful) procedure is his *signature-table* procedure, in which the evaluation function need no longer be linear but is defined in a less restrictive way which takes account of some possible interactions among features (Samuel, 1967). It seems plausible that an optimal evaluation function of a given form (linear or signature table) will do well, even in positions not occurring in the book. Unfortunately, no practical procedure is known for finding such optimal evaluation functions. However, Samuel has specified practical procedures for finding a good (though not optimal) signature-table evaluation function, which chooses the book move about 38 percent of the time. It gets this relatively high percentage despite the fact that the procedure is searching only to level 1 for an ordinary successor and deeper for a successor with jumps. The actual playing program, which searches much deeper than one level, chooses the book move a much higher percentage of the time. For comparison, a procedure which chooses at random would choose the book move about 12 percent of the time.

Samuel has programmed the computer to "learn by rote" book moves as well as positions which have already been evaluated by the program and which occur frequently in actual games. At the option of the programmer (under the control of a sense switch on the computer), the program makes the book move, if any, which is stored on magnetic tape. The fact that such a move is made in less than 1 sec is very disconcerting to some human players. After having decided upon its move in a game, the computer learns by rote (stores in its memory) the position from which it moves and its assigned value. The search procedure is modified so that, if a position to be evaluated has been learned by rote, the remembered value is taken as value. These remembered positions and values are kept on magnetic tape in approximately the order in

Table 2-1

Game move	*Black (computer)*	*White (Nealey)*	*Game move*	*Black (computer)*	*White (Nealey)*
1	11–15		28		27–23
2		23–19	29	15–19	
3	8–11		30		23–16
4		22–17	31	12–19	
5	4–8		32		32–27
6		17–13	33	19–24	
7	15–18		34		27–23
8		24–20	35	24–27	
9	9–14		36		22–18
10		26–23	37	27–31	
11	10–15		38		18–9
12		19–10	39	31–22	
13	6–15		40		9–5
14		28–24	41	22–26	
15	15–19		42		23–19
16		24–15	43	26–22	
17	5–9		44		19–16
18		13–6	45	22–18	
19	1–10–19–26		46		21–17
20		31–22–15	47	18–23	
21	11–18		48		17–13
22		30–26	49	2–6	
23	8–11		50		16–11
24		25–22	51	7–16	
25	18–25		52		20–11
26		29–22	53	23–19	
27	11–15			White concedes	

which the positions might occur in actual play. When there are more than some preset number of such positions, the least used ones are deleted.

Typically the program makes its move in about a minute. (For purposes of standardization throughout these chapters, times are given as if the program was run on the IBM 7094 digital computer.) The power of the program was increased by the introduction of the alpha-beta procedure, marginal and convergence forward pruning, and shallow search, which was used for both plausibility ordering of moves and *n*-best forward pruning. The performance of the program was further improved by tapering the marginal and *n*-best forward pruning. The program is an excellent checker player, although the world champion beat it four games out of four. The program beats its own programmer and once beat the champion of Connecticut in the game shown in Table 2-1.

2.5 PROGRAMS THAT PLAY KALAH

The kalah program of John McCarthy and some of his students is a fixed-ordering alpha-beta procedure which uses marginal forward pruning. The termination criteria used are game over, minimum depth, maximum depth, and dead position. The evaluation function uses a feature k called the *kalah advantage*. By definition, the kalah advantage is the number of stones in the program's kalah minus the number of stones in the man's kalah. At the option of the programmer, the evaluation function is either $k+d$ or simply k. Since the distribution feature d does not help much, it will not be described. The kalah program of John Dixon and the author (1969) is a dynamic-ordering alpha-beta procedure. In fact, it is an *A-B* alpha-beta procedure with a reluctance parameter R. The termination criteria are game over and maximum depth. The evaluation function is simply the kalah advantage.

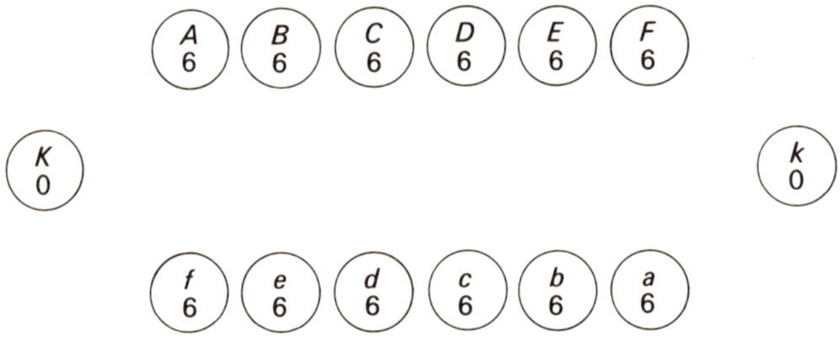

Figure 2-8 Starting position in kalah. There are six stones in each hole and none in each kalah.

The Rules of Kalah The initial kalah position is shown in Figure 2-8. The players are called *P* and *p*. Player *P* owns one kalah *K* and six holes A, B, C, D, E, and F. Similarly, *p* owns a kalah *k* and six holes a to f. The game begins with six stones in each of the 12 holes. A player wins if he gets more than half the stones in his kalah. If all the holes of one player become empty (even if it is not his turn to move), the stones remaining in the holes of the opponent are put in the kalah of that opponent, and the game ends.

Player *p* makes the first move. (This paragraph describes how a player makes his move. A later paragraph describes a game illustrating various moves.) A player begins his move by picking up the stones in one of his holes. Proceeding counterclockwise around the board, he puts one of the picked-up stones in each hole, and his own kalah (skipping the opponent's kalah), until no picked-up stones remain. Three outcomes are possible, depending on where the last picked-up stone lands. If the last stone lands in the (player's) kalah, the player goes again. If the last stone lands in an empty hole owned by the player and if the opponent's hole directly across the board contains at least one stone, the player puts his stone and all the stones in the opponent's hole into the player's kalah, and the opponent moves next. In the third case, nothing special happens, and the opponent moves next.

The rules are well illustrated by the game shown in Table 2-2. The man *p* moves first and is beaten by the computer program *P* of McCarthy et al. The man's move was 1.a, which means he picked up the six stones in hole a, put one stone in his kalah and one in each of the holes F, E, D, C, and B. The man's third move 3.a,f means that he made move a (a go-again move) and then move f.

Performance of the Programs Typically, each of the programs makes its move in a game in about a minute. They almost always beat humans. The only way for a human to beat one of the programs consistently is to find a sequence of moves which wins and make this sequence over and over. The programs do not learn, and so will keep playing the identical losing sequence of moves. The human can discover such sequences by trial and error or by having the program play against itself. Various procedures that, when introduced, increased the power of the program of McCarthy et al. include the alpha-beta procedure, shallow search (for plausibility ordering), and marginal forward pruning. McCarthy et al. have used their program to prove that the first player can force a win in the three variations of kalah in which each hole starts with one, two, or three stones rather than six. The power of the program of John Dixon and the author was increased when a fixed-ordering procedure was replaced by an *A-B* alpha-beta procedure with a suitable reluctance parameter *R*.

Table 2-2 The program of John McCarthy et al. beats a man in a game of kalah

Move number	*Position*	*Move by man p*	*Position*	*Move by program P*
1	0 6 6 6 6 6 6 6 6 6 6 6 6 0	a	0 6 7 7 7 7 7 6 6 6 6 6 0 1	A
2	1 0 7 7 7 7 7 7 7 7 7 7 0 1	f	1 0 7 7 7 7 8 0 8 8 8 8 1 2	B
3	2 1 0 7 7 7 8 1 9 9 9 9 1 2	a,f	2 1 0 7 7 7 8 0 10 9 9 9 0 3	A,C
4	4 1 1 0 7 7 8 1 11 10 10 9 0 3	b	4 2 2 1 8 8 9 2 11 10 10 0 1 4	B,C
5	17 3 0 0 8 8 9 2 0 10 10 0 1 4	a,d	17 4 1 1 9 9 10 2 0 0 11 1 1 6	D
6	18 5 2 2 0 9 10 3 1 1 12 2 1 6	a,b,d	18 5 2 2 0 9 10 3 1 0 13 0 1 8	B,E
7	20 7 1 3 1 0 10 4 2 1 14 0 1 8	a,c	20 8 2 4 2 1 11 5 3 2 1 2 1 10	A
8	21 0 2 4 2 1 12 6 4 3 2 3 2 10	f,c,d,a	21 0 3 5 3 2 13 0 0 1 2 7 0 15	F
9	24 1 4 6 4 3 0 1 1 2 3 8 0 15	b	24 2 5 7 5 4 1 1 1 2 3 0 1 16	C
10	25 3 6 0 5 4 1 2 2 3 4 0 1 16	a,f	25 3 6 0 5 4 1 0 3 4 4 0 0 17	B
11	26 4 0 0 5 4 1 1 4 5 5 0 0 17	e	26 4 0 0 5 4 0 1 0 6 6 1 0 19	A
12	27 0 0 0 5 4 0 2 1 7 6 1 0 19	f	27 0 0 0 5 4 0 0 2 8 6 1 0 19	D
13	28 1 1 1 0 4 0 1 2 8 6 1 0 19	c	28 1 1 1 1 5 1 1 2 8 0 2 1 20	A,E,A,B,D
14	35 1 0 3 0 0 1 1 0 8 0 2 1 20	a,b,a,d	35 1 0 4 1 1 2 1 0 0 1 1 1 24	F
15	35 1 0 4 2 2 0 1 0 0 1 1 1 24	a,c	35 1 0 4 2 2 0 1 0 0 0 2 0 25	A,C
16	37 1 1 0 2 2 0 2 0 0 0 2 0 25			

2.6 A PROGRAM THAT PLAYS CHESS

A chess program written by Richard Greenblatt, Donald Eastlake III, and Stephen Crocker (1967) at the Massachusetts Institute of Technology uses the alpha-beta procedure. For the sake of efficiency, the procedure evaluates the *moves* from a position and not the resulting positions (successors), as would be done in a shallow search of one level; it uses the results for plausibility ordering of moves and for tapered *n*-best forward pruning of moves. The termination criteria are game over, minimum depth, tapered *n*-best forward pruning of moves, and dead position. The program looks for duplicate positions on the game tree in order to detect draws by repetition of positions and to avoid duplicate searches. The program uses book openings and much other "chess knowledge," which is described in the article by Greenblatt et al.

Various procedures that, when introduced, increased the power of the program include the alpha-beta procedure, the evaluation of moves from a position (for plausibility ordering and tapered n-best forward pruning), looking for duplicate positions, and the use of book openings and other chess knowledge. Typically, the program makes its move in a game in about a minute. A good player (not to mention an expert or master) usually beats this or any other chess program. The program is an honorary member of the United States Chess Federation and the Massachusetts Chess Association under the name of Mac Hack Six. The program plays in tournaments and is operated via telephone lines from a teletype at the tournament site. In an April, 1967, tournament, the program won the Class D trophy. Table 2-3 gives two tournament games played by Mac Hack Six. In the first game, white's rating of 2190 means that he is an expert and almost a master. His first move is pawn to king knight three (P–KN3); that is, he moves the pawn in front of his king's knight from the second to the third rank. The reply of Mac Hack Six is pawn to king four (P–K4). White plays knight to king bishop three, etc. BxR means bishop takes rook. For castling O–O denotes king side, and O–O–O denotes queen side.

Other Programs That Play Chess The program of Greenblatt et al. is better than all previous chess programs, some of which are described below. A. N. Turing's procedure (1951) was hand-simulated but never actually programmed for a computer. It was a depth-first minimax procedure. The termination criteria included the dead-position idea. Turing called a position dead if there were no immediate captures available. The Los Alamos program (Kister et al., 1957) was a depth-first minimax procedure for a 6×6 chessboard. Alex Bernstein's program (1958) was a depth-first minimax procedure. The termination criteria were game over, a maximum depth of 4, and 7-best forward pruning. The 7-best forward pruning consisted of searching below only the seven most plausible (as determined by the move generator) successors at the top four levels. Thus, $7^4 = 2401$ terminal positions occurred at level 4.

A. L. Bastian's program (1959) was a depth-first minimax procedure. The termination criteria were game over, a maximum depth of 6, and tapered n-best forward pruning. Instead of searching below the seven most plausible moves at each level, as in Bernstein's program Bastian's program searched seven successors at level 1, five at level 2, four at 3, three at 4, three at 5, and two at 6. Thus, $(7)(5)(4)(3)(3)(2) = 2520$ terminal positions occurred at level 6. The move generator determined move plausibility and made moves that had more than one purpose very plausible.

Table 2-3 Two Tournament Games played by Mac Hack Six[1]

First game
White is a human rated 2190; black is Mac Hack Six

Move number	*White*	*Black*	*Move number*	*White*	*Black*
1	P–KN3	P–K4	29	R–Q3	R–K7
2	N–KB3	P–K5	30	R–Q2	RxR
3	N–Q4	B–B4	31	QxR	N–K4
4	N–N3	B–N3	32	R–Q1	Q–QB2
5	B–N2	N–KB3	33	B–Q5	K–N3
6	P–QB4	P–Q3	34	P–QN4	B–N3
7	N–B3	B–K3	35	Q–B2	N–B3
8	P–Q3	PxP	36	B–K6	N–Q5
9	BxP	QN–Q2	37	RxN	BxR
10	PxP	R–QN1	38	QxPch	K–N2
11	B–N2	O–O	39	Q–N4ch	K–R3
12	O–O	B–N5	40	QxB	Q–K2
13	Q–B2	R–K1	41	Q–R4ch	K–N3
14	P–Q4	P–B4	42	B–B5ch	K–N2
15	B–K3	PxP	43	QxRPch	K–B1
16	NxP	N–K4	44	Q–R8ch	K–B2
17	P–KR3	B–Q2	45	Q–R8	Q–B2
18	P–N3	B–QB4	46	Q–Q5ch	K–N2
19	QR–Q1	Q–B1	47	K–N2	Q–K2
20	K–R2	N–N3	48	P–KR4	K–R3
21	B–N5	R–K4	49	P–N4	K–N2
22	BxN	PxB	50	P–R5	Q–K7
23	N–K4	P–B4	51	P–R6ch	K–B1
24	N–KB6ch	K–N2	52	P–R7	QxKBPch
25	NxB	QxN	53	KxQ	K–K2
26	N–B6	QR–K1	54	P–R8queen	P–R3
27	NxR	RxN	55	Q–K6mate	
28	Q–B3	P–B3			

Second game
White is Mac Hack Six; black is a human rated 1510

Move number	*White*	*Black*	*Move number*	*White*	*Black*
1	P–K4	P–QB4	12	QxQP	B–Q2
2	P–Q4	PxP	13	B–R4	B–N2
3	QxP	N–QB3	14	N–Q5	NxP
4	Q–Q3	N–B3	15	N–B7ch	QxN
5	N–QB3	P–KN3	16	QxQ	N–B4
6	N–B3	P–Q3	17	Q–Q6	B–KB1
7	B–B4	P–K4	18	Q–Q5	R–B1
8	B–N3	P–QR3	19	NxP	B–K3
9	O–O–O	P–QN4	20	QxNch	RxQ
10	P–QR4	B–R3ch	21	R–Q8mate	
11	K–N1	P–N5			

[1] The first game (a loss) was the first tournament game ever played by a computer (January 21, 1967). The second was the first tournament game ever won by a computer.

Allen Newell's program (1959) starts by selecting a set of features (for example, king safety) relevant to the top position. Next, an alpha-beta search is made with termination criteria of game over and dead position. This program was the first to use the alpha-beta procedure. A position is dead if it is inactive with respect to each feature in the originally selected set of features. For any live position in the tree, a move is plausible if it is relevant to an originally selected feature which is still active in that position. Plausibility ordering of moves is used, and multipurpose moves are given high priority. His program is based on the psychological experiments performed by Adriaan De Groot on chess players, including world champions.

The chess program of Professor John McCarthy at Stanford University and some of his students is an alpha-beta procedure which uses shallow search for plausibility ordering of moves and for *n*-best forward pruning. The termination criteria are game over, maximum depth, *n*-best forward pruning, and dead position. The program uses a linear evaluation function. At the Moscow Institute of Theoretical and Experimental Physics, G. M. Adelson-Velskiy et al. wrote a chess program similar to the Stanford program. However, the Moscow program embodies a few more ideas, including better searching of forcing (checking and capturing) moves. Actually, there are two versions of the Moscow program. In a 1967 to 1968 correspondence match, the stronger version of the Moscow program beat the Stanford program two games out of two.

2.7 CONCLUSIONS FROM PROGRAMS THAT PLAY CHECKERS, KALAH, AND CHESS

Peformance The programs described in this chapter take only 1 min per move, whereas tournament rules in chess and checkers allow 4 or 5 min per move. The checker and kalah programs play an excellent game, whereas the chess programs play only a fair game. In checkers and kalah, successful performance can be obtained from fast and accurate searching of rather large trees. In chess, the successful player is very good at inventing and using strategies. He mixes abstract thinking with move-by-move analysis. He is very selective and therefore needs to search a relatively small tree. Researchers are working to mechanize these and other heuristics used by expert human chess players.

Search Procedures The alpha-beta procedure has a great theoretical advantage over the depth-first minimax procedure. This advantage has been borne out by experience with computer programs. The alpha-beta programs were helped by the introduction of shallow search programs for plausibility ordering of moves and for *n*-best forward pruning. They were further helped by the introduction of optimistic-pessimistic forward pruning (actually only marginal forward pruning) and convergence forward pruning. Tapered *n*-best forward pruning and tapered marginal forward pruning were even better than their untapered counterparts. In the one comparison made, a dynamic-ordering procedure (actually an *A-B* alpha-beta procedure with suitable reluctance *R*) was superior to a fixed-ordering procedure. Search techniques similar to the above should be used in the solution of other complex problems.

Computer Learning The checker program can perform successfully a kind of generalization learning and a kind of rote learning. The generalization learning (learning evaluation functions of certain types) is applicable to many problems besides games. Practical procedures have been specified for finding good (but not optimal) evaluation functions of certain types. Most Artificial Intelligence researchers agree that it is important and desirable to get machines to learn. The ability to learn is an important component of natural intelligence. For a computer which truly learned, people would not, as they do now, have to specify separate and lengthy programs for each new intellectually difficult task. Unfortunately, it seems very difficult to get computers to learn, even half as well as people do. To date, no program learns better than the checker program described above.

EXERCISES

1. Fill in the blank with the correct word ("sometimes," "always," or "never").

a. The alpha-beta procedure will ______ choose to move to a position with higher backed-up value than will the corresponding depth-first minimax procedure.

b. A (static) evaluation function is ______ linear.

2. What is the main reason for plausibility ordering of moves in an alpha-beta search procedure?

3. Suppose that a simple search procedure searches to a depth (level) of 2 in a game in which any position has 30 successors. Neglecting shallow search, forward pruning, game over, etc., and not counting the top position, answer the following questions:

a. How many positions are generated by a depth-first minimax procedure?

b. What is the largest possible number of positions that can be generated by an alpha-beta procedure?

c. What is the smallest possible number of positions that can be generated by an alpha-beta procedure?

4. In Figure 2-6, why is 4 the value of the position obtained from *C* (15–18)?

5. Construct an analysis similar to that in Section 2.3 for white's next move under the assumption that black replied 16–19.

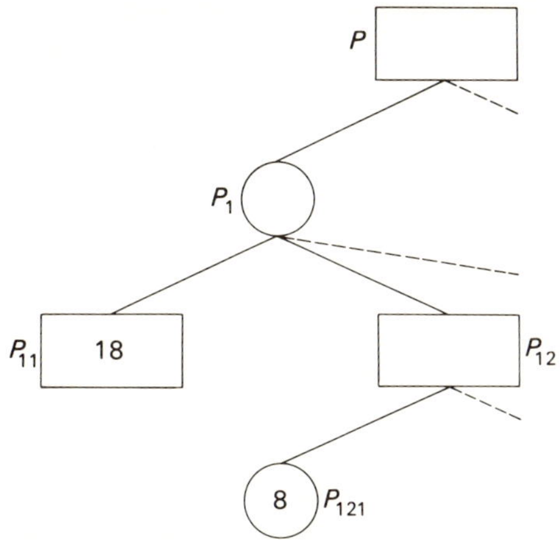

Figure 2-9

6. Assuming that square is the maximizing player in the tree shown in Figure 2-9, which one of the following would an alpha-beta procedure generate next?

a. P_2 because there is an alpha cutoff.
b. P_{13} because there is a beta cutoff.
c. P_{122}.
d. P_2 because there is a beta cutoff.
e. P_{13} because there is an alpha cutoff.

7. The rules of the two-person game tic-tac-toe may be described as follows. Player square moves first by marking an X in one of the nine spaces on a 3×3 board. Then player circle marks an O in one of the eight remaining spaces. Then player square marks an X in one of the seven remaining spaces. Play continues to alternate. A player wins if he is the first to get three of his marks in a row—horizontally, vertically, or diagonally. The game is a draw if neither player has won after nine moves. Suppose the evaluation function is $y_1 + 5y_2 + 25y_3$, where y_1 is the unblocked-one-in-a-row advantage, y_2 is the unblocked-two-in-a-row advantage, and y_3 is the three-in-a-row advantage. For example, in the top position in Figure 2-10, $y_1 = 4 - 1 = 3$. Player square (X) has four unblocked-one-in-a-rows, namely, one diagonal, the first row, the second column, and the third column. Player circle has one unblocked-one-in-a-row, namely, the bottom row. Similarly, $y_2 = 0 - 1 = -1$. Square has no unblocked-two-in-a-rows. Circle has an unblocked-two-in-a-row in the first column. Since neither player has a three-in-a-row, $y_3 = 0 - 0 = 0$. Hence the value of the position is $3 + 5(-1) + 25(0) = -2$. Suppose that the implicit tree shown in Figure 2-10 is searched by a simple alpha-beta

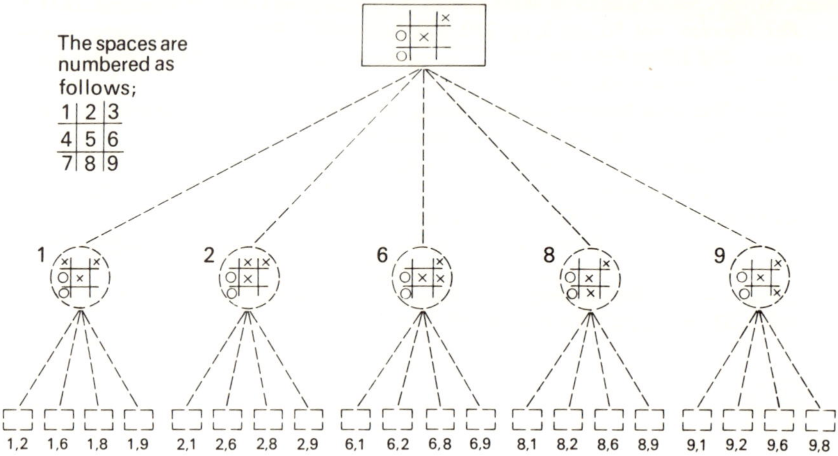

Figure 2-10 Tic-tac-toe tree for Exercise 7.

procedure with a termination criterion of a maximum depth of 2. Use a heavy solid line to trace the portion of the tree that is searched. Do not trace any portion which is not searched. For each level-2 position evaluated during the search, write its value in the center of the corresponding square.

8. In the above exercise, the number of the move chosen by the alpha-beta procedure is:

a. 1.
b. 2.
c. 6.
d. 8.
e. 9.

BIBLIOGRAPHY

Bernstein, Alex, and Michael Roberts: Computer Versus Chess Player, *Sci. Am.*, June, 1958.

De Groot, Adriaan D.: "Psychological Studies for Thought and Choice in Chess," Mouten & Company, The Hague, 1965.

Greenblatt, Richard, Donald Eastlake, III, and Stephen Crocker: The Greenblatt Chess Program, *Proc. AFIPS Annu. Fall Joint Computer Conf.*, 1967, pp. 801–810.

Kister, J., P. Stein, S. Ulam, W. Walden, and M. Wells: Experiments in Chess, *J. ACM*, pp. 174–177, April, 1957.

Newell, Allen, J. C. Shaw, and Herbert Simon: Chess Playing Programs and the Problems of Complexity, *IBM J. Res. Develop.*, pp. 320–335, October, 1958. Reprinted in Edward Feigenbaum, and Julian Feldman (eds.), "Computers and Thought," McGraw-Hill Book Company, New York, 1963.

Nilsson, Nils J.: A New Method for Searching Problem-Solving and Game-Playing Trees, *Proc. IFIP Congr.*, 1968.

Samuel, Arthur: Some Studies in Machine Learning Using the Game of Checkers, *IBM J. Res. Develop.*, vol. III, no. 3, pp. 210–229, July, 1959. Reprinted in Edward Feigenbaum, and Julian Feldman (eds.), "Computers and Thought," McGraw-Hill Book Company, New York, 1963.

———: Some Studies in Machine Learning Using the Game of Checkers, II, Recent Progress, *IBM J. Res. Develop.*, vol. XI, no. 6, November, 1967.

Slagle, James: Game Trees, m & n Minimaxing, and the $m \times n$ Alpha-Beta Procedure, *Artificial Intelligence Group Rept.* 3, University of California, Lawrence Radiation Laboratory, Livermore, Calif., November 8, 1963.

———, and John Dixon: Experiments with Some Programs That Search Game Trees, *J. ACM*, vol. XVI, no. 2, pp. 189–207, April, 1969.

———, and ———: "Experiments with the m & n Tree-searching Program," *J. ACM*, vol. XIII, no. 3, pp. 147–154, March, 1970.

3
Programs for Five-in-a-Row, Qubic, and Card Games

This chapter describes some successful programs that play five-in-a-row, qubic, contract bridge, draw poker, and hearts. Programs which were used to find practical winning strategies in Nevada baccarat and blackjack are touched on.

Roughly speaking, the five-in-a-row and qubic programs are search procedures with a linear evaluation function and with a termination criterion of a maximum depth of 1. In the general description of game-playing programs that was given in Section 1.6, the evaluation step (step F) in the five-in-a-row and qubic programs is usually performed by a static evaluation function rather than by a search procedure. In these games, the evaluation function dominates in importance because tree searching is impractical. Each of the two programs adjusts its own evaluation function according to the observed skill of the opponent. Actually, there are two programs that play five-in-a-row; only one of these programs (that of Joseph Weizenbaum and R. C. Shepherdson) adjusts its evaluation function.

3.1 PROGRAMS THAT PLAY FIVE-IN-A-ROW

Since the five-in-a-row programs written by Joseph Weizenbaum (1962) (with the help of R. C. Shepherdson) and Deena Koniver (1963) are similar, no

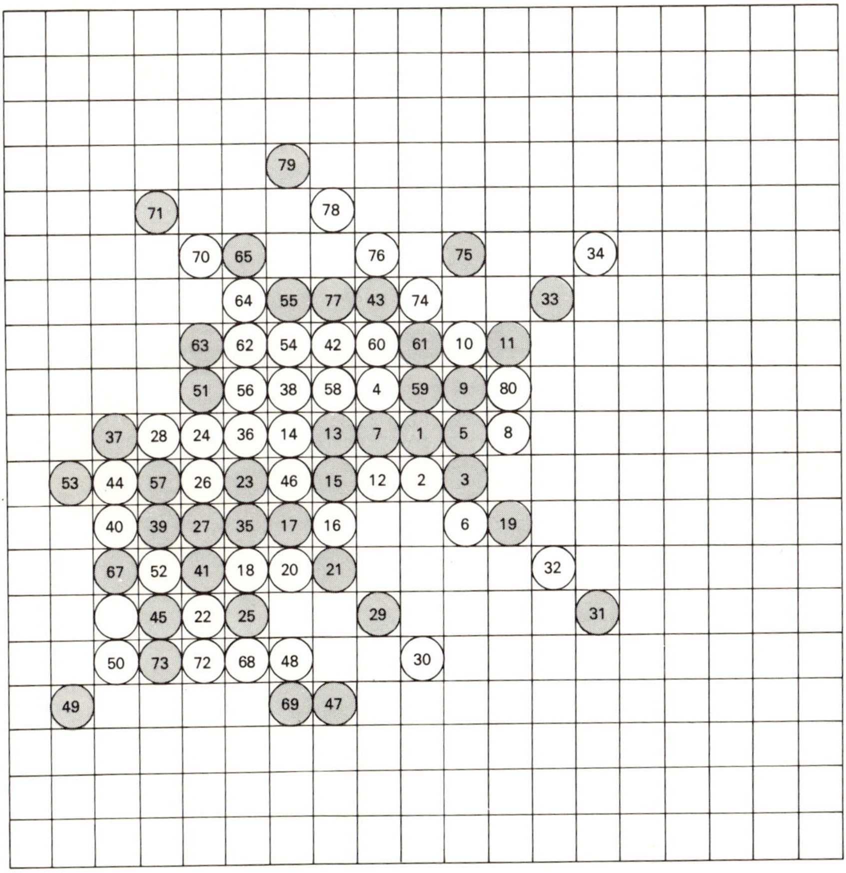

Figure 3-1 A man (white) beats the program (black) at five-in-a-row.

distinction will be made between them in the discussion that follows. Five-in-a-row is a two-person, strictly competitive game played on a (go) board which has 19 × 19 squares. A player wins if he gets five of his stones consecutively in a row—horizontally, vertically, or diagonally. The players alternate their moves, just as in tic-tac-toe.

The rules are illustrated in Figure 3-1, which shows a game actually played by the program. The program moved first (an advantage) and was beaten by the man. The program's first move was to put one of its stones in the tenth row and tenth column as shown by the numeral 1 in that square in Figure 3-1.

Performance of the program improved when the program adjusted its evaluation function to make the program play more aggressively when it was winning. The program takes only a few seconds to move and beats novices. In fact, novices tend to use a playing procedure similar to that of the program

Table 3-1 The program beats a man at qubic

Move number	*Human move*	*Machine move*	
1	322	111	
2	222	141	
3	232	441	
4	332	241	
5	341	121	
6	131	221	
7	331	321	
8	421	231	
9	411	211	Machine wins

and are beaten by the superior bookkeeping ability of the program. Better players beat the program and sometimes use procedures quite different from those of the program. These players, for example, seem to search below any position which is not "dead." Performance would probably improve if the program used a similar dead-position termination criterion.

3.2 A PROGRAM THAT PLAYS QUBIC

William Daly programmed a computer to play qubic. Qubic is a three-dimensional form of tic-tac-toe, which is played on a board having $4 \times 4 \times 4$ squares. The rules are illustrated in Table 3-1, which shows a game actually played by the program written by William Daly (1961). No moves were ever made into planes 3 or 4, which are therefore not shown in Figures 3-2 and 3-3. The human opened with move 3,2,2, which means the third row, second column, second plane.

The qubic program is a depth-first minimax procedure with a linear evaluation function. The termination criterion is a maximum depth of 1 except for a "forcing" search to a maximum depth of 10. The program searches for a "forced" win; that is, a win preceded by a sequence of computer moves, each causing a three-in-a-row which the opponent is forced to block. If the program cannot force a win in this manner, it pretends that it makes no move and the forcing search is again performed, this time for the opponent. If the opponent can force a win, the forcing search acts as a move generator. These moves are arranged in order of plausibility by a shallow (level-1) search. The program chooses the most plausible move, if any, against which the opponent cannot still force a win.

X			X
			X
			O
			X

plane 1

	O	O	
	O	O	

plane 2

Figure 3-2 Position after human's fifth move.

X	X	O	X
X	X	X	X
	X	O	O
O	O		X

plane 1

	O	O	
	O	O	

plane 2

Figure 3-3 Position at end of game.

Performance of the program was improved by introduction of the forcing search. Performance was also improved by the program's adjusting its evaluation function according to the win-loss record of its opponent. Other game-playing programs would perform better if they would take into account the strengths and weaknesses of their opponents. The qubic program makes its move in a few seconds and plays very well. Although the program usually went second (a disadvantage), it won over 80 percent of the more than 100 games it played. No tie was ever played. The program was weak in opening strategy; however, openings could be improved by rote learning, as in the checker program. Performance would probably improve by searching to a level of 2 or 3 rather than level 1.

3.3 PROGRAMS THAT PLAY CARD GAMES

Card-playing programs roughly fit the general description of game-playing programs that was given in Section 1.6 but unfortunately have very little else in common. Such programs are special-purpose. Section 1.6 gives the general purposes of programming a computer to play a game. Card games have been selected by some researchers because they are more like "real life"; chance plays a part and the players do not know exactly what position they are in.

A program written by Gay Carley (1962) bids and plays the cards in contract bridge. The bidding is poor. It plays the cards about as well as would an average player. A program written by T. N. Thiele, R. R. Lemke, and K. S. Fu (1963) to play modified hearts is better than the average player. A program written by Donald Waterman (1970) learns to play a fairly good game of draw poker.

3.4 PROGRAMS FOR WINNING AT NEVADA BACCARAT AND BLACKJACK

Edward Thorpe wrote programs to help him find winning "systems" in Nevada baccarat and blackjack. (See the article by O'Neil, 1964.) As these games are played in the gambling casinos, the deck of cards is not shuffled after each deal. The winning system consists of betting high when the remainder of the deck becomes favorable as a result of the proportion of key cards remaining in the deck. Professor Thorpe has used his systems to win many thousands of dollars from Nevada casinos. Incidentally, using a second timer in his shoe, he won on the 40 to 1 bet on the wheel of fortune. He developed these systems because it was interesting (he is a mathematician), fun, and, of course, profitable.

Blackjack The blackjack program is given a description of a remainder of a deck; that is, the number of cards and key cards (for example fives or tens) remaining in the deck. The program finds the best possible strategy and the corresponding expectation for the player. To get his system, Thorpe memorized a strategy corresponding to a favorable deck description which occurs sufficiently frequently in actual play.

The history of Professor Thorpe's system is very interesting. In January, 1961, he (then a professor of mathematics at the Massachusetts Institute of Technology) presented his paper "Fortune's Formula, A Winning Strategy for Blackjack," at the American Mathematics Society meeting in Washington, D.C. In the spring of 1961, he ran \$10,000 (provided by two New York backers) into \$21,000, and one of the backers lost \$11,000 by playing without the system. In the summer of 1961, Thorpe, to his bewilderment, could barely break even. Fortunately for him, he joined forces in the winter of 1962 with Michael (Mickey) MacDougal, a former investigator for the Nevada

Gaming Control Board. Mickey solved the mystery. Dealers were cheating Thorpe! Since taking suitable counter measures, he now wins about $100 per hour, despite the fact that he does not stick to his system, which dealers can now spot. In order not to get thrown out of the casinos, he has sometimes resorted to disguises. At the time of this writing, he is over $25,000 ahead in blackjack.

Baccarat Thorpe discovered that there was a practical winning system for the side bet on natural 9 and natural 8 in Nevada baccarat. He figured out that his capital would double in an average of only 25 hr. Just as with blackjack, the system consists in making the side bets when the remainder of the deck becomes favorable. He programmed a computer to tabulate the probabilities of winning given the distribution of nines and eights in the deck. In this way he obtained a betting system which allowed fast growth of capital with negligible risk of going broke. In the spring of 1963 he used his baccarat system against the casinos and won thousands of dollars. The casinos no longer have these side bets!

EXERCISES

1. Give two reasons why the games played by the card-playing programs are more like real life than are the other games played by programs.

2. In the man's first move in Figure 3-1, into which row and column did he put his stone?

3. Give the position after the human's seventh move in the qubic game in Table 3-1.

BIBLIOGRAPHY

Carley, Gay: "A Program to Play Contract Bridge," master's thesis, Department of Electrical Engineering, Massachusetts Institute of Technology, Cambridge, Mass., June, 1962.

Daly, William: "Computer Strategies for the Game of Qubic," master's thesis, Department of Electrical Engineering, Massachusetts Institute of Technology, Cambridge, Mass., January, 1961.

Koniver, Deena: "Computer Heuristics for Five-In-A-Row," master's thesis, Department of Mathematics, Massachusetts Institute of Technology, Cambridge, Mass., June, 1963.

O'Neil, Paul: The Professor Who Breaks the Bank, *Life*, March 27, 1964.

Thiele, T. N., R. R. Lemke, and K. S. Fu: A Digital Computer Card Playing Program, *Behavioral Sci.*, vol. VIII, pp. 362–368, 1963.

Waterman, Donald A.: Generalized Learning Techniques for Automating the Learning of Heuristics, *Artificial Intelligence*, vol. 1, no. 1–2, Spring 1970.

Weizenbaum, Joseph: How to Make a Computer Appear Intelligent; Five-in-a-row Offers No Guarantee, *Datamation*, pp. 24–26, February, 1962.

———, and R. C. Shepherdson: Gamesmanship, *Datamation*, p. 10, April, 1962.

4
Programs that Solve Problems in Chess, Geometry, and Calculus

Many kinds of intellectually difficult problems seem to have a certain structure in common. Two equivalent kinds of implicit trees can represent many kinds of problems, including problems in chess, geometry, and indefinite integration. Heuristic programs were written to search such trees. Experiments with working computer programs for chess (Baylor and Simon, 1966), geometry (Gelernter et al., 1959, 1960), and integration (Slagle, 1963) led to certain conclusions. The programs are able to solve fairly difficult problems. The speed of each program compares favorably with that of a good human problem solver. Research should be directed toward extending these successes to the solution of important real problems that are even more difficult.

4.1 REPRESENTATION OF A PROBLEM AS AN IMPLICIT TREE

Geometry and chess problems are good examples of a fairly general kind of problem that can be represented by two kinds of implicit trees. These two representations will be shown to be equivalent. A chess problem may be represented as an implicit, two-person, strictly competitive game tree. The problem is to search (make explicit) enough of the game tree to prove that white

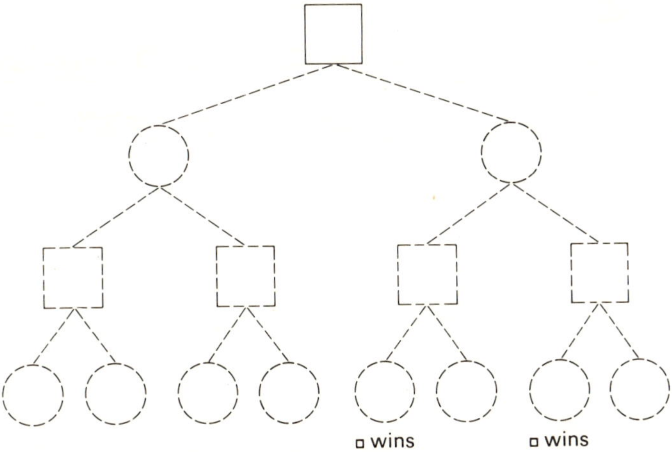

Figure 4-1 Top three levels of an implicit game tree.

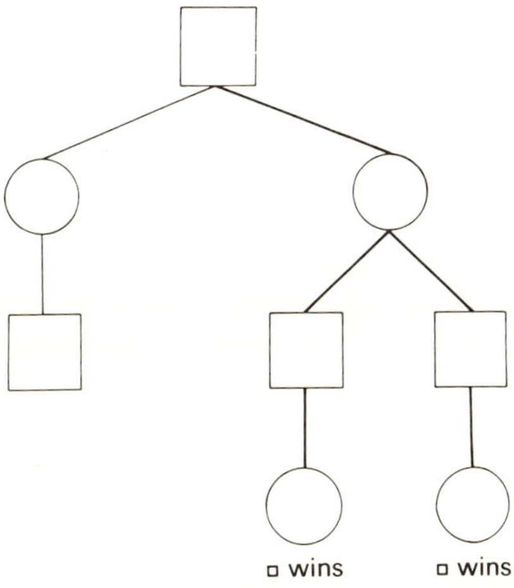

Figure 4-2 Explicit game tree and proof. Heavy solid lines represent the proof.

(square) can force a win. Figure 4-1 depicts the top three levels of an "implicit" game tree. Making explicit the tree shown in Figure 4-2 solves the problem. The heavy solid lines represent a proof.

A geometry problem may be represented as an implicit, disjunctive-conjunctive goal tree. The problem is to prove some geometric conclusion, for example, that two angles are equal, given certain hypotheses. Looking for a proof corresponds to searching an implicit, disjunctive-conjunctive goal tree whose top goal (node) G is "to prove the originally given conclusion."

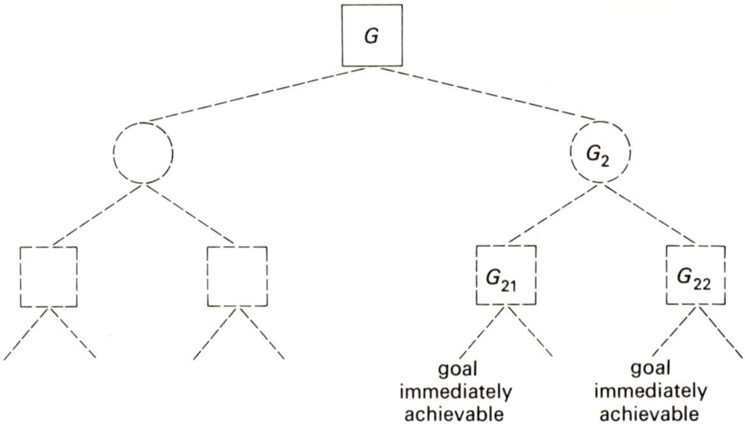

Figure 4-3 Top three levels of an implicit goal tree.

In Figure 4-3 the top goal G is achievable if the disjunction of the goal G_1 and the goal G_2 is achievable, that is, by definition of disjunction, if either G_1 or (inclusive) G_2 is achievable. This disjunction is represented by the square shape of G. In the example of proving two angles equal, the goal G_1 might be to prove that the angles are corresponding parts of congruent triangles, and the goal G_2 might be to prove that the angles are alternate interior angles of parallel lines. In Figure 4-3 the goal G_2 is achievable if the conjunction of G_{21} and G_{22} is achievable, that is, by definition of conjunction, if both G_{21} and G_{22} are achievable. This conjunction is represented by the circular shape of G_2. Making explicit the tree shown in Figure 4-4 proves the originally given conclusion. The heavy solid lines represent the proof.

Comparison of Figure 4-1 with Figure 4-3 and Figure 4-2 with Figure 4-4 shows that the two representations are equivalent. The chess problem could just as well have been represented by an implicit, disjunctive-conjunctive goal tree. The geometry problem could be represented as an implicit, two-person, strictly competitive game tree. We shall see that an indefinite integration problem can also be represented in either way.

4.2 PURPOSES OF PROGRAMMING COMPUTERS TO SOLVE PROBLEMS IN CHESS, GEOMETRY, AND INDEFINITE INTEGRATION

As with most problems so far handled by heuristic programs, chess, geometry, and indefinite integration problems have the advantage of being simpler than and yet resembling important real problems. Section 1.6 discusses this point. In addition, the programmers wished to determine the

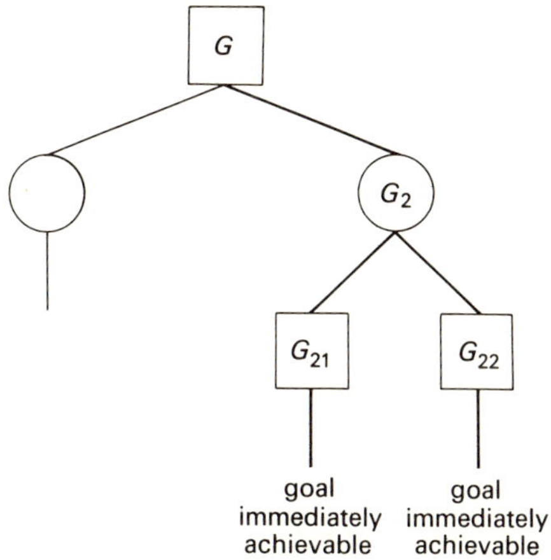

Figure 4-4 Explicit goal tree and proof. Heavy solid lines represent the proof.

level of difficulty of problems which their programs could solve on present-day computers. This determination is facilitated by the fact that many people are familiar with these kinds of problems. The person who is familiar with the particular problem domain can evaluate the solutions given by a program, and the performance of the program can be compared with that of humans. The researchers wanted to develop procedures, including tree search procedures, to handle a fairly general kind of problem, namely, those problems which can be represented by an implicit, two-person, strictly competitive game tree, or, equivalently, by an implicit, disjunctive-conjunctive goal tree. Developing procedures for a general rather than a specific kind of problem has two important advantages. It is a more efficient way to get the computer to solve several kinds of problems, and it is more likely to yield general insights into the problem-solving process.

As for purposes specific to each program, the geometry program studies the use of models, and the integration program is potentially useful in itself. The end of this chapter discusses performance and conclusions relevant to the specific purposes (for example, how the indefinite integration program was extended to a calculus program which handles definite and multiple integration). Since solving such integration problems is important in science and engineering, a descendant of the calculus program will have commercial applications. The geometry program uses a diagram as a model and rejects subgoals which do not conform to this model. This is very important, since humans use models to great advantage in successful problem solving.

4.3 GENERAL DESCRIPTION OF THE PROGRAMS

Goal-tree notation will be used throughout the description of the procedures used by the three programs to search the implicit trees described in Section 4.1. What is common among the three programs will be emphasized, since this is a beginning (well-grounded in computer experiments) of a general theory of how to solve problems. This problem-solving theory will become very important in the future. It will be used to improve the problem-solving abilities of both men and machines, and it will provide a standard of comparison against which specific problem-solving performances can be measured.

Executive Organization of the Programs The general procedure used by each of the three programs consists of the following steps, to be taken in order except where otherwise indicated. The subsections given after the procedure describe ideas needed for a more detailed understanding of the procedure. Before the procedure starts, it is given the original goal and the resource allotment. Within the allotted resources the procedure tries to decide the original goal, that is, achieve the goal or show that it cannot be achieved by transformations available to the procedure.

A. If the try for an immediate solution with the original goal succeeds, print the answer and stop.
B. If the resource allotment has been exceeded, print this fact and stop.
C. If no untried goals remain, print this fact and stop.
D. Select an untried goal from which to try to sprout (generate).
E. If no more goals can be sprouted from the selected goal, go to step B.
F. Sprout the next untried goal *G* from the selected goal.
G. If the try for an immediate solution with the newly sprouted goal *G* fails, go to step E. If the try succeeds, prune the goal tree with respect to *G*. The pruning will have one of the following three results:

1. If the original goal is decided, print the answer and stop.
2. If the original goal is not decided but if the selected goal is decided, go to step B.
3. If the selected goal is not decided, go to step E.

Goals How goals are generated, transformed into other goals, and decided is described later. Every goal in the geometry program consists of proving some proposition, given certain assumptions. Three typical kinds of propositions are that two angles are equal, that two sides are equal, and that two triangles are congruent. Each goal in the mate (chess) program consists of proving that, in a given chess position, one player, say white, can force a checkmate of the other. It need not be white's turn to move. Each goal in the indefinite integration program consists of performing some indefinite integration, for example,

$$\int \frac{x^4}{(1 - x^2)^{5/2}} \, dx$$

A Procedure That Tries for an Immediate Solution For any new goal G, the procedure uses its straightforward methods in an attempt to decide it. If G is decided, an attempt is made to decide the original goal.

In geometry, the try for an immediate solution with a goal consists of seeing whether the corresponding proposition is either given, obviously true, or obviously false. For example, a proposition which can be proved by "identity" or "vertical angles are equal" is obviously true. A proposition which does not conform to the diagram supplied with the original goal is obviously false.

In chess, the try for an immediate solution with a goal consists of looking for a checkmate or stalemate in the position corresponding to the goal. If white has checkmated black, that goal has been achieved. If a stalemate occurs or if black has checkmated white, that goal cannot be achieved.

In the indefinite integration program, the try for an immediate solution is more complicated than in the geometry or mate programs. The program uses a combination of *standard forms* and *immediate transformations*. Whenever an integrand of a newly generated goal is of standard form, that goal is immediately achieved by substitution. An integrand is said to be of standard form when it is a substitution instance of one of a certain set of forms. For example, $\int 2^x \, dx$ is an instance of $\int c^v \, dv = c^v/(\ln c)$ and hence has the solution $2^x/(\ln 2)$. The indefinite integration program used 26 standard forms. Whenever the procedure finds that an integrand is not of standard form, a test is made to see if an immediate transformation can be applied. By definition, an immediate transformation, when applicable, is always or almost always appropriate. For a goal, a transformation is called appropriate if it is the correct next step toward bringing that goal nearer to achievement. Three of the eight immediate transformations used in the indefinite integration program are the following:

A. Factor constant; that is,

$$\int cg(v) \, dv = c \int g(v) \, dv$$

B. Decompose; that is,

$$\int \sum g_i(v) \, dv = \sum \int g_i(v) \, dv$$

C. Use linear substitution; that is, if the integral is of the form

$$\int f(c_1 + c_2 v)\, dv$$

substitute $u = c_1 + c_2 v$ and obtain an integral of the form

$$\int \frac{1}{c_2} f(u)\, du$$

For example, in

$$\int \frac{\cos 3x}{(1 - \sin 3x)^2}\, dx$$

substitute $y = 3x$.

The Role of the Resource Allotment The resource allotment is a side condition of the original goal and is given as an input to the program. Before selecting an untried goal, it must be verified that the resource allotment has not been exceeded. If the resource allotment has been exceeded, the program reports this fact as its final answer. The resource allotment in the programs consists of time or total amount of work space. For hand simulation, the work space can be measured by the number of pages or lines used for final and all intermediate results.

Selection of the Untried Goal to Try to Sprout from Next In step D, the executive procedure selects an untried goal to try to sprout from next. Obviously, this is a crucial decision for the procedure. So far, researchers have had to settle for procedures with more or less obvious deficiencies because no one has succeeded in stating a precise and practical theory of how such selections should be made. It is very important to observe that the main deficiency of the selection procedures used in these three programs is that they do not properly take into account how relevant each untried goal is to the decision concerning the top goal. Although much more research needs to be done on selection procedures, some progress has been made by the author with his MULTIPLE program, described in Chapter 7. The geometry program selects the untried goal estimated to be "nearest to being decided." A goal is near to being decided to the extent that the corresponding proposition is simple and resembles the given hypotheses. The chess program selects an untried goal either because it is shallow on the goal tree or because black has very few moves (because he is in check or threatened with mate in one). The indefinite integration program selects the untried goal estimated to have the lowest relative cost. Although other estimates could and should be tried for the relative cost estimate of a goal, the program uses simply the depth of its integrand. The depth of an integrand is the maximum level of function composition which occurs in that expression: x is of depth 0; x^2 is of depth 1; e^{x^2} is of depth 2; xe^{x^2} is of depth 3. This makes use of the fact that, ordinarily, the deeper the integrand, the more will be the resources needed to investigate that goal.

Transformations A transformation transforms a goal into one of its subgoals (successors). In a disjunctive-conjunctive goal tree, a goal can be related to its subgoals either by disjunction or conjunction. In geometry, a transformation is represented by a theorem. For example, suppose the goal is to prove that two angles are equal. The theorem "Corresponding angles of congruent triangles are equal" transforms the goal into the subgoal of proving that certain triangles are congruent. Similarly, the theorem "Alternate interior angles of parallel lines are equal" transforms the goal into the subgoal of proving that the angles are alternate interior angles of parallel lines. The goal is related to these two subgoals by disjunction. In chess, a legal move transforms a goal into a subgoal. The 10 types of transformation used by the indefinite integration procedure are designed to generate plausible subgoals by substitution or by the method of integration by parts or by making a change in the form of the integrand. Below is given only the most successful type of transformation, "substitution for a subexpression whose derivative divides the integrand." Let $g(v)$ be the integrand. Let the main connective of some nonconstant nonlinear subexpression $s(v)$ be different from (unary) minus. Let $s(v)$ not be a product containing a constant factor. Let the number of nonconstant factors of $g(v)/s'(v)$ (after cancellation) be less than the number of factors of $g(v)$. For each such $s(v)$, try substituting $u = s(v)$. Thus in $\int x \sin x^2 \, dx$, substitute $u = x^2$.

Pruning of the Goal Tree Whenever some goal G has been decided, the goal tree is pruned; that is, certain closely related goals are automatically decided and certain other goals newly rendered superfluous are discarded. The pruning procedure will be clarified by an example. In Figure 4–5(a), the achieving of G_{221} allows G_{22} to be achieved (since, as indicated by the two $*$, G_{222} has already been achieved). In turn, the achieving of G_{22} allows G_2 to be achieved (since there is a disjunctive relationship). Since the achievement of G_2 has now rendered G_{23} superfluous, G_{23} is discarded. However, another of G_2's subgoals, G_{12}, is not discarded because it is still relevant to the achievement of the original goal G. The original goal G cannot be achieved from the achieving of G_2, since there is a conjunctive relationship and G_1 has not yet been achieved. Therefore, the result of the pruning process is as shown in Figure 4-5(b). If either G_{11} or G_{12} is later achieved, the original goal could and would be achieved.

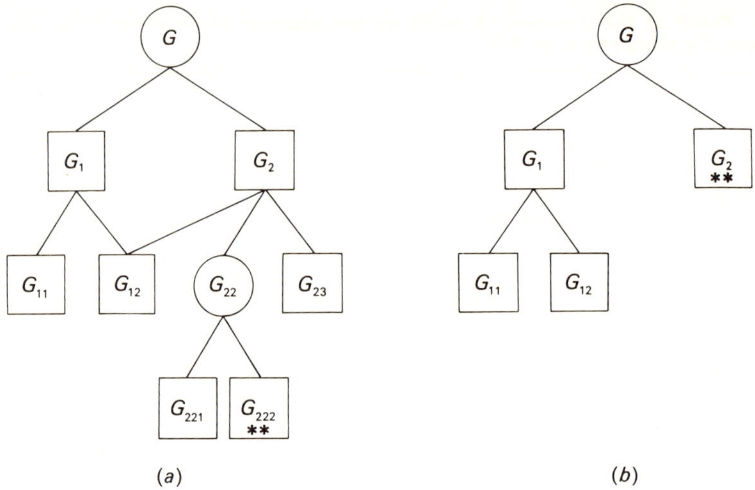

Figure 4-5 The pruning of the goal tree (*a*) after the achieving of the goal G_{221} results in the goal tree (*b*). Later, achieving of G_{11} or G_{12} would result in the achieving of the original goal G.

4.4 A PROGRAM THAT SOLVES PROBLEMS IN GEOMETRY

A program by Herbert Gelernter et al. (1959, 1960) proves geometry theorems at the level of a very good high school student. The program uses many of the methods and heuristics of students attacking the same theorems. As explained previously, the geometry program searches an implicit, disjunctive-conjunctive goal tree. Gelernter's specific purpose was to study the use of models. He expected that the use of models would greatly improve search programs, since it is a common observation that successful human problem solvers make extensive use of models. The geometry program uses a geometric diagram as a model and rejects goals which do not conform to this model.

In a typical example of the program's external behavior, the program reads some punched cards containing (in a suitable notation) the diagram shown in Figure 4-6 and the theorem "A point on the bisector of an angle is equally distant from the sides of the angle." After 5 sec the program prints out the proof shown in Table 4-1.

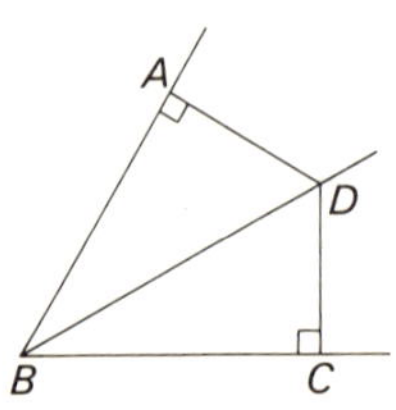

Figure 4-6

Table 4-1 Proof of the theorem "A point on the bisector of an angle is equally distant from the sides of the angle"

Premises
Angle *ABD* equals angle *DBC* Segment *AD* perpendicular segment *AB* Segment *DC* perpendicular segment *BC*
Definition
Right angle *DAB* Right angle *DCB*
Goals
Segment *AD* equals segment *CD*
Solution

Angle *ABD* equals angle *DBC*
  Premise
Right angle *DAB*
  Definition of perpendicular
Right angle *DCB*
  Definition of perpendicular
Angle *BAD* equals angle *BCD*
  All right angles are equal
Segment *DB*
  Assumption based on diagram
Segment *BD* equals segment *BD*
  Identity
Triangle *BCD*
  Assumption based on diagram
Triangle *BAD*
  Assumption based on diagram
Triangle *ADB* congruent triangle *CDB*
  Side-angle-angle
Segment *AD* equals segment *CD*
  Corresponding elements of congruent triangles are equal

As for the program's typical observed behavior, it is much more powerful when it uses a diagram than when it does not. The program is more powerful in the sense that it is much faster and consumes much less space in the computer's memory. Typically the program uses the diagram to reject all but a handful of the several thousand subgoals sprouted from a selected goal.

The program has proved over 50 theorems, including the following difficult one. "If the segment joining the midpoints of the diagonals of a trapezoid is extended to intersect a side of the trapezoid, it bisects that side."

Gelernter's work on his geometry program has led to several important specific conclusions. Section 4.7 gives general conclusions concerning such search procedures. A computer has been programmed to prove fairly difficult theorems in geometry, and the speed of the program compares very favorably with the speed of a good high school student. The program is much more powerful when it uses a model than when it does not; this suggests that other heuristic programs should also use models.

4.5 A PROGRAM THAT FINDS CHECKMATES

A program written by George Baylor and Herbert Simon (1966) solves chess problems at the level of a good player. The program uses many of the methods and heuristics of good players attacking the same problems. As explained previously, the mate program searches an implicit, disjunctive-conjunctive goal tree.

In a typical example, the program reads some cards containing the chess problem shown in Figure 4-7. The program prints out the following six-move mate:

	White	*Black*
1.	RxPch	K–N1
2.	R3xPch	K–R1
3.	RxNch	K–N1
4.	R–R8ch	KxR
5.	N–N6dblch	K–N1
6.	R–N7mate	

Some specific conclusions may be drawn from work on the mate program. A computer has been programmed to solve fairly difficult chess problems. To find a mate, the program often considers fewer than 20 variations, and

Figure 4-7 White to move and mate.

almost always fewer than 100. The speed of the program compares very favorably with the speed of good players. In short, Baylor and Simon have been fairly successful in developing a procedure for searching implicit trees in the specific case of chess problems. Section 4.7 gives some conclusions concerning search programs in a more general case.

4.6 A PROGRAM THAT SOLVES CALCULUS PROBLEMS

A program written by the author (1963) solves elementary symbolic integration problems at the level of a good college freshman. The program is called SAINT, an acronym for Symbolic Automatic INTegrator. SAINT uses many of the methods and heuristics of students attacking the same problems. The indefinite integration program includes, as a trivial part, a program that differentiates elementary expressions. As explained previously, the indefinite integration program searches an implicit, disjunctive-conjunctive goal tree. The general purposes of writing such search programs are discussed in Section 4.2. An additional purposes of the author was to determine if a practical calculus program could be written.

To illustrate SAINT'S external behavior, suppose that SAINT reads a card containing (in a suitable notation) the symbolic integration problem, $\int xe^{x^2}\,dx$. In less than $1\frac{1}{2}$ min, SAINT prints out the answer, $\frac{1}{2}\,e^{x^2}$. (Note that SAINT omits the constant of integration, and we too shall ignore it throughout this section.) After working for less than 1 min on the problem, $\int e^{x^2}\,dx$ (which cannot be integrated in elementary form), SAINT prints out that it cannot solve the problem.

As a concrete example, we sketch how SAINT solved

$$\int \frac{x^4}{(1-x^2)^{5/2}}\,dx$$

in 11 min. (SAINT'S average performance is better than the impression given by this example, in which the program has an unusually difficult time. The problem was chosen to illustrate the inner workings of the program.) SAINT'S only try at a first step is to try the substitution $y = \arcsin x$, which transforms the original problem into

$$\int \frac{\sin^4 y}{\cos^4 y}\,dy$$

For the second step, SAINT makes three alternative tries:

A. By trigonometric identities

$$\int \frac{\sin^4 y}{\cos^4 y}\,dy = \int \tan^4 y\,dy$$

B. By trigonometric identities.

$$\int \frac{\sin^4 y}{\cos^4 y}\, dy = \int \cot^{-4} y\, dy$$

C. By substituting $z = \tan(y/2)$

$$\int \frac{\sin^4 y}{\cos^4 y}\, dy = \int 32 \frac{z^4}{(1+z^2)(1-z^2)^4}\, dz$$

SAINT immediately brings the 32 to the left of the integral.

After estimating that A is the cheapest of these three problems to investigate, SAINT tries the substitution $z = \tan y$, which yields

$$\int \tan^4 y\, dy = \int \frac{z^4}{1+z^2}\, dz$$

SAINT immediately transforms this into

$$\int \left(-1 + z^2 + \frac{1}{1+z^2}\right) dz = \int -\,dz + \int z^2\, dz + \int \frac{dz}{1+z^2}$$

$$= -\,z + \frac{z^3}{3} + \int \frac{dz}{1+z^2}$$

Estimating incorrectly that B is cheaper than $\int dz/(1+z^2)$, SAINT temporarily abandons the latter and goes off on the following tangent. By substituting $z = \cot y$, we obtain

$$\int \cot^{-4} y\, dy = \int -\frac{dz}{z^4(1+z^2)} = -\int \frac{dz}{z^4(1+z^2)}$$

Now SAINT estimates that $\int dz/(1+z^2)$ is cheap and tries the substitution $w = \arctan z$, which yields $\int dw$. Immediately SAINT integrates this, substitutes back, and solves the original problem:

$$\int \frac{x^4}{(1-x^2)^{5/2}}\, dx = \arcsin x + \tfrac{1}{3}\tan^3 \arcsin x - \tan \arcsin x$$

SAINT can perform some definite integrations by first finding the corresponding indefinite integrals. Thus, for example, for the problem

$$\int_0^3 x\sqrt{x^2+16}\, dx$$

SAINT first finds the indefinite integral

$$\int x\sqrt{x^2+16}\, dx = \tfrac{1}{3}(x^2+16)^{3/2}$$

SAINT substitutes the limits and obtains the answer, $\frac{61}{3}$.

SAINT can perform multiple integration when it can perform the required definite integrations, for example,

$$\int_{-1}^{1} \int_{y^2}^{2-y^2} dx\, dy$$

Performance The experiments to measure SAINT'S behavior involved 86 problems. Designed largely for the purpose of debugging, 32 of the problems were selected or constructed by the author, who fully expected SAINT to solve them all. More objectively, the remaining 54 problems were selected by the author's assistant from M.I.T. freshman final examinations in calculus. He was instructed to select the more diverse and difficult problems, provided that the method of partial fractions was not needed for the solution. (In order to save computer memory space, this method was not put in the program.)

The SAINT program described previously selected untried goals in order of increasing depth (relative cost estimate). It tried to solve all 86 problems selected by the author and his assistant. As the author expected, SAINT solved all 32 of his problems. It took an average of 3.3 min per problem. Of the 54 M.I.T. problems, SAINT solved 52 and quickly (in less than 1 min each) reported failure on the other two. In order to save computer memory space, the two fairly specialized methods required to solve the problems on which the program failed were not put into the program. For the 52 successes, it took an average of 2 min. Some examples of SAINT'S extreme behavior are now given. For this purpose only M.I.T. problems are considered, since they were selected more objectively. SAINT seemed to find

$$\int_{1}^{2} \frac{dx}{x}$$

the easiest problem, since it generated no subgoals at all and took the least time, namely 0.03 min. SAINT took the most time, 18 min, for

$$\int \frac{\sec^2 t}{1 + \sec^2 t - 3 \tan t}\, dt$$

SAINT generated the most subgoals, 18, for

$$\int (\sin x + \cos x)^2\, dx$$

Instead of trying untried goals in order of increasing depth (relative cost estimate), breadth-first SAINT tries such goals merely in the order in which they were generated. Unmodified SAINT was faster than breadth-first SAINT in three of the four problems which caused a difference in behavior.

Conclusions Specific to the Integration Program A computer has been programmed to solve fairly difficult symbolic integration problems. The speed of the program compares favorably with the speed of a good college freshman. A compiled SAINT program would run about 20 times faster than the author's (interpreted) program. The program is more powerful when it selects untried goals in order of increasing depth (relative cost estimate) rather than in order of generation. SAINT'S performance showed that a practical calculus program could be written. A solution of an average M.I.T. final examination problem with a compiled but otherwise unimproved program on a new computer would cost a few cents and take a fraction of a second. SAINT could be made even more practical; for example, one could add both a program for numerical evaluation of definite integrals and more standard forms. One useful approach would be for an engineer or a scientist to use a mathematical manipulation system (including symbolic integration) via computer time sharing. In fact, as discussed in Chapter 6, Joel Moses has written a practical integration program which is included in such a system.

4.7 GENERAL CONCLUSIONS

Computers have been programmed to solve fairly difficult problems in chess, geometry, and integration. The speed of each program compares favorably with that of a good human problem solver. Procedures have been developed to handle a fairly general kind of problem, namely, many problems which can be represented by an implicit, two-person, strictly competitive game tree, or, equivalently, by an implicit, disjunctive-conjunctive goal tree. The procedures developed search the tree by using transformations and by trying for immediate solutions. What is common among the three programs represents a beginning of a general theory of how to solve problems. An important unsolved research problem is to develop general procedures for making good decisions about where to sprout next on the tree. As described in Chapter 7, the author has made some progress on this problem. Other research should be directed toward extending the successes in chess, geometry, and integration to the solution of important real problems that are similar but more difficult.

EXERCISES

1. Which of the following untried goals would the indefinite integration program select first? Why?

a. $\int \sin x^2\, dx$.

b. $\int x \cos x^2\, dx$.

2. Integrate:

a. $$\int \frac{\sec^2 t}{1 + \sec^2 t - 3 \tan t} \, dt.$$

Compare your time with the 18 min taken by SAINT.

b. $\int \cos x \sec^2 \sin x \, dx.$

3. Consider the following game. The two players are square and circle. The initial position has five stones. Square moves first, then circle, then square, etc. Each move consists of removing one or two stones. The player to remove the last stone wins. Draw with light broken lines the complete game tree.

4. Is it true or false that in Exercise 3, the first player (square) can force a win?

5. In heavy solid lines, draw a proof of your answer to Exercise 4. Try to make your proof as small as possible. You should draw your heavy solid lines right over your light broken lines in your answer to Exercise 3.

6. Assuming that the goal A in the following disjunctive-conjunctive goal tree (Figure 4-8) is achieved, draw the tree that results after pruning.

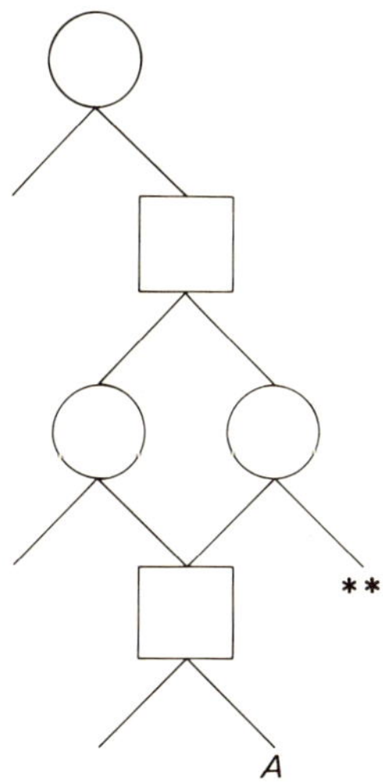

Figure 4-8

BIBLIOGRAPHY

Baylor, George, and Herbert A. Simon: A Chess Mating Combinations Program, *Proc. AFIPS Annu. Spring Joint Computer Conf.*, 1966, pp. 431–447.

Feigenbaum, Edward, and Julian Feldman (eds.): "Computers and Thought," McGraw-Hill Book Company, New York, 1963. Contains the following articles:

a. Gelernter, Herbert: Realization of a Geometry Theorem Proving Machine. Reprinted from *Proc. Intern. Conf. Information Processing*, 1959.

b. Gelernter, H., J. R. Hansen, and D. W. Loveland: Empirical Explorations of the Geometry Theorem Machine. Reprinted from *Proc. Western Joint Computer Conf.*, 1960, pp. 143–147.

c. Slagle, James R.: A Heuristic Program That Solves Symbolic Integration Problems in Freshman Calculus. Reprinted from *J. ACM*, vol. 10, pp. 507–520, 1963.

5
Automatic Theorem Proving Using the Resolution Principle

The two approaches to automatic theorem proving are proof finding and consequence finding. A proof-finding program, such as the one written by Dr. Lawrence Wos et al. (1964), attempts to find a proof for a certain given theorem. A consequence-finding program, such as that written by Richard Char-tung Lee (1967), is given some axioms and then tries to deduce consequences from the axioms and to select "interesting" consequences. Both programs use the resolution principle, which is a natural and powerful rule of inference that will be explained later.

Some of the purposes of programming a computer to prove theorems concern Artificial Intelligence and deduction. Artificial Intelligence researchers point out that proving a nontrivial theorem is an intellectually difficult problem. The theorem-proving programs we shall study in this chapter use mathematical logic or, to be specific, first-order predicate calculus. In mathematical logic, one can express fairly conveniently almost all kinds of deductive arguments. Writing a theorem-proving program which uses mathematical logic allows the researcher to study deduction in its purest form. Deduction is important because it plays a major role in solving many kinds of problems (not just in mathematics). A program which can prove some theorems has what Prof. John McCarthy (1959) has called common sense, that is, the ability to make deductions from given facts. This kind of common sense is an important part of human intelligence. As we shall see in Chapter 10, a program that uses mathematical logic to find proofs can be extended to deduce answers to questions.

The other purposes of programming a computer to prove theorems concern mathematics and mathematical logic. Mathematicians point out that a program of the future which proves new and interesting theorems would be useful in itself. It would be a tremendous achievement if some program of the future proved or disproved the famous Fermat or Goldbach conjecture. Mathematical logic is well suited to computers, since logicians have striven for decades to make their rules of inference "mechanical." It is an attractive idea to write a program based on mathematical logic, since this is a well-formulated and well-studied branch of mathematics. In addition, programming a computer to prove theorems is a way to study mathematical logic. For example, the programmer may develop powerful, natural, intuitive inference rules to which heuristics can be added easily.

P. C. Gilmore (1960), H. Wang (1965), as well as M. Davis and H. Putnam (1960), are among those who programmed a computer to find proofs in first-order predicate calculus (also called *quantification theory*). (Roughly speaking, each of their programs substituted many constant terms for the variables and then checked to see if the theorem had been proved. If not, more constant terms were added and another check was made, etc.) After these programs had been written, J. A. Robinson (1965) developed an inference rule which he calls the *resolution principle*. Roughly speaking, the resolution principle draws the most general possible conclusion from two given statements; the conclusion and the two statements generally contain variables. The resolution principle is more natural, more intuitive, and easier for people to use than are the inference rules used by the previous programs. Furthermore, it is easier to think of heuristics to add to the resolution principle. Wos et al. then wrote a proof-finding program embodying the resolution principle. This program is more powerful than the preresolution programs. Lee then wrote a consequence-finding program based on the resolution principle. Later sections of this chapter describe the resolution principle, the proof-finding program of Wos et al., the consequence-finding program of Lee, and some conclusions.

5.1 THE RESOLUTION PRINCIPLE

The resolution principle is a rule of inference. Before defining it precisely, three examples are given illustrating various aspects of the rule. This section concludes with a discussion of the fact that the resolution principle is effective, sound, and complete.

Example 1 Suppose that we want to find a proof of the following theorem by use of the resolution principle. Note that the statements are understood to hold for all values of their variables; for example, the statement P1 holds for all x, for all v, and for all y. This is the same sense in which the identity $x^2 - y^2 = (x + y)(x - y)$ holds for all x and for all y. (The reader who is familiar with mathematical logic will have an advantage in reading this chapter. See, for example, the excellent logic book by Stephen Kleene, 1967.)

THEOREM 1 *Suppose*

P1 *If* x *is part of* v, *and if* v *is part of* y, *then* x *is part of* y.

P2 *A finger is part of a hand.*

P3 *A hand is part of an arm.*

P4 *An arm is part of a man.*

From P1 through P4, we may conclude that a finger is part of a man.

Proof of Theorem 1 A procedure which tries to find proofs using the resolution principle first takes the denial of the conclusion and then tries to deduce a contradiction. In this example, this denial is the following:

P5 A finger is not part of a man.

A resolvent of P1 and P2 is:

P6 If a hand is part of y, then a finger is part of y.

P6 is a consequence of P1 and P2. The term *resolvent* is defined by example now and more precisely later. P6 is obtained by first "matching" (making identical) the clause P2 and the first portion of clause P1 by letting x be finger and by letting v be hand. This substitution in P1 gives the following intermediate result, which is a logical consequence of P1.

P1′ If a finger is part of a hand and a hand is part of y, then a finger is part of y.

This is indeed a logical consequence of P1, since P1 is asserted to be true for all x and for all v (and for all y) and therefore must be true in the special case when x is finger and v is hand. The clause P6 is an immediate consequence of P1′ and P2. Usually the resolvent P6 would be given directly without expressing the intermediate result P1′.

Each of the three portions of the clause P1 is called an *atom*. For example, the second atom in P1 is "v is part of y." Each of the clauses P2, P3, and P4 consist of one atom. Clause P6 consists of two atoms.

Returning to the proof, we match the clause P3 and the first atom in P6 by letting *y* be arm. This yields the intermediate result

P6′ If a hand is part of an arm, then a finger is part of an arm.

This, together with P3, yields the resolvent

P7 A finger is part of an arm.

Similarly, the resolvent obtained by matching P7 and the first atom of P1 is

P8 If an arm is part of *y*, then a finger is part of *y*.

The resolvent of P4 and the first atom of P8 is

P9 A finger is part of a man.

Matching this with P5 gives a contradiction, which completes the proof of Theorem 1.

This proof is outlined in the first and second columns of Table 5-1. In this table, the corresponding proof in symbols is self-explanatory, except for the following. The expression *r*[P3,P6a] denotes the resolvent obtained by matching the clause P3 and the first atom in clause P6. The symbol & means "and." The symbol → means "if . . . then . . ." or "implies." The symbol – means "not."

Table 5-1 Proof of Theorem 1

Clause name	*Proof in words*	*Proof in symbols*	
		Clause	*Reason*
P1	If *x* is part of *v* and if *v* is part of *y*, then *x* is part of *y*.	Part (*x*,*v*) & Part (*v*,*y*)→ Part (*x*,*y*)	Given
P2	A finger is part of a hand.	Part (finger, hand)	Given
P3	A hand is part of an arm.	Part (hand, arm)	Given
P4	An arm is part of a man.	Part (arm, man)	Given
P5	A finger is not part of a man.	–Part (finger, man)	Denial of conclusion
P6	If a hand is part of *y*, then a finger is part of *y*.	Part (hand, *y*)→ Part (finger, *y*)	*r*[P1a,P2]
P7	A finger is part of an arm.	Part (finger, arm)	*r*[P3,P6a]
P8	If an arm is part of *y*, then a finger is part of *y*.	Part (arm, *y*)→ Part (finger, *y*)	*r*[P1a,P7]
P9	A finger is part of a man.	Part (finger, man)	*r*[P4,P8a]
P10	Contradiction.	Contradiction	*r*[P5,P9]

Example 2 The resolution principle consists of only factoring and resolution. This example illustrates factoring, disjunctive notation, and how theorems are formulated for the resolution principle. The reader unfamiliar with abstract algebra should still read this section to get these key ideas about the resolution principle.

THEOREM 2 *In any associative system which has left and right solutions* s *and* t *for all equations* s·x = y *and* x·t = y, *there is a right identity element.*

Proof Below are given some notes on the formulation of the first four clauses given in Table 5-2.

Table 5-2 Proof of Theorem 2

Clause name	*Clause*	*Reason*
A1	$g(x,y)\cdot x = y$	Given (existence of a left solution)
A2	$x \cdot h(x,y) = y$	Given (existence of a right solution)
A3	$(x\cdot y = u)$ & $(y\cdot z = v)$ & $(x\cdot v = w) \rightarrow (u\cdot z = w)$	Given (part of associativity)
A4	$k(x)\cdot x \neq k(x)$	Denial of conclusion
A5	$(x\cdot y = u)$ & $(y\cdot z = y) \rightarrow (u\cdot z = u)$	f[A3,a,c]
A6	$(y\cdot z = y) \rightarrow (u\cdot z = u)$	r[A1,A5a]
A7	$y\cdot z \neq y$	r[A4,A6b]
A8	Contradiction	r[A2,A7]

A1 Existence of a left solution. This means that for all x and for all y there is an s such that $s\cdot x = y$. In other words, there exists a function $g(x,y) = s$ such that $g(x,y)\cdot x = y$.

A2 Existence of a right solution. This means for all x and for all y there exists t such that $x\cdot t = y$. In other words, there is a function $h(x,y) = t$ such that $x\cdot h(x,y) = y$.

A3 Associativity. This means $(x\cdot y)\cdot z = x\cdot(y\cdot z)$. Actually we need and use only the following:

$$(x\cdot y = u) \;\&\; (y\cdot z = v) \;\&\; (x\cdot v = w) \;\rightarrow\; (u\cdot z = w)$$

A4 Denial of conclusion. There is no right identity element. For any proposed right identity element x there exists u such that $u\cdot x \neq u$. In other words, there exists a function $k(x) = u$ such that $k(x)\cdot x \neq k(x)$.

In the proof given in Table 5-2, clause A5 is obtained from clause A3 by "factoring" A3 with respect to its first and third atoms. The clause A3 implies its special case A5, and A5 is called a factor of A3. This factor is obtained by matching (making identical) the first atom, $x \cdot y = u$, and the third atom, $x \cdot v = w$, of A3. This is done by substituting y for v and u for w throughout A3 and canceling the third atom, which has become identical (and therefore redundant) to the first. In general, factoring a clause with respect to two or more of its atoms is performed as follows:

A. Find the minimal substitution (if any) which makes the atoms identical. (What it means for a substitution to be minimal is described later.)

B. Make the substitutions throughout the clause and cancel all but one of the redundant atoms.

Example 2 is also used to illustrate implication and disjunction. Representing $x \cdot y = z$ by $P(x,y,z)$ transforms the mathematical notation of Table 5-2 into the (implication) symbolic logic notation of Table 5-3. In Table 5-3, the "disjunctive notation" is logically equivalent to the implication notation and is the computer formalism recommended by J. A. Robinson and used in the programs of L. Wos et al. and R. Lee. The symbol $\vee$ means *disjunction* (the *inclusive or*).

To illustrate minimal substitution, let us try to factor the following clause with respect to its first two atoms:

$$P(f(w),w) \vee P(y,g(x)) \vee P(w,f(y))$$

We simply try to match the two atoms from left to right. The first required substitution is $f(w)$ for y. [Of course, it would not be valid to substitute y for $f(w)$.] Substituting $f(w)$ for y throughout the clause yields $P(f(w),w) \vee P(f(w),g(x)) \vee P(w,f(f(w)))$. The next required substitution is $g(x)$ for w. [The nonminimal substitution of $h(z)$ for x and $g(h(z))$ for w also leads to a match, but the "factor" thus obtained would be a special case of and therefore

Table 5-3 Symbolic logic (predicate calculus) proofs of Theorem 2

Clause name	*Implication notation*	*Disjunctive notation*	*Reason*
A1	$P(g(x,y),x,y)$	$P(g(x,y),x,y)$	Given (existence of a left solution)
A2	$P(x,h(x,y),y)$	$P(x,h(x,y),y)$	Given (existence of a right solution)
A3	$P(x,y,u)$ & $P(y,z,v)$ & $P(x,v,w) \rightarrow P(u,z,w)$	$-P(x,y,u) \vee -P(y,z,v) \vee -P(x,v,w) \vee P(u,z,w)$	Given (part of associativity)
A4	$-P(k(x),x,k(x))$	$-P(k(x),x,k(x))$	Denial of conclusion
A5	$P(x,y,u)$ & $P(y,z,y) \rightarrow P(u,z,u)$	$-P(x,y,u) \vee -P(y,z,y) \vee P(u,z,u)$	f[A3,a,c]
A6	$P(y,z,y) \rightarrow P(u,z,u)$	$-P(y,z,y) \vee P(u,z,u)$	r[A1,A5a]
A7	$-P(y,z,y)$	$-P(y,z,y)$	r[A4,A6b]
A8	Contradiction	Contradiction	r[A2,A7]

worse than the factor we shall obtain.] Substituting $g(x)$ for w yields $P(f(g(x)), g(x)) \vee P(f(g(x)),g(x)) \vee P(g(x),f(f(g(x))))$. Thus the substitution of $g(x)$ for w and $f(g(x))$ for y in the original clause is minimal. The factor, obtained by deleting one of the two redundant atoms, is $P(f(g(x)),g(x)) \vee P(g(x),f(f(g(x))))$. If the nonminimal substitution mentioned above were used, the "factor" would be as above, except that $h(z)$ would be substituted for x throughout the factor. It happens that there are no other factors of the original clause, since the third atom cannot be matched with the first or second atoms.

Example 3 Example 3, given in Table 5-4, illustrates the minimal-substitution aspect of resolution. The list of arguments of B1 and the list of arguments of B2 can be made to match by making minimal substitutions. Each list of arguments becomes: $s,g(s),m(g(s)),h(s,m(g(s))),n(g(s),h(s,m(g(s)))), k(s,m(g(s)),n(g(s),h(s,m(g(s)))))$. The resolution procedure, first described in a paper by J. A. Robinson (1965), produces the proof in one simple calculation which takes a few minutes by hand. A procedure he gave in an earlier paper would have made 10^{256} substitutions before encountering the contradiction.

Precise Definition of the Resolution Principle The resolution principle, that is, resolution and factoring, is now defined more precisely. The definition is given in terms of disjunctive notation. Roughly speaking, the resolution principle combines the following two ideas:

1. *The syllogism principle of propositional calculus.* This principle states that from $a \vee b$ and $-a \vee c$ one may infer $b \vee c$.
2. *The instantiation principle of predicate calculus.* This principle states that from the formula $F(v_1, v_2, \ldots, v_n)$ (which is understood to hold for all values of its variables $v_1, v_2, \ldots, v_n$) one may infer the formula $F(t_1, t_2, \ldots, t_n)$ obtained by substituting the "terms" $t_1, t_2, \ldots, t_n$ for the variables $v_1, v_2, \ldots, v_n$, respectively. By definition, a term is either:

1. An individual constant, for example, finger.
2. An individual variable, for example, x.
3. A function of the other terms, for example, $g(x,y)$ and $h(s,m(g(s)))$.

Table 5-4 Illustration of the minimal-substitution aspect of resolution

Clause name	*Clause*	*Reason*
B1	$P(s,g(s),t,h(s,t),u,k(s,t,u))$	Given
B2	$-P(v,w,m(w),x,n(w,x),y)$	Denial of conclusion
B3	Contradiction	r[B1,B2]

We shall explain *general resolution* (part of the resolution principle). A (disjunctive) clause consists of the disjunction of literals. By definition, a literal is an atom or the negation (denial) of an atom. The resolvent, if any, of a literal in one clause and a literal in another clause is implied by the two clauses taken together. The resolvent is obtained as follows:

A. Rename variables so that all the individual variables in one clause are distinct from all the individual variables in the other clause.
B. Find the minimal substitution, if any, which makes the literals identical, but opposite in "sign."
C. Make the substitution *throughout* both clauses.
D. If exactly the same literal occurs more than once in a clause after the substitution, cancel all but one copy of that literal in that clause.
E. Delete the two literals which were made identical but opposite in sign.
F. The resolvent is the disjunction of the literals remaining in the first clause and the literals remaining in the second clause.

General factoring (part of the resolution principle) is now explained. The factor, if any, of two or more literals in a clause is implied by that clause. The factor is obtained as follows:

A. Find the minimal substitution, if any, which makes the literals identical (and the same in sign).
B. Make the substitution *throughout* the clause.
C. Cancel all but one copy of the literals which were made identical by the substitution.
D. The factor is the disjunction of the remaining literals.

The Resolution Principle Is Effective, Sound, and Complete J. A. Robinson (1965) was the first to prove that the resolution principle is effective and sound, and, for proof finding, is complete. R. Lee (1967) was the first to prove that resolution is complete for consequence finding. That the resolution principle is effective means that one can write a computer program, which, in a finite number of steps, will find the factors of any clause and the resolvents of any two clauses. That such a program can be written should be plausible to any computer programmer. Indeed, Wos et al., Lee, and others have written and run such programs. That the resolution principle is sound means that a clause logically implies each of its factors and that two clauses, taken together, logically imply each of their resolvents. That the resolution principle is sound should be plausible to the careful reader.

The resolution principle is complete for proof finding and consequence finding. Remember that a procedure which uses the resolution principle for proof finding tries to show that the negation of the given theorem to be proved is unsatisfiable (contradictory, inconsistent). The resolution principle is complete for proof finding in the sense of the following theorem, first proved by J. A. Robinson: *If a finite set of clauses is unsatisfiable, then a contradiction can be found in a finite number of applications of the resolution principle.* The resolution principle is complete for consequence finding in the sense of the following theorem, first proved by R. Lee.

THEOREM *If a clause* C *is a consequence of a finite nonempty set of clauses, then a clause* T *can be found in a finite number of applications of the resolution principle such that* C *is an immediate consequence of* T *alone.*

Several researchers have strengthened these theorems by showing that certain restricted forms of the resolution principle are still complete. This is of practical importance to automatic theorem proving because theoretical considerations and computer experiments indicate that restricted and complete resolution tends to be more efficient than is unrestricted resolution. Some of these restricted yet complete forms of the resolution principle are *set-of-support resolution* (Wos et al.), *hyper-resolution* (Robinson), and *semantic resolution* (Slagle, 1967). Roughly speaking, set-of-support resolution corresponds to working backward from the conclusion toward the hypotheses of the theorem to be proved. Semantic resolution generalizes set-of-support resolution, hyper-resolution, and the way that the geometry program of H. Gelernter et al. discards propositions which are false on the given geometric diagram (model). Except for unit resolution, described in the next paragraph, further theoretical discussion of the various restricted forms of the resolution principle is beyond the scope of this book.

Unit Resolution Unit resolution is a restricted form of resolution. It is of great practical importance and is present in most recent theorem-proving programs. A unit is defined as a clause consisting of one literal. Suppose one resolves a unit clause U_1 with the first literal in a clause, and then resolves a unit U_2 with the descendant of the second literal in the clause. It has been proved (Slagle, 1967) that one will obtain the same resolvent if instead one first resolves U_2 with the second literal in the clause and then U_1 with the descendant of the first literal in the clause. Hence, in this case, unit resolution restricts resolution to only one of the two possible orders in which the resolvent could be obtained.

In general, if there are q units to be resolved with a clause, unit resolution restricts resolution to one of the $q!$ possible orders in which the resolvent could be obtained. Unit resolution is a special case of semantic resolution, which under certain conditions restricts to one of $q!$ possible orders even when the U's are not necessarily units.

5.2 STRATEGIES FOR THEOREM PROVING WITH THE RESOLUTION PRINCIPLE

A strategy for theorem proving with the resolution principle is a heuristic, analogous to a generation procedure for game trees. In fact, there is a breadth-first strategy analogous to a breadth-first generation procedure. A proof-finding or a consequence-finding program based on the resolution principle must have a strategy (rule) for choosing what to do next, namely, whether to factor or resolve which clauses and which literals. Below are described three strategies—breadth-first, unit-preference, and set-of-support. The set-of-support strategy is applicable only to proof finding, whereas the other two strategies could be applied to both kinds of theorem proving. In proof finding, a strategy terminates if a contradiction is found or if other termination criteria are met.

The breadth-first strategy is described for three reasons. It is simple to understand; it is the basic strategy used in Lee's consequence-finding program; and it was used by Robinson for theoretical purposes, for example, in his proof of the completeness of the resolution principle for proof finding. The strategy begins by generating all the factors of the originally given clauses. The originally given clauses and their factors are defined to have level 0. From these level-0 clauses, the strategy generates level 1 by obtaining resolvents and the factors of these new resolvents. From previous (level-0 and level-1) clauses, the strategy generates level 2 by obtaining resolvents and the factors of these new resolvents. The strategy then generates level 3, etc.

The unit-preference strategy (Wos et al., 1964) tries to deduce clauses with as few literals as possible. One advantage of this strategy is that short clauses are easier to work with than are long ones. The main point of this strategy for proof finding is that the contradictory clause, which the program is trying to derive, can be considered as a clause consisting of no literals. Although this strategy has not been implemented for consequence finding, it would probably be useful for this purpose, since interesting consequences tend to be short. By definition, a j-clause is a clause consisting of j literals. Thus a unit is a 1-clause. The unit-preference strategy, as the name implies, gives top priority to a resolution involving a unit. In addition, this strategy gives second priority to resolving clauses whose resolvent has the fewest expected number of literals. The expected number of literals for an h-clause and a j-clause is $h + j - 2$, since at least two literals cancel during resolution. Thus, for example, the strategy prefers in order a unit versus a unit to a unit versus a 3-clause to a unit versus a 6-clause to a 2-clause versus a 2-clause to a 3-clause versus a 4-clause to a 2-clause versus a 6-clause, etc.

The unit-preference strategy starts by trying to resolve a unit with a unit. For example, in Table 5-5, a proof-finding procedure using the unit-preference strategy tries but fails to match P2 and P3. It continues trying to match the

Table 5-5 Unit-preference strategy

Clause name	*Clause*	*Reason*
P1	–Part (x,v) ∨ –part (v,y) ∨ part(x,y)	Given
P2	Part (finger, hand)	Given
P3	Part (hand, arm)	Given
P4	Part (arm, man)	Given
P5	–Part (finger, man)	Denial of conclusion
P6	–Part (hand, y) ∨ part (finger, y)	r[P2,P1a]
P7	Part (finger, arm)	r[P3,P6a]
P8	–Part (hand, man)	r[P5,P6b]
P9	–Part (x, finger) ∨ part (x, hand)	r[P2,P1b]
P10	–Part (arm, y) ∨ part (hand, y)	r[P3,P1a]
P11	Part (hand, man)	r[P4,P10a]
P12	Contradiction	r[P8,P11]

four units P2 through P5 by pairs but has no success. It next tries to match a unit with a 2-clause, but there are no 2-clauses. It next tries to match the unit P2 with the first literal of the 3-clause P1. This succeeds and yields the 2-clause P6. The strategy next tries to match the units with this new 2-clause rather than continuing with the 3-clause. The resolvent of P3 and the first literal of P6 is the unit P7. The attempt to match the other units with P7 fails. Therefore, the strategy resumes trying to match the units with the 2-clause P6 and obtains P8. The attempt to match the other units with P8 fails. Therefore, the strategy resumes trying to match the units with the 2-clause P6 but no further matches are obtained. Therefore, it resumes trying to match the units with the 3-clause P1 and obtains the 2-clause P9. The strategy next tries to match the units with the new 2-clause P9 rather than continuing with the 3-clause. No such matches exist, and so the strategy resumes trying to match units with the 3-clause P1. This yields the 2-clause P10. As usual, the strategy next tries to match the units with this new 2-clause P10 rather than continuing with the 3-clause. This yields the unit P11. Next, the strategy tries to match the other units with this new unit P11 rather than continuing with the 2-clause P10. This yields the contradiction P12, which completes the proof. The computer would print out Table 5-5 but would omit the irrelevant clauses P7 and P9.

The set-of-support strategy is used by the proof-finding program of Wos et al. but is not applicable to consequence finding. The experimenter labels certain clauses as "axioms" and all others as members of the set-of-support. The program never resolves two axioms (or their factors). All other resolutions are allowed. Wos et al. have shown experimentally that a strategy which combines the set-of-support strategy and the unit-preference

Table 5-6 A set-of-support strategy (let P5 be the only clause in the set-of-support)

Clause name	*Clause*	*Reason*
P1	–Part (x,v) ∨ –part (v,y) ∨ part (x,y)	Given
P2	Part (finger, hand)	Given
P3	Part (hand, arm)	Given
P4	Part (arm, man)	Given
P5	–Part (finger, man)	Denial of conclusion
P6	–Part (finger, v) ∨ –part (v, man)	r[P1c,P5]
P7	–Part (hand, man)	r[P2,P6a]
P8	–Part (finger, arm)	r[P4,P6b]
P9	–Part (hand, v) ∨ –part (v, man)	r[P1c,P7]
P10	–Part (arm, man)	r[P3,P9a]
P11	Contradiction	r[P4,P10]

strategy is often much more efficient than the unit-preference strategy alone. It has been proved (Slagle, 1967) (previously Wos et al. proved a slightly weaker theorem) that the set-of-support strategy is complete in the following sense. If the axioms are satisfiable (consistent), then a contradiction (assumed to be present) can be found in a finite number of steps without ever resolving two axioms (or their factors). In Table 5-6, P5 is the only clause in the set-of-support. The set-of-support strategy would not try to match any pair from the axioms P1 through P4.

5.3 A PROGRAM THAT USES THE RESOLUTION PRINCIPLE TO FIND PROOFS

Wos et al. (1964) wrote a proof-finding program embodying the resolution principle. Actually, they wrote several programs, but we shall describe only one. The program was obtained by starting with a breadth-first procedure and then introducing in turn the unit-preference strategy, the set-of-support strategy, and unit resolution. The performance of the program improved greatly as each of these changes was made. For one theorem, the breadth-first strategy took over 30 min, whereas the unit-preference strategy took less than 1 sec. As for computer time and memory requirements, the program is vastly more efficient than are the preresolution programs which find proofs in predicate calculus. The program has found proofs for theorems which are considerably more difficult than the three examples given in this chapter. It has found proofs of theorems in geometry and number theory. Mostly, however, it has found proofs for the first theorems in group theory in abstract algebra. Perhaps some successor of this program will find proofs of theorems which people have not proved.

5.4 A PROGRAM THAT USES THE RESOLUTION PRINCIPLE TO FIND CONSEQUENCES

A program written by Richard Lee (1967) uses the resolution principle to find consequences derivable from given axioms. We shall describe the best of several versions of his program. As a concrete example (discussed in more detail later in this section), suppose that the program is given as axioms the first four clauses in Table 5-7. These clauses axiomatize an associative system with a left identity and a left inverse. Almost immediately, the program starts typing consequences (conclusions) which can be derived from these axioms. The first consequences are obvious, but then the consequences become more and more difficult. The clauses actually typed by the program include clauses C5 through C13 in Table 5-7. These include the interesting consequence that the left inverse is also a right inverse (clause C10) and that the left identity is also a right identity (clause C13).

A few details about the program are now given. It uses a breadth-first strategy and unit resolution. A resolution is not attempted if the expected number of literals in the resolvent is more than some parameter n, say four. For example, a clause consisting of four literals would not be resolved with a clause consisting of three literals since the expected number of literals is $4 + 3 - 2 = 5$. The program also uses what Lee calls the axiom-resolution strategy. In this strategy, at least one of the two clauses being resolved must be an axiom. In other words, two consequences are never resolved. However, the program adds "interesting" consequences to the axioms, so that an interesting consequence will be resolved with other consequences. Lee has

Table 5-7 The consequence-finding program finds the target consequence[1]

Clause name	*Clause*	*Reason*
C1	$-P(x,y,u) \vee -P(y,z,v) \vee -P(x,v,w) \vee P(u,z,w)$	Associativity
C2	$-P(x,y,u) \vee -P(y,z,v) \vee -P(u,z,w) \vee P(x,v,w)$	Associativity
C3	$P(e,x,x)$	Left identity
C4	$P(i(x),x,e)$	Left inverse
C5	$-P(x,e,u) \vee -P(x,z,w) \vee P(u,z,w)$	r[C1b,C3]
C6	$-P(i(x),e,u) \vee P(u,x,e)$	r[C4,C5b]
C7	$-P(i(x),y,u) \vee -P(y,z,e) \vee -P(u,z,w) \vee P(w,x,e)$	r[C2d,C6a]
C8	$-P(x,z,e) \vee -P(e,z,w) \vee P(w,x,e)$	r[C4,C7a]
C9	$-P(x,z,e) \vee P(z,x,e)$	r[C3,C8b]
C10	$P(x,i(x),e)$	r[C4,C9a]
C11	$-P(i(x),z,v) \vee -P(e,z,w) \vee P(x,v,w)$	r[C2a,C10]
C12	$-P(e,x,w) \vee P(x,e,w)$	r[C4,C11a]
C13	$P(x,e,x)$	r[C3,C12a]

[1] Only the clauses relevant to the target consequence are presented.

given his program a criterion for "interest" of a consequence. Roughly speaking, a clause is considered interesting if, after possibly being simplified, it is not a trivial consequence of some axiom or previous interesting consequence. His criterion will not be described further, since it is rather detailed and specialized. The problem of defining the *interest* of a consequence is of central importance in consequence finding, and much more research should be devoted to this problem. A consequence generated by the program is discarded if it is a unit clause which is a trivial consequence of some axiom or previous interesting consequence. For example, the newly generated consequence $P(e,e,e)$ would be discarded if some axiom or previous interesting consequence was $P(e,x,x)$, where x is a variable and e is a constant.

The program was tested on 45 theorems taken from a book by W. Lederman (1964). For each "book theorem," Lee gave his program the axioms and hypotheses of that theorem, and the program tried to obtain the theorem's conclusion as a consequence. Note that this differs from generating the book theorem from the axioms alone. The program generated the target consequences in 41 of the 45 theorems. For each of the 41 theorems, it decided that the clause representing the conclusion was interesting. The main reason for the failures seems to be too many input clauses, as evidenced by the fact that each of the four failures required more than 14 axioms and hypotheses.

As an example of how the program works, suppose that the theorem under consideration is the following. *In an associative system with a left identity and a left inverse, the left identity is also a right identity.* The experimenter gives the program the first four clauses in Table 5-7. The target consequence is $P(x,e,x)$ (clause C13 in Table 5-7). Only the clauses relevant to the target consequence are presented in Table 5-7. The program first checks clause C1 and clause C2. Since it expects that the resolvent will have six literals, it ignores the clauses, since the upper-bound parameter is 4. There are three resolvents from clause C1 and clause C3, but only the one which deletes the second literal of clause C1 is relevant to the generation of the target consequence. The program generates many other clauses at this level by, say, resolving C1 and C4; C2 and C3; etc. However, according to the axiom-resolution strategy, the program does not resolve the generated clauses with one another. It will resolve C5 with an axiom. As before, C5 will not be resolved with C1 or C2 because of the bound put on the number of literals that the resolvent should contain. It will be resolved with both C3 and C4. Later, C6 can be used to resolve with C4, and the resolvent is $P(e,e,e)$. Since this is a unit, its triviality is checked. It is found to be a trivial consequence of clause C3 and is deleted from the memory. The program considers C9 to be the first interesting consequence and adds it to the axioms. Then the program generates C10 and judges it to be interesting too. Still later, the program generates C13 and decides that it is interesting. This is the target consequence.

Several conclusions may be drawn from Lee's work. A program has been written to find consequences derivable from given axioms. The program exhibits a form of what Prof. John McCarthy calls common sense; that is, the program can find simple logical consequences of what it is told. This kind of common sense is an important part of human intelligence. A better search strategy than a breadth-first, axiom-resolution strategy should be used. It helps a great deal to use the unit-resolution strategy. It also helps to discard a newly generated consequence if it is a unit clause which is a trivial consequence of some axiom or previous interesting consequence. This is about the right compromise between checking every consequence (or no consequence) to see if it is a trivial consequence of some axiom or previous consequence. It is important to guide the consequence-finding program toward areas which are relatively dense with interesting consequences. A step in this direction was made by putting a bound on the expected number of literals in any resolvent. The introduction of the axiom-resolution strategy helped, but it is not clear exactly why. It also helped to add interesting consequences to the axioms. Much more research should be done on the problem of defining the interest of a consequence. It would probably be a good idea to study how an intelligent human finds consequences. This may help in obtaining a consequence-finding program which can reason inductively, make definitions, and make conjectures.

5.5 CONCLUSIONS

Computers can be programmed to prove theorems (find proofs and find consequences), for example, the first theorems in group theory in abstract algebra. This has importance for problem solving in general, since deductive reasoning occurs in most kinds of problem solving and not just in mathematics. Chapter 10 tells how the ideas used in automatic proof finding can be directly applied to automatic deductive question answering. Work on getting computers to prove theorems has led to contributions in the field of mathematical logic. In particular, it has led to the development of the resolution principle, which has been proved to be effective, sound, and complete. Completeness theorems have been proved for several restricted forms of the resolution principle, including set-of-support resolution, hyper-resolution, and semantic resolution.

The resolution principle is more natural and powerful than are the rules of inference used by the preresolution proof-finding programs. It is powerful because the calculation of terms to use in instantiation is automatic in each application of the rule. This makes it vastly more efficient in terms of computer time and memory requirements. Because the resolution principle is so natural, it is relatively easy to add heuristics (for example, unit resolution and the unit-preference strategy), which help the theorem-proving program. The set-of-support strategy is good for proof finding. More experimenting should be done with known heuristics, including hyper-resolution and semantic resolution. In addition, more and better heuristics should be sought. One way to do this would be to study how an intelligent human proves theorems.

EXERCISES

In the following exercises, assume that s, t, u, v, w, x, and y are variables and that a, b, and e are constants.

1. Fill in the blank with the correct word—"sometimes," "always," or "never."

a. A factor of a clause is ——— implied by the clause.

b. If A, B, and C are literals, then $(A \,\&\, B) \rightarrow C$ is ——— equivalent to $-A \vee -B \vee C$.

c. A breadth-first strategy will ——— find a contradiction if the initial clauses are $Q(a)$ and $-Q(x) \vee Q(f(x))$.

d. A breadth-first strategy will ——— find a contradiction if the initial clauses are $P(x,f(y))$ and $-P(f(y),x)$.

2. By matching P4 with the first atom of P8 in Table 5-1 give the intermediate result P8′ (not the resolvent) in:

a. Words.

b. Symbols.

3. Give the disjunctive notation corresponding to the symbolic (implication) notation of Table 5-1.

4. Consider the following two clauses:

D1 $P(x,g(x),a) \vee -P(b,g(x),x)$.

D2 $P(x,y,a)$.

a. Find all resolvents between clauses D1 and D2.

b. Find all factors of clause D1.

c. Find all factors of clause D2.

5. Formulate the following as a clause and try to factor the clause. For all x and for all y there exists an s such that either $Q(a,x,y)$ or $Q(x,s,y)$.

6. Suppose that xy means x multiplied by y and that $P(x,y,u)$ means $xy = u$.

a. Write a unit clause that states that multiplication is closed. Closure of multiplication means that for all x and for all y there exists an s such that $xy = s$.

b. Write a simple completion of the following clause, so that it states that multiplication is commutative. Commutativity of multiplication means that for all x and for all y, $xy = yx$:

$-P(x,y,u) \vee$ ———————

7. Assuming no shallower proofs exist than those given, at what level would the breadth-first strategy find the contradiction in:

a. The first example.
b. The second example.
c. The third example.

8. Give the order in which the unit-preference strategy would try the following resolutions.

a. A 2-clause and an 8-clause.
b. A unit and a 2-clause.
c. A 4-clause and a 5-clause.
d. A 7-clause and a unit.
e. A 3-clause and a 2-clause.
f. A unit and a 4-clause.

9. Assuming that P, Q, and R are atoms and using the resolution principle and disjunctive notation, find a proof of the following theorem. If $P \vee Q$, $P \rightarrow R$, and $Q \rightarrow R$, then R.

10. Using the resolution principle, derive a contradiction from the following initial set of clauses:

Clause name	*Clause*	*Reason*
J1	$P(e,x,x)$	Given
J2	$P(g(x),x,e)$	Given
J3	$-P(x,y,u) \vee -P(y,z,v) \vee -P(u,z,w) \vee P(x,v,w)$	Given
J4	$-P(x,y,u) \vee -P(y,z,v) \vee -P(x,v,w) \vee P(u,z,w)$	Given
J5	$-P(a,e,a)$	Denial of conclusion

11. Using the resolution principle and disjunctive notation, find a proof of the following theorem. If there are no intelligent machines and if every ideal machine is an intelligent machine, then the ideal machine does not exist. Let $N(x)$ mean that x is an intelligent machine, and let $D(x)$ mean that x is an ideal machine.

12. Using the resolution principle and disjunctive notation, find a proof of the following theorem. If every deceitful person is a criminal and if anybody who encourages a criminal is a criminal and if there is a timid person who has encouraged a deceitful person, then some criminal is timid. Let $C(x)$ mean that x is a criminal; let $D(x)$ mean that x is a deceitful person; let $E(x,y)$ mean that the person x encourages the person y; let $T(x)$ mean that x is a timid person.

BIBLIOGRAPHY

Davis, M., and H. Putnam: A Computing Procedure for Quantification Theory, *J. ACM*, vol. VII, pp. 201–215, July, 1960.

Gilmore, P. C.: A Proof Method for Quantification Theory: Its Justification and Realization, *IBM J. Res. Develop.*, pp. 28–35, January, 1960.

Guard, James R., F. C. Oglesby, J. H. Bennett, and L. G. Settle: Semi-automated Mathematics, *J. ACM*, vol. 16, no. 1, pp. 49–62, January, 1969.

Kleene, Stephen: "Mathematical Logic," John Wiley & Sons, Inc., New York, 1967.

Lederman, W.: "Introduction to the Theory of Finite Groups," Oliver & Boyd Ltd., London, 1964.

Lee, Richard Char-tung: "A Completeness Theorem and a Computer Program for Finding Theorems Derivable from Given Axioms," doctoral dissertation, Department of Electrical Engineering and Computer Science, University of California, Berkeley, 1967.

McCarthy, John: Programs with Common Sense, in "Journal Proceedings of the Symposium on the Mechanization of Thought Processes," Her Majesty's Stationery Office, London, 1959, pp. 75–84.

Meltzer, Bernard: Theorem Proving for Computers: Some Results on Resolution and Renaming, *Computer J.*, vol. VIII, pp. 341–343, 1966.

Morris, James B.: E-Resolution: Extension of Resolution to Include the Equality Relation, *Proc. Intern. Joint Conf. Artificial Intelligence,* 1969.

Robinson, J. A.: A Machine Oriented Logic Based on the Resolution Principle, *J. ACM* vol. XII, pp. 23–41, January, 1965.

———: A Review of Automatic Theorem Proving, *Proc. Symp. Appl. Math.,* vol. XIX, 1966.

lution in Consequence Finding, *Proc. Intern. Joint Conf. Artificial Intelligence,* 1969.

Wang, Hao: Formalization and Axiomatic Theorem Proving, *Proc. IFIP Congr.* 1965, vol. 1, May, 1965, Spartan Books, Washington, D.C., pp. 51–58.

Wos, L., D. Carson, and G. Robinson: The Unit Preference Strategy in Theorem Proving, *Proc. AFIPS Annual Fall Joint Computer Conf.,* 1964, pp. 616–621.

6
Other Programs for Mathematics

Researchers have written a program that proves theorems in elementary logic, a program that verifies proofs, a heuristic regression-analysis program, a program that solves geometric analogy problems, a program that helps people manipulate mathematical expressions, and a problem-solving program that plans, finds lemmas, and learns. Such researchers have two purposes in writing heuristics programs that do mathematics. They may want to try out their Artificial Intelligence ideas on well-formulated problems, or they may be interested in eventually obtaining a *practical* program. Experiments with these programs and the other mathematical programs described in the previous two chapters lead to certain conclusions. The speed of each program compares favorably with that of a good problem solver. More research should be directed toward extending these successes to the practical solution of mathematical problems that are even more difficult and important. While writing programs for mathematics, researchers have discovered some very useful ideas in heuristic programming. These ideas may serve as a basis of a general theory of how to solve problems.

6.1 A PROGRAM THAT PROVES THEOREMS IN ELEMENTARY MATHEMATICAL LOGIC

A program called the Logic Theorist, or simply LT (Newell, Shaw, and Simon, 1957) proves theorems in propositional calculus (also called sentential calculus or boolean algebra). Propositional calculus is a special case of predicate calculus. LT uses many of the methods and heuristics of students proving the same theorems.

The purpose of these researchers was not to obtain a practical program. They were attracted by the fact that the problem of proving a theorem in propositional calculus is well defined. They wanted to develop procedures to search an implicit, disjunctive goal tree. However, their main purpose was to gain some insight into natural intelligence by trying to get the program to simulate how people solve the intellectually difficult problem of proving such theorems.

Two Typical Logic Theorems Two typical examples of LT's external behavior are now given. Let LT read cards containing five axioms, including the following one:

$$(p \lor p) \rightarrow p \qquad (1.2)^1$$

This axiom means "If either p or p, then p," where p is a variable. (Since propositional calculus will not be explained in detail in this chapter, the reader who was puzzled by the last sentence should skip to the next subsection.) Now let LT read a card containing the problem of proving the logic theorem

$$(p \rightarrow -p) \rightarrow -p \qquad (2.01)$$

This theorem means "If p implies not p, then not p." In about 2 sec, LT prints out the proof shown in Table 6-1.

Table 6-1 LT Proves Theorem 2.01

Statement number	*Statement*	*Reason*
1	$(A \lor A) \rightarrow A$	By axiom 1.2
2	$(-A \lor -A) \rightarrow -A$	By substitution of $-A$ for A
3	$(A \rightarrow -A) \rightarrow -A$	By replacement of disjunction by implication
4	$(p \rightarrow -p) \rightarrow -p$	Substitution of p for A (q.e.d.)

[1] The number 1.2 means that this is the second numbered formula in chapter I of "Principia Mathematica" by Alfred North Whitehead and Bertrand Russell (1935).

LT can prove much more difficult theorems than (2.01), but it failed in the following attempt. Suppose that the 28 theorems prior to (2.31) are given to LT (to add to the five axioms). After working for 4 min on

$$[p \vee (q \vee r)] \rightarrow [(p \vee q) \vee r] \tag{2.31}$$

LT reports that its resource allotment (4 min) has been exceeded.

Implicit, Disjunctive Goal Trees LT searches an implicit, disjunctive goal tree. Such a tree contains no conjunctive relations but is otherwise the same as an implicit, disjunctive-conjunctive goal tree. If one of the subgoals of a goal on a disjunctive tree is achieved, then that goal can be achieved. Thus, if any goal on the tree is ever achieved, the top goal can be achieved. In general, a procedure to handle a disjunctive tree is far simpler than one for a disjunctive-conjunctive tree. For example, a disjunctive procedure does not have to do complicated processing of duplicate goals or prune the goal tree. A disjunctive tree is equivalent to a one-person game tree. (A solitaire card game in which the player sees all the cards may be represented by an implicit, one-person game tree.)

The disjunctive tree of LT is analogous to the disjunctive-conjunctive tree of the geometry program. Each goal in LT consists of proving some proposition, given certain axioms and theorems. A transformation consists of a rule of inference (such as detachment, also called *modus ponens*) and a theorem (or axiom). The transformations are such that a goal is related to its subgoals by disjunction.

A General Procedure for Searching an Implicit, Disjunctive Goal Tree The procedure used by LT is a special case of the following general procedure. Note that this general procedure is almost the same as the procedure given in Section 4.3 for a disjunctive-conjunctive tree. The only difference is that the disjunctive procedure has a simpler step G than the disjunctive-conjunctive procedure has. The paragraph given after the procedure describes ideas needed for a more detailed understanding of the procedure used by LT. Before the general procedure starts, it is given the original goal and the resource allotment. Within the allotted resources, the procedure tries to achieve the original goal. The steps in the following general procedure are to be taken in order except where otherwise indicated.

A. If the try for an immediate solution with the original goal succeeds, print the answer and stop.
B. If the resource allotment has been exceeded, print this fact and stop.
C. If no untried goals remain, print this fact and stop.
D. Select an untried goal from which to try to sprout.

E. If no more goals can be sprouted from the selected goal, go to step B.
F. Sprout the next untried goal G from the selected goal.
G. If the try for an immediate solution with the newly sprouted goal G succeeds, achieve the original goal and stop. If the try fails, go to step E.

In LT, the procedure that tries for an immediate solution is like the standard forms procedure in SAINT. LT uses a breadth-first search procedure. Thus, the selection in step D is not very good. However, the reader should take careful note of the following. Suppose that a disjunctive program has a program which can make good estimates of how close each untried goal is to being achieved. In this case, the selection problem is satisfactorily solved by having the disjunctive program in step D select the untried goal nearest to being achieved. The reader should contrast this solution with the (as yet) unsolved selection problem for disjunctive-conjunctive programs such as SAINT.

Performance and Conclusions LT was asked to prove in sequence the first 52 theorems in "Principia Mathematica." With each theorem it was asked to prove, LT was given the axioms and all the theorems previously proved in the book regardless of whether LT had succeeded in proving these theorems. LT proved 38 of the 52 theorems. Of the 38 proofs, 17 used no transformations (the try for an immediate solution with the original goal succeeded); 19 used one transformation; 2 used two transformations. Since most of the 14 failures would have required at least two transformations and since the branching encountered by the breadth-first search procedure was very great, any reasonable resource allotment was exceeded by these 14 theorems. The speed of the program compares favorably with that of a student. The researchers attained their main objective, that of gaining some insight into natural intelligence by getting the program to simulate how people solve the intellectually difficult problems of proving a theorem in propositional calculus. They found that, roughly speaking, LT and many people used the same general methods. LT searches (breadth-first) the tree by using transformations and by trying for immediate solutions. In the previous subsection we have given a general procedure for making good decisions about where to sprout from next on a disjunctive goal tree or, equivalently, a one-person game tree.

6.2 A PROGRAM THAT VERIFIES MATHEMATICAL PROOFS

Paul Abrahams programmed a computer to check mathematical proofs. John McCarthy was the first to suggest that a proof-checker program be written. Part of Abrahams' (1963) program checks rigorous proofs in a predicate calculus formulation which is more complicated than the resolution principle defined in the previous chapter. His formulation has 10 elementary rules of inference, which will not be given because they have been made obsolete by the resolution principle. The other part of his program expands a proof in some branch of mathematics (such as propositional calculus or group theory) into a predicate calculus proof, which is then checked. Sometimes, this expansion program needs to do some searching by trial and error. The program reads cards containing a theorem and a proof. If it verifies the proof, it prints out the expanded proof and that the theorem is true.

Abrahams had several purposes in writing the program. The task of verifying a proof is well defined. He wanted to see what level of performance and speed his program could achieve on present-day computers. In addition, a proof checker could be useful in itself. It could help eliminate erroneous proofs and "theorems," which are sometimes published, and it could verify a proof that a certain computer program meets its specifications. A proof that a program works is superior to the present system, which is to "debug" a program. Debugging consists of making sure that the program works for some cases, usually a very small percentage of all possible cases. Over the years, a proof checker could be made more and more sophisticated where the steps in the proof are larger and larger. The program would fill in these steps. Eventually, the program would become a theorem prover.

The performance of the program is very interesting. For lack of space, the program failed to verify proofs in group theory. Hence, the rest of this paragraph discusses proofs in propositional calculus only. Abrahams punched on cards the first 67 theorems and proofs in "Principia Mathematica" and gave these cards to the program to read. Defects in some of the proofs were found. For example, one proof mentioned an irrelevant theorem; other proofs used unproved and even unmentioned derived rules of inference. Abrahams remedied all but one of the defective proofs. At the end of the experiment with proofs of the 67 theorems, 63 were checked; the attempt to check three of the proofs exhausted computer memory space; Abrahams did not bother to remedy a defective, one-step "proof" of a theorem which actually required 10 steps. The 63 verifications took an average of 17 sec each.

6.3 A PROBLEM-SOLVING PROGRAM THAT PLANS, FINDS LEMMAS, AND LEARNS

Larry Travis (1964) programmed a computer to solve knight problems. Each problem consists of moving a knight by means of a sequence of chess knight moves from a given square to another on a 20 × 20 "chessboard." A knight move consists of moving two squares in one direction (horizontally or vertically) and then one square perpendicular to this direction. Thus, from most squares (except near the boundary of the board), the knight can be moved to any one of eight squares. However, for each knight problem, the knight is forbidden to land on certain squares, called proscribed squares. A knight problem and a solution are shown in Figure 6-1. The problem is to

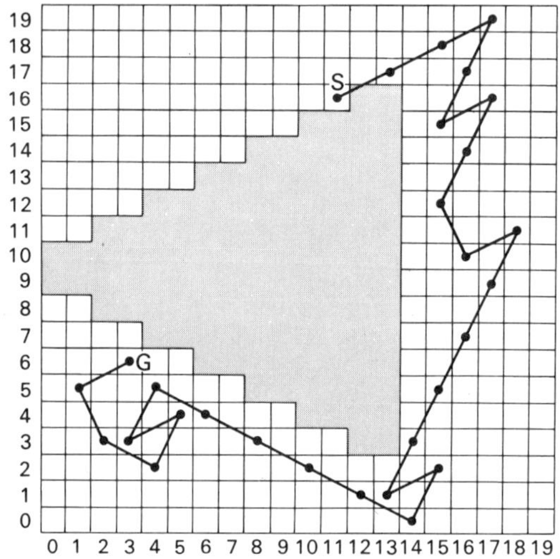

Figure 6-1 The program solves a knight problem.

move a knight from square *S* to square *G*. The filled-in squares are the proscribed squares. The program found the solution given in Figure 6-1.

Actually, the program also solved half-knight problems. A half-knight can make four basic moves as compared with the full knight which can make eight basic moves. Since everything which follows applies equally to both kinds of problems, no further mention will be made of half-knight problems.

Travis had several purposes in writing the program. Knight problems are well defined and simple. They are simple in the sense that people are good at solving them and the transformations (knight moves) are simple. Travis invented this problem domain in order to achieve his main purposes without getting bogged down in the details of some complicated problem domain. He wanted to program a computer to construct long sequences of transformations. Theorem proving or program-writing programs need to construct similar sequences. In fact, he calls his program a theorem-proving program. In addition, he wished to determine the level of difficulty of problems that his program could solve. He wanted to study how a program might plan, find lemmas, and learn. Because he calls his program a theorem-proving program and because these three abilities should be added to other theorem-proving programs, his work is described in this chapter. His program "learns" in the sense that it uses previously developed solutions of easy problems to solve difficult problems.

Description of the Program The two parts of Travis's program are the performance program and the learning program. The three parts of the performance program are the planning program, the ordering program, and the lemma-finding program.

The planning part of the performance program uses plausibility ordering and a depth-first search procedure on an implicit, disjunctive goal tree in order to look for plans. The termination criteria are n-best forward pruning and maximum depth. The experimenter supplies the parameter n to the program. A *plan* is a transformation obtained in general by combining several transformations stored in the computer's memory.

Each transformation is either basic or compound. The basic transformations are the eight knight moves. Each compound transformation is built up from basic transformations. A compound transformation is specified by means of the number of times each basic transformation occurs. The order in which the basic transformations in a compound transformation are to be applied is *not* specified. With each transformation (basic or compound) is stored its net effect, given by two integers X and Y. X gives the change in the number of columns, and Y gives the change in the number of rows. For one of the basic transformations, for example, X is 2 and Y is -1. The transformations are classified according to the signs and relative magnitudes (absolute values) of X and Y.

The original knight problem yields the top goal of transforming the knight from S to G. This goal is classified and then matched with the transformations stored in memory. The n transformations chosen consist of a transformation which brings the knight from S closest to G (ignoring the proscribed squares) and of $n-1$ closely related transformations. Suppose that the n transformations bring the knight from S to squares $S_1, S_2, \ldots, S_j, \ldots, S_n$, respectively. Each of the n subgoals is to transform S_j into G. Transforming S_1 into G is the most plausible subgoal, and the depth-first procedure works on it first. This subgoal is classified and then matched with the transformations in memory, etc. The disjunctive goal tree is searched until a sequence of "successful" transformations is found. The sequence of successful transformations is combined into a single transformation. This transformation is only a plan for solving the original problem. In fact, it may not be possible to order the basic transformations in a plan so that the knight stays on the board and off the proscribed squares.

The ordering part of the performance program tries to order the basic transformations in a plan so that the knight stays on the board and off the proscribed squares. As it tries to obtain such an ordering, the program accumulates a list of "relevant" proscribed squares, which are given to the lemma-finding program from time to time. These are the squares which are frequently blocking successful orderings. The ordering program will not be described further, since planning, lemma-finding, and learning are more important to Artificial Intelligence.

The lemma-finding part of the performance program considers the relevant proscribed squares and tries to find a "lemma" square M which might be a good square for the knight to occupy during its journey. Guessing the lemma square M, the lemma-finding program breaks the original problem into the conjunction of two problems, namely, the problem of transforming S into M and the problem of transforming M into G. Each of these problems is worked on by the planning program. Later, the lemma-finding program may be called upon to break up one or both of these problems, etc. Thus, this program generates a conjunctive goal tree. At deeper and deeper levels of this tree, the parameter n given to the planning program is made smaller and smaller.

The learning done by the learning program is somewhat similar to the rote learning in the checker program of Arthur Samuel. After the performance program has solved a knight problem, the learning program creates the corresponding transformation, classifies it, and files it away for possible later use by the planning part of the performance program. The learning program also culls (deletes) transformations from the file that have been of little use.

Performance and Conclusions A sequence of 60 problems was used to measure the program's behavior. Later problems in the sequence tended to be more difficult than earlier ones. The program described in the previous subsection solved about 60 percent of the problems posed to it. It generally failed on the later problems. For one difficult problem, the program found a solution consisting of 44 basic transformations. For comparison, a human found a solution consisting of only 28 basic transformations. The rather low level of performance of this program is doubtless due in part to the use of a depth-first search procedure on an implicit, disjunctive goal tree. As described in Section 6.1, it would probably be much better to select the untried goal on the basis of its consisting both of relatively few basic transformations (so far) and being relatively near to being achieved. Choosing a simple problem domain allowed the study of a program that constructs long sequences of transformations. Theorem-proving and program-writing programs need to construct somewhat similar sequences. The program runs faster when it has a procedure that classifies transformations and each untried subproblem than it would have without this procedure. When possible, classification procedures should be incorporated into other heuristic programs. The planning procedure works. Each plan is obtained by solving an abstraction of the original problem. Unfortunately, it is not known how to abstract many other kinds of problems. Nevertheless, when possible a heuristic program should use planning. The procedure that finds and uses lemmas is very effective. Unfortunately, it is not known how to find satisfactory lemmas for many other kinds of problems. Ordinarily, a heuristic program will perform much better if it finds and uses lemmas.

Learning works but not very well. The combination of the performance program and the learning program solved more of the 60 problems than did the performance program alone. After more easy problems were added to the beginning of the sequence of 60 problems, the combination program solved no more of the difficult problems than before.

6.4 A PROGRAM THAT HELPS PEOPLE MANIPULATE MATHEMATICAL EXPRESSIONS

Several researchers have written programs to help people manipulate mathematical expressions. William Martin (1967) and Joel Moses (1967) have written one such program for the time-shared computer at M.I.T. The program can, among other things, simplify, differentiate, and integrate mathematical expressions and solve some simple differential equations. Typically the human user types into the computer some initial mathematical expressions. He then tells the program how he wants these expressions manipulated, and the program carries out the manipulations quickly and accurately and obtains intermediate expressions. The user then tells the program how he wants the intermediate expressions manipulated. This process may be repeated many times until the user gets the final expressions he wanted to find. In this way, for example, the program can be made to simplify and differentiate very large expressions quickly and accurately. Work that used to be done with pencil and paper is now done faster and more accurately. Some jobs that are too large to be done by hand are now done with the assistance of the program. Thus the program is already practical.

As the program is augmented, it becomes a more intelligent assistant and therefore more useful. Suppose a programmer wants to write a heuristic program to do some specific task. Instead of trying to do this directly, he can program the computer to help a person to do that task. The programmer then continues to augment his program so that the computer can take over more and more of the task until finally it is able to take over the entire task.

6.5 A PROGRAM THAT SOLVES GEOMETRIC ANALOGY PROBLEMS

A program written by Thomas Evans (1964) solves a wide class of geometric analogy problems. The program is called ANALOGY. ANALOGY solves these problems at the level of a good high school student.

Each geometric analogy problem consists of eight labeled line drawings and the following question, "Drawing *A* is to drawing *B* as drawing *C* is to which of the five given answer drawings?" When given the problem illustrated in Figure 6-2, ANALOGY correctly selected the drawing labeled 4 as its answer. Geometric analogy problems appear on intelligence tests. For example, this problem is taken from the 1942 edition of the psychological test for college freshmen of the American Council on Education.

Why did Evans choose geometric analogy problems? First, he wished to study programs that processed complicated line drawings. These programs include programs to decompose a line drawing into its parts and other

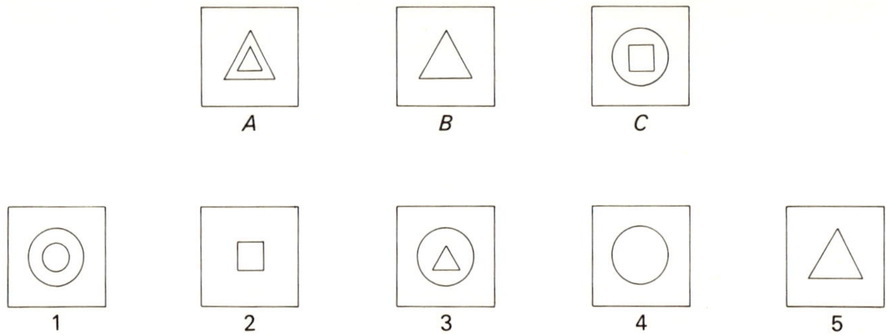

Figure 6-2 Eight line drawings used for the geometric analogy program ANALOGY.

programs that use relationships among these parts. In addition, he wished to study the use of explicit internal descriptions of drawings and transformations. Furthermore, the ability to reason by analogy may be an important component of the more powerful heuristic programs of the future. Finally, such problems appear on intelligence tests and require intelligence to solve them.

The program may be described in terms of the following eight-step procedure:

A. Read the input descriptions of the eight drawings. The input descriptions are prepared by hand. Each drawing is described in terms of straight-line segments and arcs of circles.

B. Try to decompose each drawing into its component objects. For example, drawing *A* of the problem described in Figure 6-3 is decomposed into the objects labeled P_1, P_2, and P_3. The labels P_1, P_2, etc. are for convenience in describing the program and are not given to the program.

C. Compute properties of these objects and relations among them. For example, this step computes that the object labeled P_2 in drawing *A* lies inside the object labeled P_3. It also computes that P_1 is above P_2 and P_3. In drawing *B*, it computes that P_4 is to the left of P_5.

D. For each pair of objects, determine all similarity transformations which carry one object of the pair into the other. The transformations include rotation and uniform scale change, as well as horizontal and vertical reflections. The angle of rotation represents a rotation. The scale factor represents a uniform scale change.

E. Using the information obtained in steps B through D, generate *AB*-rules. By definition, an *AB*-rule transforms drawing *A* into drawing *B*. An *AB*-rule specifies how the objects of drawing *A* are removed, added to, and altered in their properties and their relations to generate drawing *B*. To generate *AB*-rules, the program matches objects in *A* with objects in

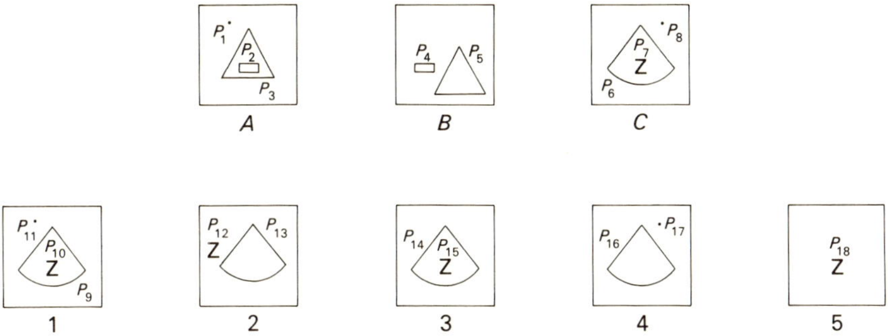

Figure 6-3 Decomposition and labeling of line drawings as done by the ANALOGY program.

B in all possible ways compatible with the similarity information. The AB-rule is very specific; that is, it qualifies the objects as much as possible with properties and relations. In the sample problem, the program finds an AB-rule which removes P_1 and which transforms P_2 into P_4 and P_3 into P_5. The program can handle the more complicated cases when objects are both added and removed.

F. Similarly, for each answer drawing X, generate CX-rules.

G. For each AB-rule and for each CX-rule try to construct "generalized rules." By definition, a generalized rule is an AB-rule and a CX-rule which does not transform C into any answer drawing except X.

H. If some generalized rule is more specific than any other generalized rule obtained in step G, print the label of the corresponding answer drawing and terminate. If there is no unique, *most specific* generalized rule, try another method.

No other methods will be described here.

In summary, a computer has been programmed to solve geometric analogy problems at the level of a good high school student. This is a significant achievement because such problems appear on intelligence tests and because the ability to reason by analogy may play a large role in more sophisticated problem-solving programs. The program can process complex line drawings; it can also decompose a drawing into its parts and then use relationships among these parts.

6.6 A HEURISTIC REGRESSION ANALYSIS PROGRAM

Floyd A. Miller (1967) wrote a practical heuristic regression-analysis program that learns. One input to the program is a set of $(n + 1)$-tuples $(x_1,x_2, \ldots,x_n,y)$, where $n \leqslant 40$. The independent variables x_j are called *predictors*. The dependent variable y is called the *response*. The other input is k, which is either 3, 4, or 5 and which does not exceed $n-2$. The program computes the model associated with each of $2n$ distinct sets of k predictors. By definition, the model associated with the k predictors x_{i_1}, $x_{i_2}, \ldots, x_{i_k}$ is the function of the form

$$y = a_0 + a_1 x_{i_1} + a_2 x_{i_2} + \ldots + a_k x_{i_k}$$

which "best fits" the sets of $(n+1)$-tuples. The a_j are called the *multiple regression coefficients*. The output of the program consists of the three best models generated by the program. Often the user of the program is primarily interested in the three good sets of k predictors which he gets as part of the three models. We shall not discuss the part of the program which, after a set of k predictors is chosen, applies a standard procedure (linear least-squares) to compute the multiple regression coefficients a_j. The main thing to notice in the procedure given below is how it learns to choose good predictors.

A. Initializing the run includes the following. Input the observational data, that is, the set of $(n+1)$-tuples. Initially set each $P_j = 1/n$, where P_j is the probability of choosing predictor x_j in step C.
B. Initialize trial. During each trial, a set of k predictors is chosen.
C. Choose a predictor probabilistically according to the probabilities P_j.
D. If the chosen predictor has already been chosen during this trial, discard this choice and go to step C.
E. If a set of k predictors has not yet been chosen, go to step C.
F. If the set of k predictors is the same as the set chosen on some previous trial, discard the set and go to step C.
G. Use regression analysis to find the model associated with the set of k predictors.
H. Save this model if it is one of the three best models obtained so far in this run.
I. Reward and punish each of the predictors, that is, adjust the probability P_j of choosing predictor x_j. (We do not present the technicalities of how this is done.)
J. If the run is not completed, that is, if fewer than $2n$ models have been generated, go to step B.
K. Print the three best models and stop.

The performance of the program is excellent. It is about four times faster than previous programs. Since 1964, it has solved more than a thousand different practical problems at various industrial companies including the Celanese Corporation of America and the Glidden Company. For example, see the articles by W. R. Blackmore et al. (1966) and by A. Drattell (1968).

The program has chosen the predictors basic to making high salaries in Canada's operations research profession and has selected important causes (predictors) of traffic deaths in Jacksonville, Florida. This heuristic program that learns is of economic importance to profit-orientated industry.

6.7 GENERAL CONCLUSIONS CONCERNING PROGRAMS FOR MATHEMATICS

As described in the last three chapters, researchers have succeeded in writing programs that prove theorems in logic and geometry, a program that verifies proofs, a program that performs integrations, a program that helps people manipulate mathematical expressions, a program that solves geometric analogy problems, a program that performs heuristic regression analysis, and a problem-solving program that plans, finds lemmas, and learns. The speed of each program compares favorably with that of a good problem solver. More research should be directed toward extending these successes to the practical solution of mathematical problems that are even more difficult and more important. The heuristic regression-analysis program and the program that helps people manipulate mathematical expressions are practical already. The program that verifies proofs and the program that performs integration could serve as the basis of practical programs.

While writing heuristic programs for mathematics, researchers have discovered some very useful ideas. For example, the importance of planning, finding lemmas, and learning has been emphasized. Procedures have been developed to handle a variety of problems; the procedures search implicit trees by using transformations and by trying for immediate solutions. These ideas may serve as the basis of a general theory of how to solve problems.

EXERCISES

1. Explain why statement 3 is a valid consequence of statement 2 in Table 6-1.

2. What is the original (top) goal in the disjunctive tree used to obtain the proof in Table 6-1?

3. Make up a knight problem of moderate difficulty and give a solution.

4. Describe in words a simple procedure which is guaranteed to find, for any given solvable knight problem, a shortest solution path.

5. Assuming that no lemmas were used, what plan did the program use in solving the knight problem in Figure 6-1?

6. Make up a geometric analogy problem of moderate difficulty and give the solution.

7. Explain in your own words the purposes of writing each of the following programs:
   a. The program that verifies mathematical proofs.
   b. The program that helps people manipulate mathematical expressions.
   c. The heuristic regression-analysis program.

BIBLIOGRAPHY

Abrahams, Paul: "Machine Verification of Mathematical Proof," doctoral dissertation, Department of Mathematics, Massachusetts Institute of Technology, Cambridge, Mass., May, 1963.

Blackmore, W. R., G. Cavadies, D. Latch, F. A. Miller, and R. Twery: Annual CORS Salary Survey for 1965, *Can. Operations Res. Soc. Bull.,* Fall, 1966.

Drattell, A.: Management Training Ground at Glidden, *Business Automation*, vol. 15, no. 4, April, 1968.

Evans, Thomas: A Heuristic Program to Solve Geometric Analogy Problems, *Proc. AFIPS Annu. Spring Joint Computer Conf.*, 1964, pp. 327–338.

Martin, William Arthur: "Symbolic Mathematical Laboratory," doctoral dissertation, Electrical Engineering Department, Massachustts Institute of Technology, Cambridge, Mass., Jan. 1967.

Miller, Floyd A.: Improving Heuristic Regression Analysis, presented at the Sixth Annual Southeastern Regional Meeting of the ACM, Chapel Hill, North Carolina, June 15–17, 1967.

Moses, Joel: "Symbolic Integration," MAC-TR-47, Project MAC, Massachusetts Institute of Technology, Cambridge, Mass., December, 1967.

Newell, Allen, J. C. Shaw, and Herbert Simon: Empirical Explorations of the Logic Theory Machine, *Proc. Western Joint Computer Conf.*, February, 1957. Reprinted in Edward Feigenbaum, and Julian Feldman (eds.), "Computers and Thought," McGraw-Hill Book Company, New York, 1963.

Travis, Larry E.: Experiments with a Theorem Utilizing Program, *Proc. AFIPS Annu. Spring Joint Computer Conf.*, April, 1964, pp. 339–358.

Whitehead, Alfred North, and Bertrand Russell: "Principia Mathematica," 2d ed., vol. I, Cambridge University Press, 1935.

7 A Multipurpose Heuristic Program

This and the following three chapters describe some multipurpose programs. Each of these programs is multipurpose in the sense that it can solve a variety of problems and not just one kind of problem. Such heuristic programs are important in Artificial Intelligence because natural intelligence is multipurpose in this same sense. A program is truly multipurpose if the same important parts of the program are used to solve different kinds of problems; that is, the program should not be a conglomeration of single-purpose problem-solving programs. It often takes less time and it is more illuminating to write a truly multipurpose program than to write the corresponding collection of single-purpose programs. The hope is that eventually a multipurpose heuristic program will be constructed that is sufficiently broad to solve some of its own "internal" problems, for example the problems of doing its own learning, planning, etc. Some multipurpose heuristic programs discussed in this book are the MULTIPLE program (described later in the present chapter) (Slagle, 1965, Slagle and Bursky, 1968, Slagle and Koniver, 1970); the General Problem Solver (GPS) (Chapter 8) of Allen Newell et al.; the general probabilistic procedure (Section 9.1) of Fred Tonge; and some question-answering programs (Chapter 10).

MULTIPLE is an acronym for MULTIpurpose Program that LEarns. It consists of two parts, the Proving Program and the Learning Program. The Proving Program (PP) searches for a constructive proof or disproof of a given proposition. In the terminology of Chapter 4, it searches for a constructive proof or disproof that a given goal is achievable. It can search a fairly general kind of implicit goal tree, including an implicit, disjunctive-conjunctive goal tree. Hence, it is an extension of components common to the three single-purpose programs described in Chapter 4, namely, the geometry program, the indefinite integration program, and the checkmate program. It uses a search procedure which efficiently selects the seemingly best proposition to work on next. It does this by alternately (1) sprouting a tree from the most meritorious untried proposition on the proposition tree and (2) backing up probability and merit from each newly generated untried proposition to the top (originally given) proposition. The probability of a proposition is the probability that the proposition can be proved. An untried proposition has merit to the extent that sprouting a tree from that proposition is expected to be cheap and to change the probability of proving the top proposition. The Learning Program (LP) has been designed but not yet programmed. When written, it will compute approximations to the functions needed by PP to compute how the probability and merit of an untried proposition depend on given features of that proposition.

In one experiment, PP was given the task of searching for proofs and disproofs of propositions about kalah end games. (See Section 2.5 for the rules of kalah.) In another experiment, the program, after some modification, *played* games of kalah. In both experiments, the program was compared with an alpha-beta program. The results were encouraging, since PP was relatively fast and efficient. Its advantage increased as the problem size was increased.

7.1 THE PROVING PROGRAM

To give the reader a good overview of the PP part of MULTIPLE, a mythical example of its operation is given before it is described abstractly.

A Mythical Example As an example, we show how PP would find a proof of a particular checker proposition. Although PP has not been given any checker propositions, the example involves checkers because that game is more familiar than kalah to most readers. (As will be seen later, the program has proved kalah propositions which are much more difficult than the trivial checker propositions given here for illustration.) Suppose that PP is trying to find a constructive proof or disproof of the proposition that white can force a win from the top position given in Figure 7-1. From the proposition G, PP sprouts the propositions G_1 and G_2. The proposition G_1 is "black to move and white to force a win" in the position given with G_1 in Figure 7-1. PP

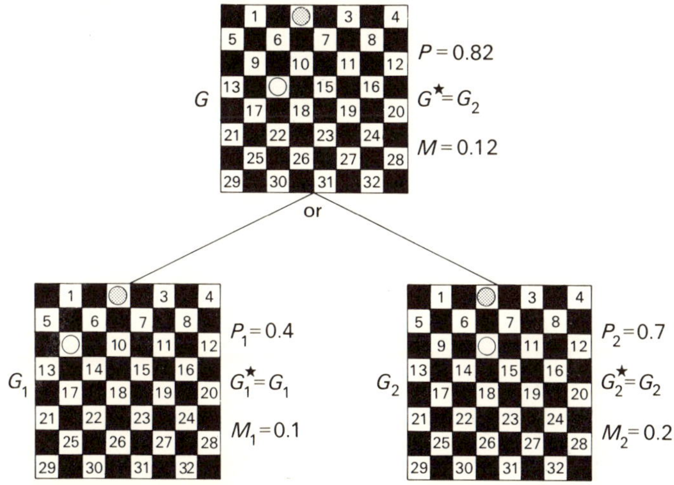

Figure 7-1 White to move and white to force a win.

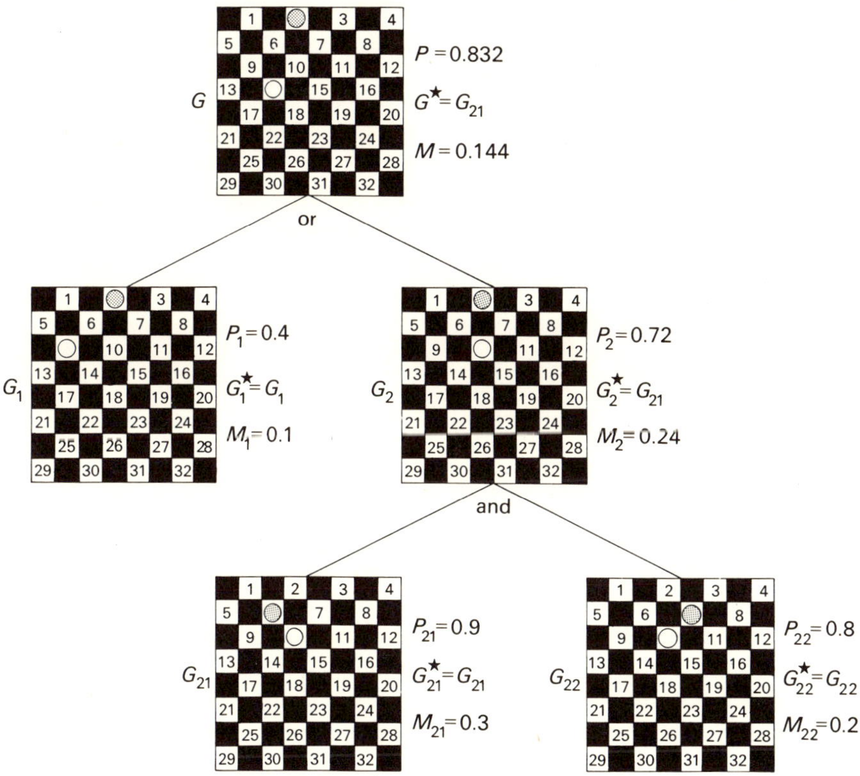

Figure 7-2

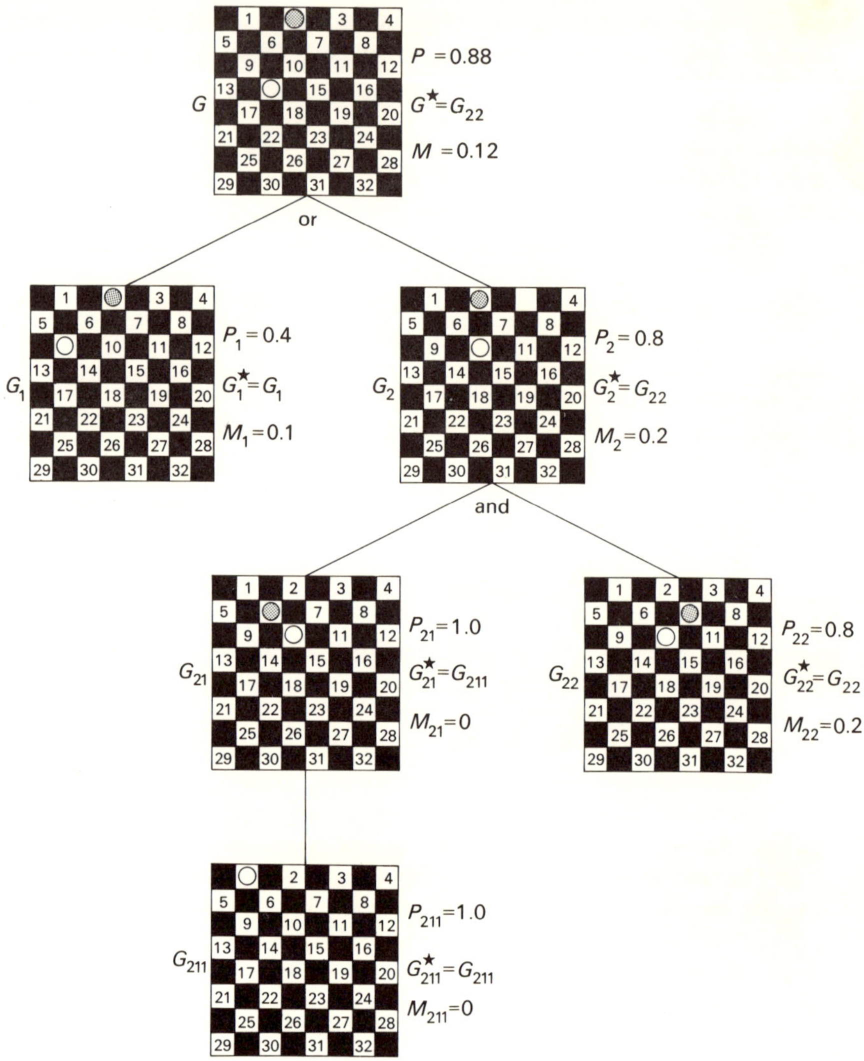

Figure 7-3

uses checker features to estimate the probability of G_1 to be 0.4. The self-merit, defined precisely later, is 0.1 and the choice G_1^* is G_1. In general, the choice at a given node on the tree is the seemingly best untried proposition on the subtree originating from the given node. Similarly, PP computes the probability, self-merit, and choice for proposition G_2. These quantities are backed up to G from G_1 and G_2. Since white can force a win in position G if and only if he can force a win in G_1 or G_2 or both and since, for simplicity, G_1

and G_2 are assumed independent, we have $p = 1 - (1 - p_1)(1 - p_2) = 0.82$. The backed-up merit is 0.12, and the backed-up choice is G_2. This means that the seemingly best untried proposition at or below G is G_2. Roughly speaking, this choice is due to the fact that G_2 has a higher probability (good for a disjunction) and a higher self-merit than does its rival G_1. Hence, PP tries to sprout from G_2, and the result is shown in Figure 7-2. PP assigns a probability self-merit, and choice to each of the newly sprouted untried propositions G_{21} and G_{22}. These quantities are backed up to G_2. Since white can force a win in G_2 if and only if he can force a win in G_{21} *and* G_{22} and since, for simplicity, G_{21} and G_{22} are assumed independent, we have $p_2 = p_{21}p_{22} = 0.72$. The backed-up merit is 0.24, and the backed-up choice is G_{21}. This new information at G_2 and the old information at G_1 are backed up to G. It is very important to note that the information at G_1 need not be recomputed and that this would be true even if G_1 were the beginning of an extremely large subtree. Thus the expense of backing up is roughly proportional to the tree depth of the selected untried proposition and not to the size of the entire proposition tree. This is important, since trees in actual practice can become extremely large.

Since the choice G^* at G is now G_{21}, the seemingly best untried proposition on the whole tree is G_{21}. PP sprouts from G_{21}, and the result is shown in Figure 7-3. In G_{211}, the probability that white can force a win is 1.0, since he already has. The information is backed up to G_{21}. The new information at G_{21} and the old information at G_{22} are backed up to G_2. The old information at G_1 and the new information at G_2 are backed up to G. PP next sprouts from G_{22}, and the result is shown in Figure 7-4. The probability that white can force a win from G_{221} is 1.0, since he already has. The information is backed up to G_{22}. The old information at G_{21} and the new information at G_{22} are backed up to G_2. The old information at G_1 and the new information at G_2 are backed up to G. From the fact that the backed-up probability to G is 1.0, PP recognizes that the top proposition has been proved. The constructive proof consists of the tree in Figure 7-4, except for G_1 and the branch leading from G to G_1.

Proposition Tree While trying to prove or disprove a given proposition, PP manipulates a proposition tree. In the proposition tree depicted in Figure 7-5, the nodes G, G_1, G_2, G_{11}, etc., represent propositions. The propositions G_1, G_2, and G_3 are called subpropositions of their superproposition G. The truth value of the proposition G is some boolean function B of the truth values of its subpropositions; that is, $G = B(G_1, G_2, \ldots, G_k)$. The experimenter tells PP how to obtain the boolean function B. Any boolean function may be used. Two boolean functions which often occur on proposition trees are conjunction and disjunction. In conjunction, $G = G_1 \ \& \ G_2 \ \& \ \ldots \ \& \ G_k$; that is, G is true if and only if G_1 is true and G_2 is true and . . . and G_k is true.

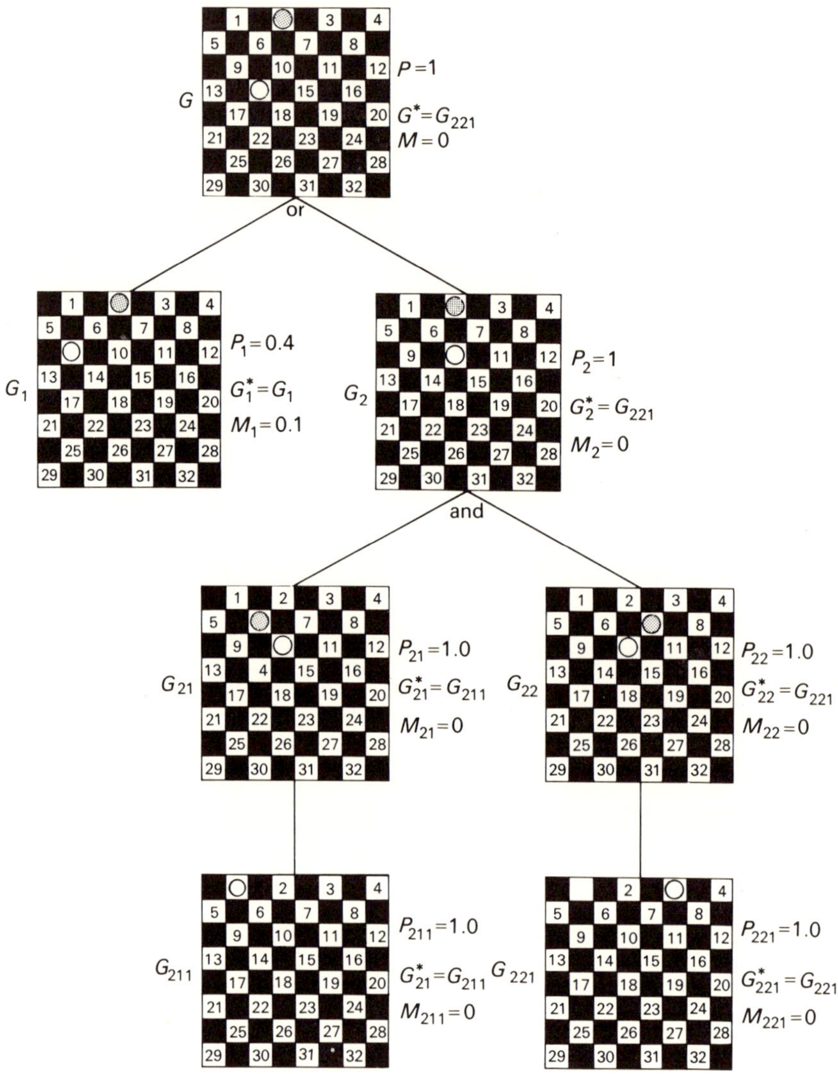
G
P = 1
G* = G221
M = 0
or
G1
P1 = 0.4
G1* = G1
M1 = 0.1
G2
P2 = 1
G2* = G221
M2 = 0
and
G21
P21 = 1.0
G21* = G211
M21 = 0
G22
P22 = 1.0
G22* = G221
M22 = 0
G211
P211 = 1.0
G21* = G211
M211 = 0
G221
P221 = 1.0
G221* = G221
M221 = 0

Figure 7-4

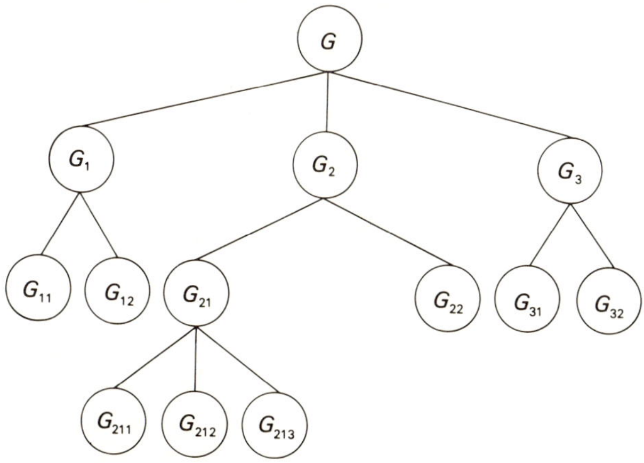

Figure 7-5 A proposition tree.

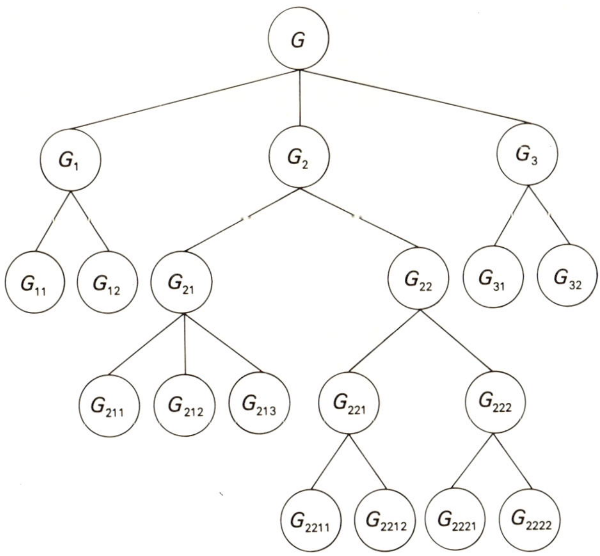

Figure 7-6 A proposition tree.

In disjunction, $G = G_1 \vee G_2 \vee \ldots \vee G_k$; that is, G is true if and only if G_1 is true or (inclusive) G_2 is true or . . . or G_k is true. The above two functions are the only ones needed for the domain of kalah.

Transformation of a Proposition The experimenter must give PP a way to transform a proposition into its subpropositions. In kalah end games, for example, he must tell PP how to make legal moves. A proposition is restricted to having only a finite number of subpropositions. This restriction is inherent in some domains. For example, in kalah end games, the number of moves from any position is finite.

Trying to Sprout a Tree from an Untried Proposition To prove or disprove the top proposition, PP alternately (1) sprouts a tree from the untried proposition having the most merit (an untried proposition is one from which PP has not tried to sprout a tree) and (2) backs up the probability, choice, and merit to the top proposition from the newly generated untried propositions. PP uses the given transformations to sprout a tree from the selected untried proposition. For example, sprouting a tree from G_{22} in Figure 7-5 might give the result shown in Figure 7-6. PP sprouts a tree large enough so that the time spent in backing up probability, choice, and merit on the entire tree is less than some given fraction A of the total machine running time. The fraction A is a parameter chosen by the experimenter.

Backing Up Probability Before backing up probability from newly generated untried propositions, PP uses a function supplied by the Learning Program LP to estimate the probability that each such untried proposition is true. After making these estimates, PP backs up probability, level by level, by using probability functions derived from the given boolean functions. The probability function is derived by proceeding as if the probabilities are independent, which they are generally not. For example, in the conjunction $G_1 = G_{11} \,\&\, G_{12}$, we have $p_1 = p_{11}p_{12}$, where p_{11} and p_{12} are the probabilities of G_{11} and G_{12}, respectively, and where p_1 is the backed-up probability of G_1. Similarly, in the disjunction $G = G_1 \vee G_2 \vee G_3$, we have $p = 1 - (1 - p_1)(1 - p_2)(1 - p_3)$.

Merit of an Untried Proposition An optimum search procedure would decide with minimum cost whether or not a given proposition is true. In this sense, PP is suboptimal, but it uses a search procedure which efficiently selects the untried proposition with the most merit. An untried proposition has merit to the extent that sprouting a tree from that proposition is expected to be cheap and to change the probability of the top proposition. PP's search procedure should approach the optimum search procedure because large changes in the probability of the top proposition at each sprouting tend to make this probability 0 or 1.

The merit of an untried proposition $G_{ij\ldots st}$ is defined as

$$\left|\frac{\partial p}{\partial c_{ij\ldots st}}\right|$$

Since p depends on p_i and since p_i depends on p_{ij}, etc., the chain rule for partial differentiation gives

$$\left|\frac{\partial p}{\partial c_{ij\ldots st}}\right| = \left|\frac{\partial p}{\partial p_i}\frac{\partial p_i}{\partial p_{ij}}\cdots\frac{\partial p_{ij\ldots s}}{\partial p_{ij\ldots st}}\frac{\partial p_{ij\ldots st}}{\partial c_{ij\ldots st}}\right|$$

The self-merit $m_{ij\ldots st}$ of the same untried proposition $G_{ij\ldots st}$ is defined by

$$m_{ij\ldots st} = \left|\frac{\partial p_{ij\ldots st}}{\partial c_{ij\ldots st}}\right|$$

Therefore, the merit of the untried proposition $G_{ij\ldots st}$ is given by

$$\left|\frac{\partial p}{\partial c_{ij\ldots st}}\right| = \left|\frac{\partial p}{\partial p_i}\frac{\partial p_i}{\partial p_{ij}}\cdots\frac{\partial p_{ij\ldots s}}{\partial p_{ij\ldots st}}\right| m_{ij\ldots st} \tag{1}$$

PP uses a function supplied by LP to estimate the self-merit $m_{ij\ldots st}$ for an untried proposition $G_{ij\ldots st}$. Actually, PP estimates

$$\left|\frac{\Delta p_{ij\ldots st}}{\Delta c_{ij\ldots st}}\right| \qquad \text{rather than} \qquad \left|\frac{\partial p_{ij\ldots st}}{\partial c_{ij\ldots st}}\right|$$

where $\Delta p_{ij\ldots st}$ is the expected change in $p_{ij\ldots st}$ as a result of sprouting a tree from $G_{ij\ldots st}$ and where $\Delta c_{ij\ldots st}$ is the expected cost of sprouting the tree from $G_{ij\ldots st}$.

Backing Up Merit and Choice The most important factor contributing to good performance by PP is that it can efficiently select the most meritorious untried proposition from which to sprout the next tree. The procedure is best described by means of an example. Suppose in Figure 7-5 that the untried proposition G_{22} is selected as having the most merit. Suppose that G_{22} sprouts a tree as shown in Figure 7-6. PP then stores the self-merit for each of the newly generated untried propositions G_{2211}, G_{2212}, G_{2221}, and G_{2222}. To initialize the backing-up procedure, PP stores the following four "choices" with the corresponding untried propositions: $G^*_{2211} = G_{2211}$; $G^*_{2212} = G_{2212}$; $G^*_{2221} = G_{2221}$; $G^*_{2222} = G_{2222}$. To back up merit from G_{2211} and G_{2212} to their superproposition G_{221}, PP computes

$$m_{221} = \max\left(\left|\frac{\partial p_{221}}{\partial p_{2211}}\right| m_{2211}, \left|\frac{\partial p_{221}}{\partial p_{2212}}\right| m_{2212}\right)$$

Note that the first quantity in the parentheses is the final portion of the expression for the merit of the untried proposition G_{2211} as given by Eq. (1), namely,

$$\left|\frac{\partial p}{\partial c_{2211}}\right| = \left|\frac{\partial p}{\partial p_2}\frac{\partial p_2}{\partial p_{22}}\frac{\partial p_{22}}{\partial p_{221}}\frac{\partial p_{221}}{\partial p_{2211}}\right| m_{2211}$$

PP also backs up the untried proposition having the most merit relative to G_{221}. G^*_{221} is either G^*_{2211} or G^*_{2212}, depending on whether the first or second quantity within the parentheses is greater. Similarly, PP backs up m_{222} and G^*_{222} from the values stored with G_{2221} and G_{2222}. Now PP backs up another level to G_{22} from G_{221} and from G_{222}. The merit is

$$m_{22} = \max\left(\left|\frac{\partial p_{22}}{\partial p_{221}}\right| m_{221}, \left|\frac{\partial p_{22}}{\partial p_{222}}\right| m_{222}\right)$$

G^*_{22} is either G^*_{221} or G^*_{222}, depending on whether the first or second quantity within the parentheses is greater. Next, PP backs up the values to G_2 from G_{21} and G_{22}. Note that the values m_{21} and G^*_{21} need not be recomputed from the tree whose source is G_{21}. Finally, PP obtains the backed-up values merit m and choice G^*. The proposition G^* is the untried proposition having the most merit. PP tries to sprout a tree from G^* and backs up probability and merit to the top proposition. This cycle is repeated again and again.

As one specific example of backing-up merit and choice, suppose PP has just sprouted from G_2 and that the result is as shown in Figure 7-2. First PP stores the self-merit for both of the newly generated untried propositions G_{21} and G_{22}. To initialize the backing-up procedure, PP stores the following choices with the corresponding propositions: $G^*_{21} = G_{21}$; $G^*_{22} = G_{22}$. Since G_2 is the conjunction of G_{21} and G_{22}, we have $p_2 = p_{21}p_{22}$. Hence,

$$\frac{\partial p_2}{\partial p_{21}} = p_{22} \qquad \text{and} \qquad \frac{\partial p_2}{\partial p_{22}} = p_{21}$$

To back up merit from G_{21} and G_{22} to their superproposition G_2, PP computes

$$\begin{aligned} m_2 &= \max\left(\left|\frac{\partial p_2}{\partial p_{21}}\right| m_{21}, \left|\frac{\partial p_2}{\partial p_{22}}\right| m_{22}\right) \\ &= \max\,(p_{22}m_{21}, p_{21}m_{22}) \\ &= \max\,(0.24, 0.18) = 0.24 \end{aligned}$$

PP also backs up the choice $G^*_2 = G_{21}$, since the first quantity within the parentheses is greater.

Next PP backs up another level to G from G_1 and G_2. Since this is a disjunction, $p = 1 - (1 - p_1)(1 - p_2)$. PP computes the backed-up merit as follows:

$$m = \max\left(\left|\frac{\partial p}{\partial p_1}\right| m_1, \left|\frac{\partial p}{\partial p_2}\right| m_2\right)$$

$$= \max\,[(1 - p_2)m_1, (1 - p_1)m_2]$$

$$= \max\,(0.028, 0.144) = 0.144$$

PP also backs up the choice $G^* = G_2^* = G_{21}$, since the second quantity within the parentheses is greater. The proposition $G^* = G_{21}$ is the untried proposition having the most merit. As in Figure 7-3, PP sprouts a tree from G_{21} and backs up probability, merit, and choice to the top proposition, etc.

7.2 THE LEARNING PROGRAM

The Learning Program LP must supply PP with functions for estimating how the probability and self-merit of an untried proposition depend on the features of that proposition. Note that LP has not yet been programmed, and so the following description is only a proposal, given here for completeness. In the experiments reported in this chapter, all functions and parameters were supplied by the experimenter. These are described in Section 7.4. A real-valued function of a proposition is called a *feature* of that proposition. For example, a feature of a proposition involving a checker position is the piece advantage of black. The experimenter gives the program a finite set of features upon which the probability p and the self-merit m depend: $p = p(x_1, x_2, \ldots, x_n)$ and $m = m(x_1, x_2, \ldots, x_n)$, where each x_j is a feature. To estimate the probability and self-merit functions, LP uses the experience of PP as well as examples and weighted data given to LP by the experimenter.

Learning How the Self-merit Depends on the Features An approximation to the self-merit function might be a polynomial in the variables $x_1, x_2, \ldots, x_n$. The experimenter may give LP a data point with co-ordinates $(M, X_1, X_2, \ldots X_n)$ with weight W. LP also uses the experience of PP to get data points. Suppose the untried proposition G having the most merit has probability P_0 and feature values $X_1, X_2, \ldots X_n$. Suppose further that the actual cost of sprouting a tree from G is ΔC and that the probability backed up to G is P_b. In this case, LP obtains the data point $(M, X_1, X_2, \ldots, X_n)$ with weight 1, where $M = |P_b - P_0|/\Delta C$.

Learning How the Probability Depends on the Features The experimenter may give LP either a data point $(P, X_1, X_2, \ldots, X_n)$ with weight W or correctly worked examples. In the latter case, LP creates a data point with weight 1 for each tried proposition which is proved or disproved. P is 1 or 0 according to whether the proposition is true or false. LP also uses the experience of PP to get data points. Each tried proposition which PP proves or disproves is handled in exactly the same manner as a tried proposition in an example given by the experimenter. In general, after PP has completed an attempt to prove or disprove a proposition, some tried propositions remain which are neither proved nor disproved. For such a proposition, LP creates a data point $(P,X_1,X_2,\ldots,X_n)$ with weight W, where P is the backed-up probability and where X_1, X_2, ..., X_n are the feature values of the tried proposition. The weight W is proportional to the total effort e spent on the tree whose source is this proposition; that is, $W = e/E$, where E is the maximum effort ever expended by PP on any tree. This gives W the desirable property of never exceeding 1.

7.3 EXPERIMENTING WITH PP

For any domain in which experiments are to be performed, the experimenter must give PP the following inputs. An illustration from the domain of checker end games is given with each input.

A Function Which, without Sprouting Any Tree, Tries to Prove or Disprove a Proposition When the function is applied to an untried proposition, it may have one of three values. The value might be a proof of that proposition. For example, in checkers, it could be "The proposition that black can force a win is true, since it is red's turn to move and red has no legal moves." The value of the function might be a disproof of the proposition. For example, in checkers, it could be "The proposition that black can force a win is false, since the game has ended in a draw." Finally, the value might be a report that the function can neither prove nor disprove the proposition. For example, in checkers it could be "It is not clear whether the proposition that black can force a win is true or not, since it is red's move and red has some legal moves." PP applies this function to a proposition as soon as it is generated.

Transformations for Untried Propositions The experimenter must tell PP how to transform an untried proposition into its subpropositions and how the proof or disproof of the superproposition depends on the proofs or disproofs of its subpropositions. In checkers, legal moves transform a previously untried proposition into its subpropositions, and the subpropositions are related to their superpropositions by either disjunction or conjunction. The experimenter classifies each transformation as either *immediate* or *mediate*. A transformation is called immediate if, when it is applicable, it should be applied without estimating the self-merit or probability of the proposition to which it can be applied. In checkers, an immediate transformation is the transforming of a proposition by making all jump moves if at least one is available. A transformation which is not immediate is called mediate. In checkers, a mediate transformation transforms a proposition in which no jump moves are available into the subpropositions which can be reached by a legal move.

7.4 EXPERIMENTAL RESULTS WITH PP

The following kalah routines were used by PP:

A. A function whose argument is a kalah position and whose value is a list of the legal moves from that position.

B. A function whose argument is a position and whose value is true or false depending on whether or not the game is over. The game is over if all the holes of either player are empty or if one player's kalah has more than half the stones. Under certain conditions where the end of the game is almost reached, it is possible for the program to decide the outcome and, in these cases, the function is true.

C. A function whose argument is a position and whose value is the probability that a given player can force a win from that position. The probability function is

$$p = \tfrac{1}{2} + \frac{1}{2.1}\,\frac{K-k}{S}$$

where p is the probability that player P can force a win, K and k are the number of stones in P's and p's kalah, and S is the number of stones still playable. This function is used only on positions which are not end-of-game positions. For these positions, $|K-k| \leqslant S$. Observe that this function has the following desirable properties. If both players have the same number of stones in their kalahs, then neither player has an advantage and the probability is $\tfrac{1}{2}$. As player P gets more stones in his kalah than does his opponent, the likelihood that P can force a win rises. When P's kalah has as many stones as his opponent's kalah plus all of the playable stones, that is, $K = k + S$, then P cannot be beaten and the probability is very close to 1. Because the game could still be a draw, the factor 1/2.1 is used instead of $\tfrac{1}{2}$ in the second term of the above expression. Thus, the probability that P can force a win is always strictly less than 1. As player p gets more stones in his kalah than does P, the likelihood that P can force a win decreases. If p's kalah has as many stones as P's kalah plus all the playable stones, that is, $k = K + S$, then P cannot force a win and the probability should be 0. However, in this case the probability is $\tfrac{1}{2} - 1/2.1 > 0$. This apparent difficulty is resolved by recalling that the probability function is never applied to end-of-game positions and hence should take values in only the open interval from 0 to 1.

D. A function whose argument is a position and whose value is the self-merit of that position. The self-merit function is defined as the reciprocal of the number of stones still playable. This function has the following desirable properties. As the number of playable stones decreases, the cost of sprouting also decreases, since there are fewer possible moves. Also the fewer playable stones there are, the closer the end of the game is. Therefore $|\Delta p|$ tends to be larger than it is for a position where the end of the game is not yet in sight.

E. A function whose argument is a position for which the game is over and whose value is 1 or 0 depending on whether or not the player in question has won.

Alpha-Beta as a Proving Program Since the alpha-beta procedure is normally used to play games, certain modifications were necessary so that it instead proved theorems concerning two-person games. These changes proved to be quite minor. When using alpha-beta as a game-playing program, the initial value of alpha is minus infinity and the initial value of beta is plus infinity. Assume that player P always goes first, that player p is his opponent and that for all practical purposes the number N is infinity and minus N is minus infinity. When the proposition to be proved is that player P can force a win from a given position, the initial value of alpha is set to $N - 1$. Thus all moves except a winning move for player P are rejected. Similarly, when the proposition to be proved is that player p can force a win from a given position, the initial value of beta is set to $-N + 1$. Thus, an initial move causes a beta cutoff if and only if it is not a losing move for player P. If all initial moves are losing moves for player P, then the proposition is proved. In both cases, the proposition is disproved if the best that the player in question can do is to obtain a tie. Alpha-beta used the same criterion for an end of game as did PP. It also used the same routine to obtain the list of legal moves from a given position. It was possible to order the moves with very little extra effort within this routine. The ordering scheme assumes that for a player to go again or to capture stones from his opponent's side is advantageous. Such an ordering scheme approximates the more costly methods of evaluating each position by using the evaluation function which computes the difference in the number of stones in the two kalahs. Plausibility ordering of moves makes alpha-beta more efficient. It does not *aid* PP but was used since it does no actual harm. This is one of several instances of "bending over backward" to be fair to alpha-beta as compared to PP. Since alpha-beta was being used as a proving program it searched to the end of the game.

Experiments Both PP and alpha-beta were asked to prove propositions concerning 23 kalah positions. Assume that player P always goes first. For each position, two propositions were posed to each search procedure. The first was that player P can force a win from this position, and the other was that player p can force a win from this position. For the purpose of these experiments, PP always sprouted a subtree of fixed depth. This depth was 1 for half the experiments and 2 for the other half. (The program is written so that the depth of each sprout may be varied without limit by the program itself.) The results are summarized in Table 7-1. The number of positions created by alpha-beta does not include those positions actually generated by the program but then not used because of an alpha or beta cutoff. This is done even though all the generated positions were used to order the list of positions. With different methods of ordering positions, these positions might never have been created, since alpha-beta uses only one position at a time. PP, on the other hand, must use all the legal moves from a given position and so these were included in the number of created positions for PP. Results show that the total number of positions created and the total amount of time used by alpha-beta is much greater than the corresponding effort by PP. Alpha-beta actually used less effort than did PP on most of the problems. This is due to the fact that most of the problems required relatively little effort. On small problems, alpha-beta is more efficient, while PP is faster for more difficult problems. This is illustrated in Table 7-2, where the results of two positions are shown. The first position is quickly solved by alpha-beta, but this procedure needs much more effort for the second position.

PP requires a large amount of space to store its tree, and so only smaller problems could be run. As can be seen from Table 7-1, PP was still not successful on all the propositions, as it did not have enough space. Alpha-beta

Table 7-1 Results of experiments on two search procedures as proving programs (23 positions used)

Sprouting depth for PP	1	1	2	2
Player who is to prove a win	P	p	P	p
Total time, sec				
PP	111	63	111	84
Alpha-Beta	183	222	353	389
Total number of positions created				
PP	4,035	2,638	4,821	4,064
Alpha-Beta	9,184	10,673	16,058	17,606
Number of positions for which PP succeeded	21	21	21	22
Number of positions for which alpha-beta succeeded	23	23	23	23
Number of times each procedure created fewer positions than the other procedure				
PP	6	8	7	9
Alpha-Beta	14	11	13	12
Tie	1	2	1	1

Table 7-2 Two examples of propositions that were proved (PP sprouting depth 1)

Player who is to prove a win	*Initial position*	*Time, sec PP*	*Time, sec Alpha-Beta*	*Positions created PP*	*Positions created Alpha-Beta*
P	7 770000 001150 8	1.2	0.4	71	10
p		3.2	0.4	184	10
P		3.1	69.6	160	3708
	10 900102 101002 10				
p		3.1	86.0	151	4032

succeeded on every proposition. Table 7-1 includes only those propositions for which PP was successful. Because of this, the time and number of positions created by alpha-beta in columns 1 and 3 and in columns 2 and 4 are different. There is a trade-off between the two procedures in the sense that alpha-beta uses more time and PP uses more space. PP's advantage will increase as computers with larger and larger memories become available. It is also felt that PP can use auxiliary storage units without taking much more time. The fact that PP, on some of the large problems, uses less than one-tenth the effort that alpha-beta uses is very encouraging. It is therefore believed PP is a useful search procedure for difficult propositions.

Comparison of PP with the Problem-solving Methods of People Eight propositions were chosen and solved by hand to compare PP with the problem-solving methods used by humans. (Note that PP is not intended to be a model of human problem-solving behavior. These comparisons are intended to indicate possible avenues of improvement for PP.) Any general conclusions are difficult to make, but the program did create, on the average, an order of magnitude more positions. It was found that a human was very good at analyzing a position without formally creating a subtree below the position. PP must actually create the subtree in order to obtain the same information. Of course, the program can do this more quickly than people, and its bookkeeping is much more reliable. PP would be much better if its evaluation function for probability and self-merit were better. Furthermore, the search by the human often has subtrees that are deep and narrow. Once the person has an idea in mind, he carries it out without any diversion. The program jumps around on the tree much more, and the resulting tree is wider. The program could be changed in two ways to keep its tree narrower. PP now creates all the legal moves from a position at once. It could instead just make the most promising moves. In addition it could sprout a deep subtree with very little branching by using an immediate transformation.

7.5 EXPERIMENTS WITH A VARIATION OF PP AS A GAME-PLAYING PROGRAM

PP was changed so that it could *play* kalah. This was accomplished by allowing PP to create only a predetermined number of nodes. It then chose to move to the position which has the highest probability for forcing a win. The only other change that was necessary was to give tie positions a probability of $\frac{1}{2}$.

Experiments PP played alpha-beta 156 games of kalah. For each of 13 initial positions, alpha-beta was given three maximum search depths (4, 5, and 6), and PP was given two sprouting depths (1 and 2). Once these depths were fixed, each procedure was allowed to go first, giving a total of 12 games for each starting position. The games were played as follows. The search depth for alpha-beta and the sprouting depth for PP were fixed, and then alpha-beta made the opening move. For making its response, PP was permitted to create three-fourths of the nodes that alpha-beta had created. A factor less than 1 was picked, as succeeding moves in a game become simpler to make and therefore both search procedures use less effort as the game progresses. Then alpha-beta moved again, and the game continued in this manner until completion. PP's effort was always limited to three-fourths of alpha-beta's effort on the latter's most recent move. As in the proving program, the number of nodes created by alpha-beta includes only those actually used and not all those generated. When the game was finished, PP made an opening move from the original position, being permitted the same number of nodes as alpha-beta used when the latter made its opening move. Then alpha-beta moved, and the game continued as before.

When PP proved or disproved the proposition that it could force a win, it printed this information but continued playing. In one game, PP actually proved a win for itself and then obtained only a tie because it made a foolish move later in the game. This illustrates the disadvantage PP had as a result of being forced to use a fixed percentage of its opponent's effort on the previous move. In this particular instance, alpha-beta searched to a depth of 4. PP's deep search was to a depth of only 1, even though the game was almost over and the complete search would have taken only a little more effort.

The results of these experiments are summarized in Table 7-3. These results were obtained by subtracting one point from a player if he went first but lost, and by subtracting one-half point if he went first and tied. PP ran out of memory space in nine games, and these games were stopped. The results were tabulated for only those starting positions for which the games were finished when both players went first. The sums of total times and total number of positions in Table 7-4 were taken in the same way. From Table 7-4 it can be confirmed that PP spends a higher percentage of its time backing up probability and merit when each sprout is smaller, that is, when the sprouting

Table 7-3 Summary of results of games

Maximum depth for Alpha-Beta	*Sprouting depth for PP*	*PP's score*	*Alpha-Beta's score*
4	1	−3	−4
5	1	−4	$-2\frac{1}{2}$
6	1	$-2\frac{1}{2}$	$-2\frac{1}{2}$
4	2	−2	$-4\frac{1}{2}$
5	2	−3	−4
6	2	−2	$-2\frac{1}{2}$
	Total	$-16\frac{1}{2}$	−20

Table 7-4 Summary of total effort by each procedure

	PP	*Alpha-Beta*
Sprouting depth of 1 for PP:		
Time, sec	508	509
Positions created	21,371	26,332
Sprouting depth of 2 for PP:		
Time, sec	334	423
Positions created	18,303	22,240

depth is 1. A general conclusion one can reach from these tables is that the two search procedures played about the same quality game, although PP has an advantage.

7.6 CONCLUSIONS

The initial experiments with the PP part of MULTIPLE have been encouraging. The experiments indicate that PP is more efficient in searching very large disjunctive-conjunctive trees than is the alpha-beta procedure. PP's chief weakness is that it must keep all unproved portions of the tree, but this drawback can be greatly reduced by using a large auxiliary memory to store parts of the tree that are not in active use. (This is possible, since the probability and merit on a subtree do not change unless PP sprouts from some untried proposition on that subtree.) After these experiments were run, PP was augmented in two ways (Slagle and Koniver, 1970). First, a program has been added to utilize duplicate propositions. Second, PP has been run on another domain—first-order predicate calculus—using the resolution principle. A Learning Program will be added so that the program can improve its performance with experience. By periodically improving the approximations to the probability and self-merit functions, the program will learn to handle problems of increasing difficulty.

EXERCISES

1. Verify that the merit and choice are backed up correctly to G in Figure 7-1.
2. Verify that the probability, merit, and choice are backed up correctly in
   a. Figure 7-3.
   b. Figure 7-4.
3. a. Assuming that $G = G_1 \,\&\, G_2 \,\&\, \ldots \,\&\, G_k$ and that $p \neq 0$, show that the backed-up merit to G is

$$m = \max\left(\frac{p}{p_1}m_1, \frac{p}{p_2}m_2, \ldots, \frac{p}{p_k}m_k\right)$$

   b. Assuming that $G = G_1 \vee G_2 \vee \ldots \vee G_k$ and that $p \neq 1$, show that the backed-up merit of G is

$$m = \max\left(\frac{1-p}{1-p_1}m_1, \frac{1-p}{1-p_2}m_2, \ldots, \frac{1-p}{1-p_k}m_k\right)$$

4. a. What self-merit would PP assign to each of the propositions in Table 7-2?
   b. What initial probability that player P can force a win would PP assign to each of the propositions in Table 7-2?

BIBLIOGRAPHY

Slagle, James: A Multipurpose, Theorem-Proving Heuristic Program That Learns, *Proc. IFIP Congr.*, 1965, vol. II, Spartan Books, Washington, D.C., pp. 323–328.

———, and Philip Bursky: Experiments with a Multipurpose, Theorem-Proving Heuristic Program, *J. ACM*, vol. 15, no. 1, pp. 85–99, January, 1968.

———, and Deena Koniver: "Finding Resolution Proofs and Using Duplicate Goals in AND-OR Trees," Heuristics Laboratory, Division of Computer Research and Technology, National Institutes of Health, Bethesda, Md., 1970.

8
The General Problem-solver Program

A program called General Problem Solver (GPS) solved a wide variety of problems (Newell, Shaw, and Simon, 1960; Ernst and Newell, 1967; Ernst and Newell, 1969). Of the many versions that were programmed, only the "final" version (1967) is described in this chapter. Ernst and Newell (1967) say that the next version, if there is one, should be an entirely new program. J. R. Quinlan (1969) has written and experimented with a successor of an earlier version of GPS. GPS is a truly unified and multipurpose program and not merely a conglomeration of programs, each specialized to perform one task.

So that the reader can think concretely, some examples of the external behavior of GPS are now given. Suppose that GPS is given in a suitable language the following "monkey task." (This task was first specified by John McCarthy, 1963.) A monkey and a box are in a room, and some bananas are hanging from the ceiling. The monkey can walk, move the box, and climb on the box. He can get the bananas if he is on the box and the box is under the bananas. What should he do so that he gets the bananas? After working for less than 4 min, GPS gives the answer that the monkey walks to the box, moves it under the bananas, climbs it, and gets the bananas. To enable GPS to perform some simple indefinite integrations, it is given several very simple rules for performing some arithmetic, algebra, differentiation, and integration. After working for about 3 min on the specific task, $\int te^{t^2}\,dt$, GPS prints out the answer $\frac{1}{2}e^{t^2}$. After working for about 6 min on another specific task, $\int(\sin^2 ct \cos ct + t^{-1})\,dt$, GPS prints out the answer $(\sin^3 ct)/3c + \ln t$.

In general, the way that GPS works is that it searches a goal tree by trying to transform a goal into easier subgoals. Here and elsewhere we say "GPS," when actually it would be more precise to say "the problem-solving executive program," which is the top-level program in GPS. The problem-solving executive program of GPS selects subgoals, selects methods, and applies the selected methods to the selected subgoals. A task is given to GPS in terms of objects, operators, and differences. GPS uses a general technique called *means-ends analysis*, in which it selects an operator as a function of the difference between the present object and the desired one. Differences are taken between what is given and what is desired. For example, a difference between two objects is a feature which occurs in one object but does not occur, or has a different form, in the other object. GPS uses the difference to select an operator relevant to reducing that difference.

Some of the findings and conclusions concerning GPS are the following. GPS worked on 11 widely different tasks. It was able to perform tasks involving inductive and deductive reasoning. It performed the tasks very slowly. Means-ends analysis was found to be very effective on some tasks but not on others. The fact that the general techniques used by GPS resemble those used by humans is very important to those researchers for whom the psychological purpose of Artificial Intelligence is very important. GPS needed to use only four types of goals. It should have ways of viewing a task as a whole, and the way in which GPS selects the next goal to be tried will need to be improved, especially when the goal trees become large. GPS may be the forerunner of a program that will, in some significant sense, perform the task of doing its own learning.

8.1 THE REPRESENTATION OF A TASK

Each task given to GPS consists of a task environment and a specific task. Each task environment consists of all the information common to tasks of a certain type, for example, the information common to all integration tasks. Each task environment consists of operators, differences, a difference-ordering, a table of connections, details for matching objects, and miscellaneous information. Each specific task consists of a top goal and its objects. Table 8-1, which specifies the monkey task, illustrates a specific task and most parts

Table 8-1 The specification for GPS of the monkey task

I. Task Environment
  A. Miscellaneous information: The set of places (on the floor) = [place 1, place 2, under the bananas]
  B. Operators
    1. CLIMB =
      a. Pretest: The monkey's place is (the same as) the box's place.
      b. Move: The monkey's place becomes on the box.
    2. WALK =
      a. Variable: x is in the set of places.
      b. Move: The monkey's place becomes x.
    3. MOVE BOX =
      a. Variable: x is in the set of places.
      b. Pretests
        1. The monkey's place is in the set of places.
        2. The monkey's place is the box's place.
      c. Moves
        1. The monkey's place becomes x.
        2. The box's place becomes x.
    4. GET BANANAS =
      a. Pretests
        1. The box's place is under the bananas.
        2. The monkey's place is on the box.
      b. The contents of the monkey's hand become the bananas.
  C. Differences
    *D*1 is the monkey's place.
    *D*2 is the box's place.
    *D*3 is the contents of the monkey's hand.
  D. Difference Ordering: *D*3 is more difficult to reduce than is *D*2 which is more difficult to reduce than is *D*1.
  E. TABLE OF CONNECTIONS = All operators are desirable for reducing all differences.

II. Specific Task
  A. TOP GOAL = Transform the initial OBJ into the desired OBJ.
  B. Objects.
    1. INITIAL OBJ =
      a. The monkey's place is place 1.
      b. The box's place is place 2.
      c. The contents of the monkey's hand are empty.
    2. DESIRED OBJ = The contents of the monkey's hand are the bananas.

of a task environment. The table of connections and details for matching objects are well illustrated in this table, but are explained more fully in Section 8.4. In the computer, tasks are specified for GPS in a language that is similar to but more formal than the language used in Table 8-1.

8.2 THE PROBLEM-SOLVING EXECUTIVE PROGRAM

The task specification is given to the problem-solving executive program, whose main steps are given below. The antecedent goals and the difficulty of a goal, which are mentioned in the steps, are defined in Section 8.4. Generally speaking, the heart (the inner loop, steps D through L) of the procedure proceeds locally; that is, in a fairly natural way it generates subgoals and moves between supergoals and subgoals (and to antecedent goals) according to successes and failures. The exceptions to this "local" characteristic are step I and step D(1). Steps A and B represent the "desperation" case, that is, the case in which all the methods for the top goal have been exhausted [see step D(1)]. Just which goal is selected in step B will not be explained here because it is of no intrinsic interest and the case seldom occurs. The following executive procedure is given a task and starts in step C.

A. If all methods for all goals have been exhausted, print this fact and stop.
B. Select a goal that has unexhausted methods, and go to step E.
C. Select the top goal.
D. If all the methods for the selected goal are exhausted,
   1. If the selected goal is the top goal, go to step A.
   2. If the selected goal is not the top goal, select its supergoal and go to step D.
E. Select an unexhausted method for the selected goal.
F. Try the selected method on the selected goal.
G. If the selected method fails, that is, it neither achieves the goal nor generates a subgoal,
   1. If the selected goal is the top goal, go to step D.
   2. If the selected goal is not the top goal, select its supergoal and go to step D.
H. If the selected method succeeds in achieving the goal,
   1. If the goal is the top goal, print the answer and stop.
   2. If the achieved goal is not the top goal, select its supergoal and go to step D.
I. The method succeeds in generating a subgoal. If the subgoal is equivalent to some previously generated goal, go to step C.
J. If the subgoal of the selected goal is undesirable because it is more difficult than the supergoal of the selected goal, go to step D.

K. If the subgoal is undesirable because it is more difficult than the antecedent of the selected goal, select the antecedent goal and go to step D.

L. If the subgoal passes this evaluation (steps J and K), select the subgoal and go to step D.

8.3 AN EXAMPLE OF PERFORMING A TASK

Table 8-2 and Figure 8-1 show how GPS uses the executive procedure to perform the monkey task specified in Table 8-1. As with any task, the executive procedure starts at step C, which selects the top goal. Since not all methods have been exhausted, the procedure goes to step E. Since the top goal is a transform-type goal, step E selects one of the methods relevant to transform-type goals. It selects the *transform* method. Note that as a mnemonic we use the same name for a goal type as for one of its methods. The transform method matches the initial OBJ with the desired OBJ. If they already match (there are no differences), the method achieves the goal. If there are differences, the method creates the subgoal of reducing the most difficult difference. Step F tries the transform method on the top goal. Since, in step G, the selected method succeeds, the procedure goes to step H. In

Table 8-2 GPS performs the monkey task

INITIAL OBJ =

- a. The monkey's place is place 1.
- b. The box's place is place 2.
- c. The contents of the monkey's hands are empty.

DESIRED OBJ = The contents of the monkey's hand are the bananas.

OBJ 2 =

- a. The monkey's place is place 2.
- b. The box's place is place 2.
- c. The contents of the monkey's hand are empty.

OBJ 3 =

- a. The monkey's place is under the bananas.
- b. The box's place is under the bananas.
- c. The contents of the monkey's hand are empty.

OBJ 4 =

- a. The monkey's place is on the box.
- b. The box's place is under the bananas.
- c. The contents of the monkey's hand are empty.

OBJ 5 =

- a. The monkey's place is on the box.
- b. The box's place is under the bananas.
- c. The contents of the monkey's hand are the bananas.

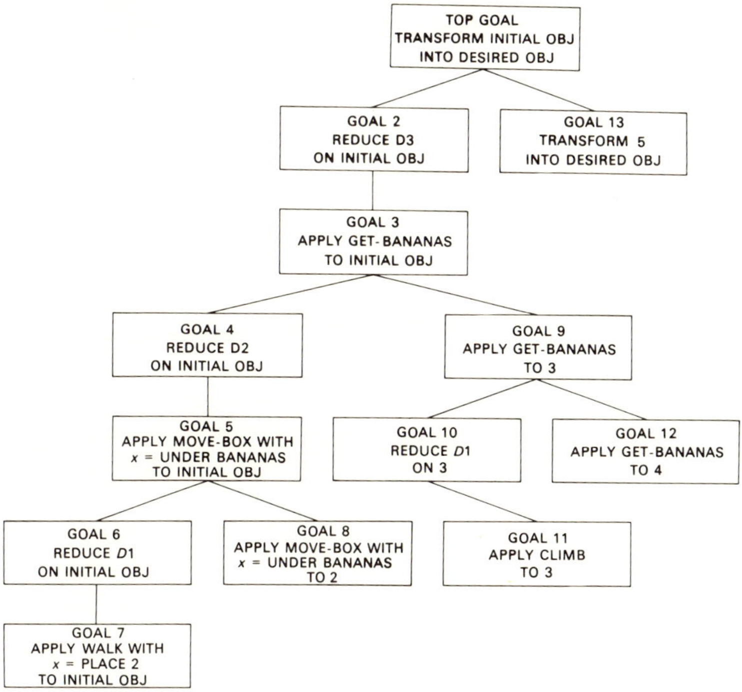

Figure 8-1

step H, the method does not succeed in achieving the goal; the initial OBJ does not match the desired OBJ, since the contents of the monkey's hand are empty in the initial OBJ and are the bananas in the desired OBJ. In step I the method succeeds in generating the subgoal, goal 2, to reduce the difference *D*3 (the contents of the monkey's hand), since this is the most difficult (and in fact the only) difference between the initial OBJ and the desired OBJ. Goal 2 passes the evaluation in steps J and K, since the selected goal (top goal) has neither a supergoal nor an antecedent goal. Step L selects goal 2 and goes to step D.

With goal 2 selected, step D is uneventful. Step E selects the *reduce* method, one of the methods relevant to reduce-type goals. If successful, the reduce method creates a subgoal of applying to the object an operator relevant to reducing the specified difference. In steps F through I, the method is applied successfully and generates goal 3, to apply the operator GET BANANAS to the initial OBJ. Since goal 3 passes the evaluation in steps J and K, step L selects goal 3 and goes to step D.

With goal 3 selected, step E selects the *apply* method, one of the methods relevant to apply-type goals. The apply method applies the operator directly if it can. If the apply method cannot apply the operator directly, it creates a subgoal to reduce the most difficult difference blocking the application of the operator. Step F tries the method on goal 3. In step H the selected method does not succeed in achieving goal 3; the operator GET BANANAS cannot be applied directly because it requires that the box be under the bananas and that the monkey be on the box. In step I, the method succeeds in generating the subgoal, goal 4, to reduce the difference $D2$ (the box's place), which is more difficult than $D1$ (the monkey's place). Step L selects goal 4 and goes to step D.

In a similar manner, the procedure next generates and selects goals 5, 6, and 7. Assume that the procedure has just selected goal 7 and goes to step D. Step E selects the apply method for goal 7. In step H, the selected method succeeds in achieving goal 7; the monkey walks to place 2; object 2 in Table 8-2 is generated. Step H(2) selects goal 6, the supergoal of goal 7, and goes to step D. Step E selects a method relevant to goal 6. This method achieves a reduce goal when its subgoal has been achieved. In steps F through H(2), the method achieves goal 6, selects its supergoal (goal 5), and goes to step D. Step E selects a method relevant to goal 5. This method for an apply goal generates another apply goal when a reduce subgoal has been achieved. In steps F through I, the method succeeds in generating goal 8, a subgoal of goal 5. Step L selects goal 8 and goes to step D.

Similarly, the procedure next generates and selects goals 9 through 13. Assume that the procedure has just selected goal 13 and goes to step D. Step E selects the transform method for goal 13. Since in step H, object 5 matches the desired OBJ, goal 13 is achieved. Step H(2) selects the top goal and goes to step D. Step E selects a relevant method for the top goal. This method achieves the transform goal if a transform subgoal has been achieved. Since in step H(1) the goal is the top goal, the procedure stops after printing the answer that the monkey walks to place 2, moves the box under the bananas, climbs the box, and gets the bananas.

8.4 GOALS, MATCHING, OPERATORS, AND THE TABLE OF CONNECTIONS

This section, together with the previous three sections, should give the reader a good idea of how GPS operates.

Goals The four kinds of goals handled by GPS are *transform object A into object B*, *reduce difference D on object A*, *apply operator Q to object A*, and *select the element of set S which best fulfills criterion C*. The first three types were illustrated in the example of the previous section. Selection criteria, which are associated with selection goals, are built into GPS in the form of programs. Although such criteria are task-dependent information, they do not appear in the task specification because of limitations in both the task-specification language and the problem-solving techniques of GPS. As will be seen later, some other task-dependent information is handled the same way because of the same limitations. It is important to note that GPS is less general to the extent that such information must be built in. It is to the great credit of GPS that only a small portion of the task-dependent information was built into GPS in the form of programs.

The antecedent goal of a goal *G* is the goal whose result is used in the statement of *G* and whose supergoal is the same as the supergoal of *G*. In Figure 8-1, for example, goal 2 is the antecedent goal of goal 13; goal 4 is the antecedent of goal 9; goal 6 is the antecedent of 8; goal 10 is the antecedent of 12. No other goal in Table 8-2 has an antecedent goal.

The difficulty of a goal is the difficulty of the difference associated with the goal. The difficulty of the difference is determined by the difference ordering given in the task environment. Since reduce goals are the only type of goals which have differences directly associated with them, a goal of any other type is considered as difficult as its most difficult subgoal. For example, in Table 8-2, the top goal does not have a difference directly associated with it, but, after goal 2 was generated, GPS considers the top goal to be as difficult as goal 2 because the difference *D*3 is the most difficult difference detected in matching the initial OBJ with the desired OBJ. Goal 4 was evaluated to be desirable because the supergoal of goal 3 is goal 2 and because the difference *D*2 was not more difficult than *D*3.

Matching Roughly speaking, the match procedure determines if two objects are the same and, if not the same, finds differences between them. The specification of the task environment often includes some details for matching objects, although the specification of the monkey task to GPS had no such details. The problem-solving executive "knows" how to match the kinds of objects which occur in the performance of the monkey task. In the specification of the task environment, the details for matching objects may tell GPS that two objects match only if they are identical. Unfortunately, some other task-dependent details for matching objects must be built into GPS in the form of programs. One program, for example, allows the matching of a variable in one object with an expression in another by means of substituting the expression for the variable.

Operators An operator transforms one object into another. Most operators are specified in the task environment, but others, called immediate operators, are built into GPS as programs. An immediate operator is applied without generating a subgoal to apply it. Each operator given in the task environment is either a move operator or a form operator. A form operator consists of two forms. An object that matches the first form may be transformed into another object according to the second form. A move operator consists of moves and possibly variables, pretests, and posttests. It has been found that move operators are usually more general than are form operators.

Table of Connections In the task environment, the table of connections tells GPS which operators are relevant to reducing each difference. The reduce method, when it is tried on a goal to reduce the difference *D* on an object, chooses an operator which the table says is relevant to *D*. The method then generates the subgoal of applying the operator to the object. Table 8-3 shows the connections that might have been used with the monkey task but were not, as explained below. The table shows that the operators CLIMB, WALK, and MOVE BOX are relevant to reducing the difference *D*1, the monkey's place. The operator MOVE BOX is relevant to reducing *D*2, the box's place. GET BANANAS is relevant to the contents of the monkey's hand. In order to make it a little harder for GPS, the actual table of connections in the monkey task environment told GPS that every operator might be relevant to every difference. However, the reduce method can examine the internal structure of move operators in order to choose operators relevant to reducing each difference.

8.5 TASKS GIVEN TO GPS

GPS was given 11 tasks and spent an average of 17 sec per goal. It is instructive for the reader to compare his performance with that of GPS.

Monkey Task As was seen previously, GPS performed this task by generating 13 goals. It spent (approximately) 221 sec.

Integration Task First, GPS was given the task environment. Six operators told the GPS how to integrate six standard forms; four other operators told how to do simple differentiating; one other operator told GPS that the integral of a sum is the sum of the integrals. To make problem solving feasible, several immediate operators had to be built into GPS in the form of programs. These immediate operators include commutativity and associativity of addition and multiplication, simplification, arithmetic, a simple integration rule, and two

Table 8-3 Possible table of connections for the monkey task

	*D*1	*D*2	*D*3
CLIMB	*R*		
WALK	*R*		
MOVE BOX	*R*	*R*	
GET BANANAS			*R*

simple differentiation rules. Concerning all the operators in the task environment, Ernst and Newell (1967) say that the transformations of SAINT are more general than the operators of GPS because each transformation corresponds to many operators and that this is a nontrivial difference in the two formulations. The first specific task given to GPS was $\int te^{t^2}\,dt$. To perform this task, GPS generated 11 goals and took 187 sec. The second specific task was $\int(\sin^2 ct \cos ct + t^{-1})\,dt$, which took 22 goals and 374 sec.

Missionaries and Cannibals Task Three missionaries, three cannibals, and a boat are on one side of a river. The only way to cross the river is in the boat, which will hold either one or two people. If the cannibals ever outnumber missionaries on a side of the river, the cannibals will eat those missionaries. (For example, if a missionary and a cannibal arrive at a side where there is a cannibal but no missionaries, the missionary will be eaten.) In every other way, the cannibals will do (operate the boat, return) what they are told to do. How can everybody and the boat get safely to the other side of the river? To perform this task, GPS generated 57 goals and took 969 sec.

Tower of Hanoi Task In the initial position in this puzzle, there are four discs of varying size on the first of three pegs as in Figure 8-2. A move consists of moving the top disc from one peg and putting it on top of the discs (if any) on another peg. A restriction is that no disc may ever be placed on top of a smaller disc. How can all four discs be moved to the third peg? To perform this task, GPS generated 46 goals. Mainly because the differences and difference ordering in this task environment are in some sense optimal, GPS made no mistakes but went directly to the solution.

Task-proving Theorems in First-order Predicate Calculus GPS was given a task environment for proving theorems using resolution (see Chapter 5). Certain information was built into GPS in the form of programs. The task

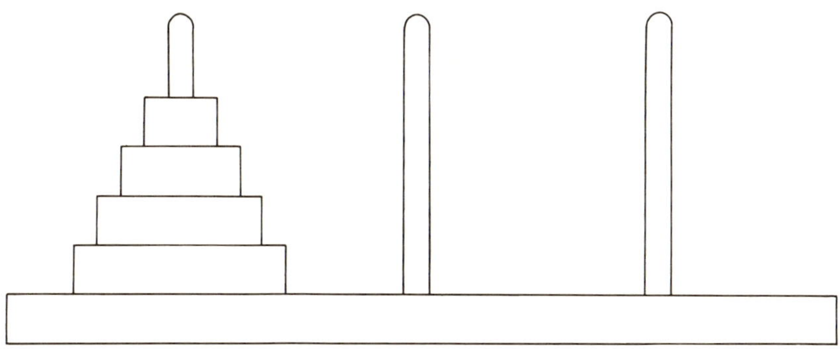

Figure 8-2 Initial position in the tower of Hanoi task.

environment was given in such a way that GPS uses a unit-preference strategy. GPS generated 59 goals in order to derive the contradiction from the following three clauses:

$$\{P(u,y)\}$$

$$\{\sim P(y,f(u,y)) \vee \sim P(f(u,y),f(u,y)) \vee Q(u,y)\}$$

$$\{\sim P(y,f(u,y)) \vee \sim P(f(u,y),f(u,y)) \vee \sim Q(u, f(u,y)) \vee \sim Q(f(u,y),f(u,y))\}$$

Father and Sons Task A father, his two sons, and a boat are on one side of the river. The only way to cross the river is in the boat, whose capacity is 200 lb. Everybody knows how to operate the boat. The father weighs 200 lb, and each son weighs 100 lb. How can they get themselves and the boat across the river? To perform this task, GPS generated 33 goals.

Three Coins Task Of three coins lying on a table, the first and third show tails, and the second shows heads. Each move consists of turning over two of the three coins. The task is to make *exactly* three moves after which all the coins show the same, either heads or tails. To perform this task, GPS generated 10 goals.

Parsing Task In the task environment given to GPS are 10 phrase-structure rules (for a simplified form of English), including the following five rules:

A. A NOUN PHRASE followed by a VERB PHRASE followed by a NOUN PHRASE followed by a period is a SENTENCE.
B. A word that can be used as an adjective is an ADJECTIVE PHRASE.
C. An ADJECTIVE PHRASE followed by a word that can be used as a noun is a NOUN PHRASE.
D. A word that can be used as a noun is a NOUN PHRASE.
E. A word that can be used as a verb is a VERB PHRASE.

The task environment tells GPS that the word "free" can be used as an adjective or verb, that "variables" can be used as a noun, that "cause" can be used as a noun or verb, and that "confusion" can be used as a noun. The specific task given to GPS is to parse the sentence (the initial OBJ):

Free variables cause confusion.

Since "free" can be used as an adjective, GPS uses rule B to transform the sentence into the object, "ADJECTIVE PHRASE variables cause confusion." Since "variables" is a noun, GPS uses rule C to transform this object into the object, "NOUN PHRASE cause confusion." Since "cause" can be used as a verb, GPS uses rule E to transform this object into the object, "NOUN PHRASE VERB PHRASE confusion." Since "confusion" is a noun, GPS

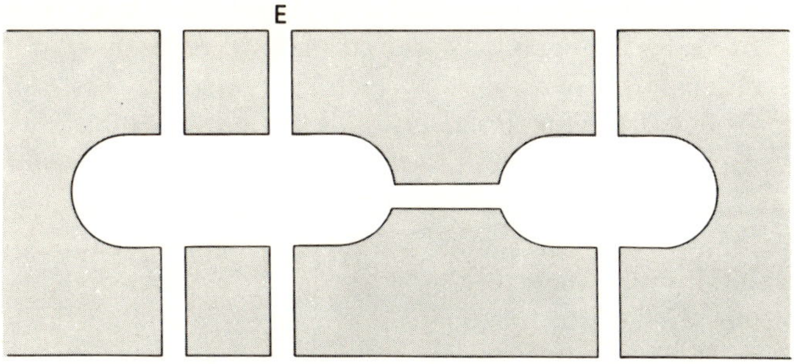

Figure 8-3 The seven bridges of Konigsberg.

uses rule D to transform this object into the object, "NOUN PHRASE VERB PHRASE NOUN PHRASE." It then uses rule A to transform this object into the final OBJ, "SENTENCE," and the parsing is complete. To perform this task, GPS generated 19 goals.

Seven Bridges of Konigsberg Task In a river in Konigsberg, Germany, were two islands connected with the mainland and with each other by seven bridges, as shown in Figure 8-3. The task is to start at point *E*, cross each bridge *exactly* once, and end at point *E*. In 1736, Euler, the famous mathematician, proved that this task is impossible. Nevertheless, this task was given to GPS. After generating 71 goals, GPS stopped because its memory was full. In its attempts it had found two ways of crossing six bridges. GPS should have ways of viewing a task as a whole instead of always just trying to apply operators within the task. After some failures on the task it should consider the possibility and perhaps even prove that the task is impossible.

Water Jug Task Given a 5-gal jug and an 8-gal jug, how can you get *exactly* 2 gal in the 5-gal jug? Since there is a sink nearby, a jug can be filled from the tap or emptied down the drain. Water can be poured from one jug to another. No measuring devices other than the jugs themselves are available. To perform this task, GPS generated 24 goals.

Letter Series Completion Task The task is to add the next two letters to the letter series BCBDBE . . . . To perform this task, GPS generated 27 goals. It finds a simple description of the given series and then adds the required two letters. This task involved inductive reasoning.

8.6 FINDINGS AND CONCLUSIONS

Tasks On the positive side, GPS can perform a wide variety of tasks. It can work on tasks involving inductive reasoning (for example, the letter series completion task) and deductive reasoning (for example, the predicate calculus task). GPS is a truly unified and multipurpose program and not merely a conglomeration of programs, each specialized to perform one task. One piece of evidence for this assertion is that each method is used for an average of half the tasks. It may be the forerunner of a program that will, in some significant sense, perform the task of doing its own learning. Newell, Shaw, and Simon (1960) present a very detailed hand simulation of how GPS might learn, although they acknowledge that some difficulties remain. We have already stressed the great value in getting a program to be general enough to do its own learning. On the negative side, GPS performs tasks very slowly. It should have ways of viewing a task as a whole instead of always just trying to apply operators within the task.

Problem-solving Techniques Means-ends analysis works very well on some tasks but not on others, depending on the suitability of the differences and difference ordering given in the task specification. The general techniques used by GPS resemble those used by humans. GPS needed to use only four types of goals, an amazingly small number. It was found that the problem-solving techniques strongly interact with the way tasks are represented. For the problem-solving techniques of GPS, certain properties of a good representation of a task were found. For example, it is generally better to represent operators as move operators (with variables, pretests, moves, and posttests) rather than as form operators. The way in which GPS selects the next goal to be tried will need to be improved, especially when the goal trees become large. GPS usually makes a local selection, but sometimes makes the somewhat arbitrary selection of the top or some other goal. The author believes that a goal-selection scheme analogous to that used in MULTIPLE would help GPS.

EXERCISES

1. List the principal similarities and differences between MULTIPLE and GPS.

2. Suppose that the difference ordering in a task environment specification says that the difference $D3$ is more difficult than is $D2$, which is more difficult than is $D1$.

a. Suppose that the problem-solving executive procedure of GPS selects goal 3 (see Figure 8-4), generates the subgoal G, and soon will go to step D. When the procedure arrives at step D, which is the selected goal, if G is to

(1) Reduce $D1$ on INITIAL OBJ.

(2) Reduce $D3$ on INITIAL OBJ.

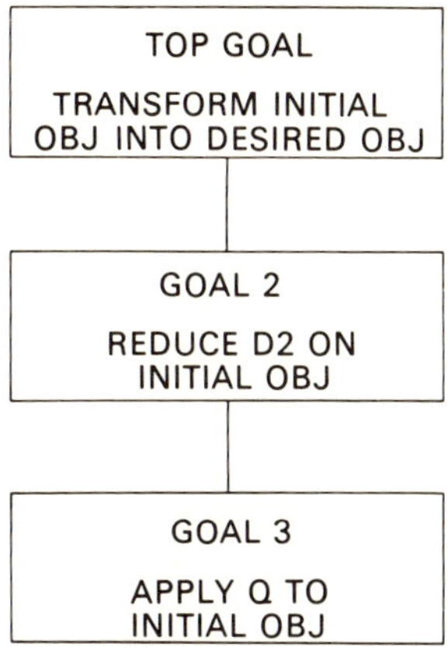

Figure 8-4

Explain your answers.

b. Suppose that the problem-solving executive procedure of GPS selects goal 4 (Figure 8-5), generates the subgoal *G*, and soon will go to step D. When the procedure arrives at step D, which is the selected goal, if *G* is to

(1) Reduce *D*1 on 2.

(2) Reduce *D*3 on 2.

Explain your answers.

3. In the seven bridges of Konigsberg task, show how one can, after starting at *E*, cross six bridges exactly once and not cross the other bridge.

4. Perform the following tasks and tabulate your times against the corresponding times taken by GPS.

a. Integrations.
b. Missionaries and cannibals.
c. Tower of Hanoi.
d. First-order predicate calculus.
e. Father and sons.
f. Three coins.
g. Water jug.
h. Letter series completion.

5. Give a step-by-step explanation of how the problem-solving executive procedure generates and selects goals 5, 6, and 7 in Figure 8-1.

6. Give a step-by-step explanation of how the problem-solving executive procedure generates and selects goals 9 through 13 in Figure 8-1.

7. With the aid of a goal tree, give a step-by-step explanation of how GPS would use the problem-solving executive procedure to perform the task ob-

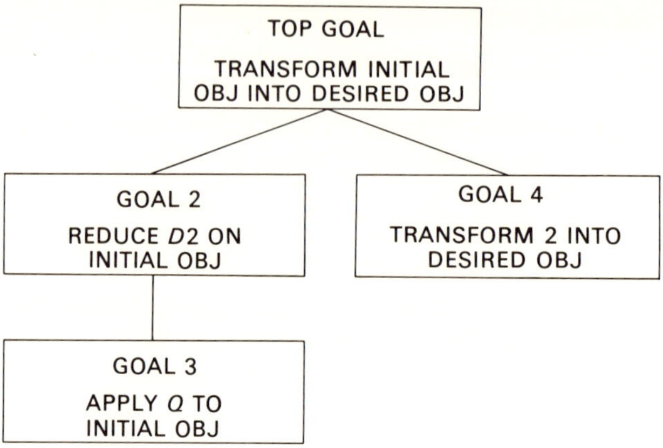

Figure 8-5

tained by having the following objects replace the objects in the specific monkey task in Table 8-1:

INITIAL OBJ =

a. The monkey's place is place 1.
b. The box's place is under the bananas.
c. The contents of the monkey's hand are empty.

DESIRED OBJ = the monkey's place is under the bananas.

8. With the aid of a goal tree, give a step-by-step explanation of how GPS would use the problem-solving executive procedure to perform the task obtained by having the following objects replace the objects in the specific monkey task in Table 8-1.

INITIAL OBJ =

a. The monkey's place is under the bananas.
b. The box's place is under the bananas.
c. The contents of the monkey's hand are empty.

DESIRED OBJ =

a. The monkey's place is place 2.
b. The box's place is place 1.

9. Give an example of a specific task which, when taken together with the monkey task environment in Table 8-1, would constitute a task that GPS would perform without generating any goal other than the top goal.

10. Are there any specific monkey tasks which would require GPS to generate more than 13 goals? Give a brief proof of your answer.

11. Let CLIMB DOWN be the MOVE operator that is the inverse of the operator CLIMB in the monkey task environment in Table 8-1; that is, CLIMB DOWN is the operator in which the monkey starts on the box and climbs down from the box.

a. Complete the following definition: CLIMB DOWN =
(1) Pretest.
(2) Move.

b. Give the row for CLIMB DOWN that should be added to the possible table of connections in Table 8-3 in order to make it easiest for GPS to handle CLIMB DOWN.

12. Suppose that the difference ordering in the monkey task environment in Table 8-1 were reversed; that is, the difference *D*1 is more difficult than is *D*2, which is more difficult than is *D*3. Which would be the first goal to be different from the corresponding goal in Figure 8-10? Explain your answer.

BIBLIOGRAPHY

Ernst, George W., and Allen Newell: "Generality and GPS," Center for the Study of Information Processing, Carnegie-Mellon University, Pittsburgh, Pa., January, 1967.

———, and ———: Some Issues of Representation in a General Problem Solver, *Proc. AFIPS Annu. Spring Joint Computer Conf.*, 1967, pp. 583–600.

———, and ———: "GPS: A Case Study in Generality and Problem Solving," *ACM Monograph*, Academic Press, Inc., New York, 1969.

McCarthy, John: "Situations, Actions, and Causal Laws," *Stanford Artificial Intelligence Project Memo* 2, Palo Alto, Calif., July, 1963.

Newell, Allen, J. C. Shaw, and Herbert Simon: A Variety of Intelligent Learning in a General Problem-solver, in M. C. Yovits and S. Cameron (eds.), "Self-Organizing Systems," Pergamon Press, New York, 1960, pp. 153–189.

Quinlan, J. R.: A Task-independent Experience Gathering Scheme for a Problem Solver, *Proc. Intern. Joint Conf. Artificial Intelligence*, 1969, pp. 193–198.

9
Programs That Balance Assembly Lines, Write Programs, Compose Music, and Find Chemical Structures

This chapter ties up some loose ends concerning multipurpose and problem-solving programs. A generalization of the program that balances assembly lines is a multipurpose program in much the same sense that GPS and MULTIPLE are. The program shows promise of being a computationally efficient way of balancing assembly lines in actual practice. A program that could write nontrivial programs could improve itself by improving one of its own programs and then using the improved program. The two program-writing programs to be described are only preliminary attempts to take the first step in reaching this long-range goal. The Heuristic Compiler writes programs in a manner similar to the way that GPS solves problems. A program was written that composes music obeying counterpoint rules which are approximately those of Palestrina; when this music is performed, it does sound something like that of Palestrina. The chemistry program finds an ordered list of structural formulas which explain a given empirical formula and mass spectrum of some acyclic organic molecule. The performance of the program approaches or exceeds that of postdoctoral laboratory workers in mass spectrometry for certain classes of organic molecules.

9.1 A PROGRAM THAT BALANCES ASSEMBLY LINES

Fred Tonge (1965) designed a computer program that balances assembly lines. A generalization of this program, called the general probabilistic procedure, is multipurpose in much the same sense that GPS (Chapter 8) and MULTIPLE (Chapter 7) are. The program found very good solutions in a relatively small number of trials. It shows promise of being a computationally efficient way of balancing assembly lines in actual practice.

The Assembly Line Balancing Problem An assembly line balancing problem consists of a cycle time, a set of tasks U_i each requiring a known operation time t_i, and a partial ordering among the tasks. Figure 9-1 shows a problem with a cycle time of 21 and a partially ordered set of tasks where each node represents a task and its associated time and where the arrows represent the partial ordering. Task U_1 has an operation time $t_1 = 4$ and must be performed prior to tasks U_2 and U_3. The solution of a problem consists of an assignment of tasks to work stations such that:

A. Each task is assigned to exactly one station.
B. The sum of the times of all tasks assigned to any station does not exceed the cycle time.
C. The stations can be ordered in a line so that the partial ordering of the tasks is preserved.

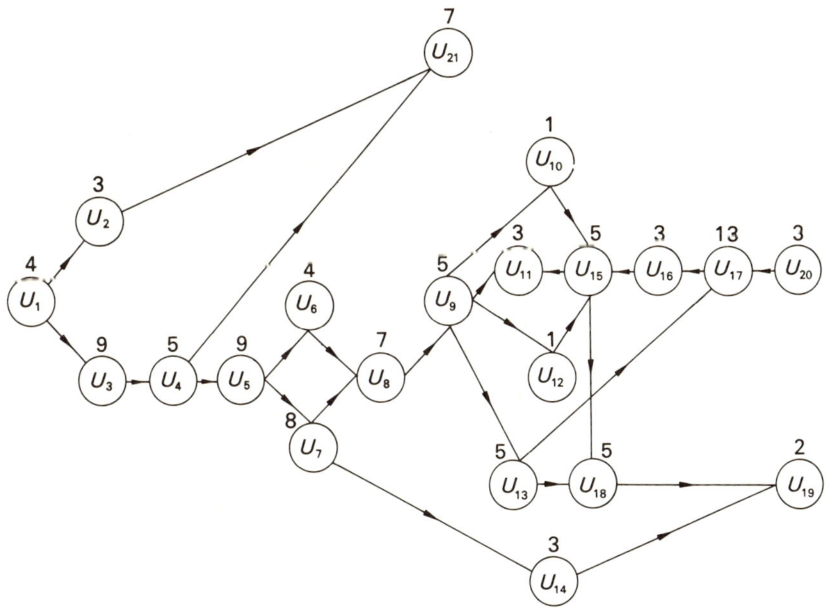

Figure 9-1 An assembly line balancing problem. The cycle time is 21.

An optimal solution is one in which the number of stations is a minimum. Many procedures which try to find optimal solutions add tasks one by one to a station. As soon as a task which is too long to fit at a station is chosen, that task is made the first task in a new station. Two of the many simple heuristics for choosing the next task to be added are:

Heuristic A: Choose the task with the largest operation time.

Heuristic B: Choose the task with the most immediate successors.

The General and Specific Probabilistic Procedures The general probabilistic procedure is stated below. It will be explained in the specific case of assembly line balancing.

A. Initialize run.
B. Initialize trial.
C. Characterize (categorize) situation.
D. Choose rule probabilistically.
E. Apply rule to modify situation.
F. If the trial is not completed, go to step C.
G. Evaluate solution. If the solution is better, then reward the corresponding rules in the sequence of categorizations. If the solution is worse, then punish the corresponding rules.
H. If the run is not completed, go to step B.
I. Print the best solution and stop.

The specific probabilistic procedure assigns tasks to work stations along the assembly line by probabilistically selecting a heuristic to choose the next task to be added to the current station. The specific procedure is described in terms of the general probabilistic procedure stated above. The situation is characterized by the number of the next task to be assigned. Thus for the illustrated problem, there are 21 characterizations (first assignment, second assignment, . . ., twenty-first assignment) with a pair of rules (heuristics A and B) and probabilities assigned with each. In the example, since both selection rules were assigned with each of the 21 categorizations, there are 42 probabilities. A run was stopped after 20 trials.

As for learning, each rule at each categorization initially had a weight of 50. Rewarding a rule occurrence consisted of adding 10 to its weight. Punishing consisted of subtracting 10. Weights could not go below plus 5. The probability of choosing a rule in a particular characterization was its weight divided by the sum of the weights of the rules associated with that categorization.

Findings and Conclusions The specific probabilistic procedure described above was tried on many assembly line balancing problems. It found very good solutions in a relatively small number of trials. It shows promise of being a computationally efficient way of balancing assembly lines in actual practice. In the small number (20) of trials used in a run, the learning procedure had little effect. Thus it will take experiments with some problems requiring more trials to test the merit of the learning procedure.

The performance of the specific probabilistic procedure on many assembly line balancing problems was compared to that of three other procedures on the same problems. One procedure used heuristic A alone; another, B alone. The probabilistic combination of heuristics produced as good or better balances (in all problems but one) than did the heuristics taken individually. The specific probabilistic procedure also outperformed the third procedure, which randomly chose tasks rather than heuristics.

The author believes that an even better assembly balancing program could be obtained from some modification of the following basic procedure, which carries out many "inner" disjunctive searches within a single "outer" disjunctive search. Each assembly line balancing problem may be represented as a disjunctive goal tree, but this tree is generally too large to handle directly. Each such problem may be factored in a natural manner into an outer problem and inner problems. The outer problem consists of assigning stations to an assembly line. Each inner problem consists of assigning tasks to a station. If this factoring idea succeeds for assembly line balancing, it should be extended to other kinds of problems, even if the factoring is not so "natural." The outer search and the inner searches should be simple modifications of the disjunctive search procedure (given in Section 6.1) which keeps an ordered list of different subgoals from best to worst. The top goal G of the outer disjunctive tree is to balance a given assembly line. Each link corresponds to the assignment of a set of tasks to a station. Corresponding to each distinct way of making an assignment to the first station is a level-1 subgoal G_i, namely, the goal of balancing the assembly line consisting of the tasks that remain unassigned after the task assignment represented by the link leading from G to G_i. Each level-2 goal is to balance the assembly line that remains after the assignment of two stations etc.

In the outer disjunctive search procedure, emphasis should be given to selecting the "best" subgoal to work on next. The elimination of duplicates will play a less important role. Each inner search finds all the distinct ways that sets of tasks may be assigned to a station. The input to each inner search is an untried goal on the *outer* tree. The output consists of all the outer successors of the outer goal. In an inner tree, each link corresponds to the assignment of a task to the station. If the assembly line balancing problem is "sufficiently large," the inner search should obtain only the n-best outer successors of an outer goal. With the inner disjunctive search, the emphasis should be on the elimination of the many duplicate subgoals which will occur.

The general probabilistic procedure designed by Tonge is a multipurpose procedure in much the same sense that GPS and MULTIPLE are. Thus it has the advantages discussed in Chapter 7 for multipurpose procedures. The general probabilistic procedure seems quite promising, since it succeeded so well in the specific domain of assembly line balancing.

9.2 A PROGRAM THAT WRITES PROGRAMS

This and the next section describe two programs that write programs. We are not talking here about the usual type of compiler (such as the FORTRAN compiler), which is given the description of a program in the source language (such as FORTRAN) and writes a program in machine language. The problem of writing a nontrivial program is intellectually difficult and is of great interest for that reason and because a program that could write nontrivial programs could improve itself by improving one of its own programs and then using the improved program. In particular, the program could improve the programs that write programs. The two programs to be described are only preliminary attempts to take the first step in reaching this long-range goal. Resolution-principle programs (Green, 1969; Waldinger and Lee, 1969) have also been used to write programs.

The Heuristic Compiler, written by Herbert Simon (1963) is actually two more or less independent programs called the State Description Compiler and the Descriptive Name Compiler. Both parts write programs in a manner similar to the way that GPS solves problems. Both parts write programs in the IPL-V progamming language (Newell, 1961), which was designed for the manipulation of symbolic expressions such as lists. Simon wanted to deepen his understanding of the kind of problem-solving activity that is involved in computer programming and the kinds of language and representational means that are needed to produce more sophisticated compilers.

The State Description Compiler part of the Heuristic Compiler deals with input and output state descriptions. An input and output state description of an IPL-V program is a description of the contents of the relevant cells before and after the program has been executed. The State Description Compiler is originally given a list of elementary operators (IPL-V instructions). With each such instruction is given an input state description I and an output state description O and a difference which that instruction tends to remove. Then this compiler is given a series of program-writing goals. Each goal consists of writing an IPL-V program which will transform a given input state description I_a into a given output state description O_a. If I_a is the same as O_a, the compiler reports success. Working much like GPS, this compiler finds a difference between I_a and O_a and then a relevant IPL-V instruction which tends to remove this difference. If this instruction transforms input state description I_b into output state description O_b, then the original goal is transformed into the conjunction of two goals, namely, transform I_a into I_b and transform

O_b into O_a. Often one or both of these goals can be made immediately achievable by matching, for example, by making O_b the same as O_a by substituting a constant for a variable in O_b. This compiler is recursive, that is, one or both of the goals may be transformed into the conjunction of two other goals, etc. The State Description Compiler has written a two-instruction IPL-V program.

The input to the Descriptive Name Compiler part of the Heuristic Compiler is a verbal description of an IPL-V program to be written. The verbal description is a sentence in a restricted form of natural English. In the initial phase, the Descriptive Name Compiler searches a list of IPL-V programs to find one whose verbal description is as similar as possible to the verbal description of the program to be written. In the final phase, this compiler transforms, in a manner similar to GPS, the verbal description of the IPL-V program (that was found) into the verbal description of the desired program. The compiler makes the corresponding transformation of the IPL-V program (that was found) into the desired program. The Descriptive Name Compiler has written two-instruction and seven-instruction IPL-V programs.

9.3 A PROGRAM THAT LEARNS TO WRITE PROGRAMS

A program written by Friedberg, Dunham and North (1958, 1959) learns in a weak sense to write programs. The program writes programs to solve very simple problems for a very simple hypothetical computer. Actually, there are three program-writing programs, called "students," which are experimentally compared with one another. Each student submits "his" program to his "teacher," which is another program. In the experiments, learned behavior was much inferior to random behavior, and the ability to partition problems and to deal with parts in order of difficulty did prove helpful.

A program for the hypothetical computer consists of 64 "machine" instructions. The program acts upon the data in 64 locations. Each instruction has one of four simple operation codes. The first instruction is executed first. The instructions are executed in sequence except when the operation code is a TRANSFER. If the sixty-fourth instruction is executed within a given time specified by the experimenter, the program is considered to have finished.

Each problem consists of input locations, an output location, and a criterion by which the teacher judges between success and failure. In the IDENTITY problem for example, the output bit (that is, a 0 or a 1) is to be made identical to the input bit. In the AND problem, the output bit is to be made the logical AND of the two input bits; that is, the output bit is to be made 1 if and only if both the input bits are 1.

The teacher, but not her students, knows what the problem is. The student submits his program to his teacher. She runs the program and tells him whether his program succeeded or failed. Actually there are two teachers, one for Homer and Teddy and the other for Ramsey. (Homer, Teddy, and Ramsey are the students.) The teacher for Homer and Teddy runs each submitted program for each possible combination of input data. Thus each submitted program is run four times for the AND problem. After each failure, Homer simply replaces his random program by another random program. He does this until he hits upon a perfect program.

Teddy tries to learn to write a program to solve a given problem. Two instructions, chosen initially at random, are on record at any time for each location so that there are, altogether, 128 instructions on record. One of the two instructions is active, and the other is inactive. In each trial, Teddy submits his program to his teacher, who executes it on all possible combinations of inputs for the problem. The program executed during the trial consists of the 64 active instructions. Teddy has two ways of altering his program. He frequently interchanges the two instructions on record for a single location, so that first one and then the other becomes the active instruction. This process is called *routine change.* Occasionally he makes a random change, that is, erases one of the 128 instructions on record and replaces it with a new instruction chosen at random. The routine changes enabled Teddy to accumulate data on the relative success of the two instructions on record for each location and gradually favor the more successful instruction. The random changes are made in order that Teddy not be restricted to the 2^{64} programs that can be made from the instructions on record at any one time. Both the routine and the random changes are governed largely by a number associated with each instruction on record. This number is called the *success number.* Each time a success or failure is recorded, the success number of each participant instruction is increased or decreased. The ratio between the success numbers of the two instructions governs the relative frequency with which each instruction emerges as active. After a failure, the modification of success numbers continues until one of the inactive instructions becomes active. There are two kinds of random changes. An instruction whose success number drops below some predetermined number is replaced by a new random instruction. In addition, an instruction is replaced after every sixty-fourth failure.

For each problem, Ramsey's teacher makes him succeed on the most difficult input situation before she tries to add in the easier parts of the problem. Experiments not reported here show that it is better to give the most difficult parts first rather than vice versa. If the program submitted by Ramsey succeeds on a given run, he "binds" all the participants and re-submits his program for the next part of the problem. If his program fails on a given run, he replaces all the unbound participants with new random instructions. Ramsey does not change bound instructions unless he gets stuck. He is said to be "stuck" when no participant can be replaced after a failing run because

Table 9-1 Performance of the students*

Problem	*Homer*	*Ramsey*	*Teddy*
IDENTITY	321	60	1,360
AND	19,445	1,758	24,898
Inclusive OR	7,208	216	44,539
NOT IF THEN	14,247	6,820	18,633

* Each entry gives the average number of trials before success was reached.

all are bound. When Ramsey becomes stuck, the problem is begun again and Ramsey submits 64 new random instructions.

The performance of the three "students" is summarized in Table 9-1. Ramsey is much better than Homer, which is much better than Teddy.

Several conclusions may be drawn from this work. Experiments with Ramsey (the best student) indicate that the ability to partition problems and to deal with parts in order of difficulty does prove helpful. This conclusion is not too surprising. We have seen many times before that analyzing a problem into subproblems is a good idea. Thus, in a very weak sense, a computer has been programmed to learn to write programs. In Section 9.2 we discussed the great importance of getting a program to write programs. Getting a program that learns to write programs is even better. Unfortunately, the program that learns to write programs—Teddy—is very weak. In the experiments reported, learned behavior was inferior to random behavior; Teddy was much worse than Homer. The experiments should be interpreted as meaning that Teddy's learning mechanisms, although plausible and somewhat complicated, are inadequate.

9.4 A PROGRAM THAT COMPOSES MUSIC

A program that composes music obeying counterpoint rules approximating those of Palestrina was written at the University of Illinois by Lejaren A. Hiller and Leonard M. Isaacson (1959) for the ILLIAC (ILLInois Automatic Computer). The program starts at the beginning of the composition and composes one note at a time until it either writes the last note or gets stuck. It makes a pseudorandom choice of the next note, which is then tested to see if it obeys the counterpoint rules. If 50 attempts to compose the next note fail, the entire composition up to that point is erased and the program starts again from the first note. It would probably be better to use a depth-first search procedure; that is, after 50 straight failures, the program would delete the previous note and continue, etc. It would be better if the program did some planning. The program has written the fairly well-known "Illiac

Suite," which has been performed and does sound something like the music of Palestrina.

9.5 A PROGRAM THAT FINDS CHEMICAL STRUCTURES

Heuristic Dendral is a program designed by Edward Feigenbaum (1968) and others at Stanford University. The input to the program is the empirical formula (number of carbon atoms, hydrogen atoms, etc.) and the mass spectrum of some acyclic (nonringed) organic molecule. The output is a list of structural formulas (molecular graphs) that explain the given data in the light of the program's model of mass spectrometry and stability of organic molecules. The list is ordered from most to least satisfactory. The performance of the program approaches or exceeds that of postdoctoral laboratory workers in mass spectrometry for certain classes of organic molecules.

The four parts of Heuristic Dendral are the preliminary inference maker, the hypothesis generator, the predictor, and the evaluator. The preliminary inference maker embodies a set of pattern recognition heuristic rules. It makes a preliminary interpretation of the data in terms of the presence of key functional groups, absence of other functional groups, weights of radicals attached to key functional groups, etc. Its activity paves the way for the hypothesis generator.

The hypothesis generator knows the valences of atoms and is capable of generating all the topologically possible isomers (same empirical formula, different structural formulas) of the empirical formula. The hypothesis generator and an empirical formula determine an implicit tree. At the top node, all the atoms are found but no structure. At the terminal nodes, complete structures are found but no unallocated atoms. The search within this tree is guided by various heuristic rules and chemical models, namely, the outputs from the preliminary inference maker, the a priori model, and the zero-order theory of mass spectrometry. The a priori model is a model of the chemical stability of organic molecules based on the presence of certain denied and preferred subgraphs of the chemical graphs. The zero-order theory is a very crude but efficient theory of the behavior of molecules in mass spectrometry. It screens out whole classes of structures because they are not valid with respect to the data, even within a crude approximation.

The output from the preliminary inference maker and hypothesis generator is a list of molecular structures that are candidate hypotheses to explain the empirical spectrum. The predictor makes a detailed prediction of the mass spectrum for each candidate hypothesis. It embodies a complex theory of mass spectrometry. The evaluator is a heuristic nonlinear hierarchy which matches the predicted spectrum for each candidate with the empirical spectrum. After discarding some candidates, it prints out the remainder from most to least satisfactory.

EXERCISES

1. Name three multipurpose programs.

2. Suppose that the assembly line balancing problem in Figure 9-1 has a cycle time of 21.

- **a.** Find a (not necessarily optimal) solution.
- **b.** Find a nonoptimal solution. Prove that your solution is not optimal.

3. Suppose that the specific procedure is using two selection rules to balance an assembly line containing 18 tasks.

- **a.** How many categorizations are there?
- **b.** What is the total number of probabilities used?

4. In the specific probabilistic procedure, suppose that each of the two rules, *A* and *B*, for a categorization has its usual weight of 50. If rule *A* is rewarded once and rule *B* is punished once, then for rule *A* give the resulting

- **a.** Weight
- **b.** Probability.

5. Match the letter of each GPS item in the first column with the number of the corresponding State Description Compiler item in the second column.

a. Object	(1) IPL-V program
b. Operator	(2) State description
c. Transform-type goal	(3) IPL-V instruction
d. Solution	(4) Program-writing goal.

6. How many times does the teacher of Homer and Teddy run each submitted program for the "identity" problem?

7. What would be the advantage of having the music composition program use a depth-first search procedure?

BIBLIOGRAPHY

Feigenbaum, Edward: Artificial Intelligence: Themes in the Second Decade, *Proc. IFIP Congr.*, vol II, Spartan Books, Washington, D.C., 1968, pp. 1000–1008.

Friedburg, R. M., B. Dunham, and J. H. North: A Learning Machine, *IBM J. Res. Develop.* part 1, vol. II, no. 1, pp. 2–12, January, 1958; part 2, vol. III, no. 3, July, 1959.

Green, Cordell: Application of Theorem Proving to Problem Solving, *Proc. Intern. Joint Conf. Artificial Intelligence*, 1969, pp. 219–240.

Hiller, Lejaren A., and Leonard M. Isaacson: "Experimental Music, Composition with an Electronic Computer," McGraw-Hill Book Company, New York, 1959.

Newell, Allen (ed.): "Information Processing Language V Manual," Prentice-Hall, Inc., Englewood Cliffs, N.J., 1961.

Simon, Herbert A.: Experiments with a Heuristic Compiler, *J. ACM*, vol. 10, pp. 493–506, October, 1963.

Tonge, Fred M.: Assembly Line Balancing Using Probabilistic Combinations of Heuristics, *Management Sci.*, vol. 11, no. 7, pp. 727–735, May, 1965.

Waldinger, Richard J., and Richard C. T. Lee: PROW: A Step toward Automatic Program Writing, *Proc. Intern. J. Conf. Artificial Intelligence*, 1969.

10
Automatic Deductive Question Answering

Many people have programmed computers to answer questions and give facts. It is usually best for such a program to be on a time-sharing system, with interaction between the computer and the human user. A program which can deduce the answers to a wide variety of questions has the long-term potential of a multipurpose program. Another long-term goal is to make such a deductive question-answering program into an intelligent conversationalist or communicator. Such a program would be able to ask questions of the user. A deductive question-answering program is useful in the short term as well. It can deduce an answer requiring the combination of several facts, whereas an ordinary information-retrieval program cannot.

When the amount of data becomes large, it must be stored in the computer's memory in such a way that a question-answering program can efficiently retrieve data relevant to the given question. Otherwise the program will spend most of its time searching for relevant data. When the amount of data is small, it is sufficient to use the simple scheme of keeping the data as a list of facts. Some but not all kinds of data are conveniently kept in tables.

Many kinds of data are conveniently kept in a network or graph, where, roughly speaking, each node is a concept linked to other nodes by various relations. A network which (partially) describes a domain is called a *model* of that domain. For example, a network describing the real world is a model of the real world. A question-answering program can find relevant facts in such a model far more efficiently than in a mere list of facts. M. Ross Quillian (1966) wrote a program (not yet a deductive question-answering program) which uses an advanced model consisting of a kind of dictionary of definitions. Each concept (node) is defined in terms of other concepts. A large computer memory could conveniently hold an intermediate amount of data in such a model. When the amount of data becomes even larger, however, more efficient models will need to be found.

10.1 PROGRAMS THAT ANSWER QUESTIONS STATED IN RESTRICTED ENGLISH

Most of these programs can also be told facts stated in restricted English, but in some other programs, the data must be "built in." Much of the program is involved in finding the syntax and meaning of English sentences. Bert Green, et al. (1962), Robert Lindsay (1963), Robert Simmons (1965), and Fred Thompson (1966) are some of the many people who have written question-answering programs emphasizing English rather than deduction. William Cooper (1964) wrote a program which answers true-false questions. The facts and questions are stated in restricted English.

Daniel Bobrow (1964) wrote a program called STUDENT which solves high school algebra word problems stated in restricted English. It transforms the problem into a set of simultaneous equations. If STUDENT fails to solve this set of equations, various heuristics are used to change the equations, and the store of global information is searched for formulas that may be useful. An example of a formula in the store of global information is the fact that distance equals speed times time. STUDENT has solved a wide variety of algebra word problems. When it solves a problem, it is usually at least as fast as are humans on the same problem. Bobrow states that STUDENT cannot solve most textbook problems exactly as written. This is due to the fact that STUDENT can handle only restricted English. A similar program, written by Eugene Charniak (1969), solves calculus word problems.

10.2 PROGRAMS THAT DEDUCE ANSWERS TO QUESTIONS STATED FORMALLY

The facts and questions are presented to these programs in predicate calculus or extended predicate calculus, and natural language is not involved. The emphasis is on generality and deduction. The first work in this direction was the proposal by John McCarthy of a program called the Advice Taker

(1959, 1963, 1969). This program was to manipulate formal descriptions of the kinds of problems encountered in everyday life. He said that the program should have "common sense" when it reasons about such problems. Fischer Black (1964) wrote a program embodying some of McCarthy's ideas, and it solved several problems. It uses a depth-first search and works backwards from the conclusion toward the hypotheses in the same manner as the geometry program of Gelernter (page 50). In the same tradition, a program was written called DEDUCOM (DEDUctive COMmunicator) (Slagle, 1965), which, when given 68 facts, answered 10 questions answerable from the facts.

A Deductive Question-answering Program Based on the Resolution Principle

Now the author proposes a program, to be called DEDUCOM-II. It is based on the idea that a program can find the values associated with specified variables by first quantifying such variables existentially and then proving the corresponding theorem while keeping track of the substitutions made for the variables of interest. This idea was discovered by John McCarthy and then independently by Cordell Green and Bertram Raphael. Green and Raphael (1968) wrote a program embodying this idea, and the program proposed here is an extension of their program. Similar programs have been written by J. L. Darlington (1969) and by R. E. Levien and M. E. Maron (1967). The latter program uses a large data base. The five kinds of questions answerable by DEDUCOM-II are elementary, alternative, continue, factual, and proof. The user sets a time limit T (say 10 sec) for answering the first two types of questions. After describing all five kinds of questions, we give a mythical example of the behavior of the proposed program.

An elementary question is preceded by a Q and is of the form PM. The prefix P consists of a sequence of quantified variables, each quantifier being either FOR ALL, THERE EXISTS, or FIND. The matrix M is quantifier free. Suppose that the variables whose values are to be found are $X_1, X_2, \ldots, X_n$, where $n \geqslant 0$. The answer to the elementary question is one of the following:

A. "I AM STOPPING SINCE I SPENT T WITHOUT SUCCESS."
B. "I CANNOT PROVE THE STATEMENT FROM THE FACTS I KNOW."
C. YES WHEN X_1 IS EITHER $t_{11}, t_{12}, \ldots, t_{1k_1}$ BUT I DO NOT KNOW WHICH, WHEN X_2 IS EITHER $t_{21}, t_{22}, \ldots, t_{2k_2}$ BUT I DO NOT KNOW WHICH, . . ., WHEN X_n IS EITHER $t_{n1}, t_{n2}, \ldots, t_{nk_n}$ BUT I DO NOT KNOW WHICH," where the t's are terms.

Several things should be noted about an answer of type C. Many of the subordinate (WHEN) clauses may be simplified in practice. For example, instead of printing out the clause, "WHEN X_2 IS EITHER (G A X_4), (F A C),

(G X_3 B) BUT I DO NOT KNOW WHICH," the program would print the clause, "WHEN X_2 IS EITHER (G A B), (F A C) BUT I DO NOT KNOW WHICH," where the term (F A C) REPRESENTS $f(a, c)$, etc. It does this by combining the first and third terms into their most general common instance, (G A B). For any variable X_j which remains unassigned (that is, $k_j = 0$), the program replaces the subordinate clause, "WHEN X_j IS EITHER BUT I DO NOT KNOW WHICH," by the clause, "WHEN X_j IS ANYTHING." For any variable X_j which has only one assignment, the corresponding subordinate clause is replaced by "WHEN X_j IS t_{j1}." Note that if no variables need to be found (that is, $n = 0$), then the question is really "VERIFY PM." A type C answer to such a question degenerates correctly into "YES."

An alternative question is preceded by a Q and is of the form P(ALTS $Q_1Q_2 \ldots Q_n$) where, for each i, PQ_i is an elementary question. The answer to an alternative question is one of the following:

A. "I AM STOPPING SINCE I SPENT T WITHOUT SUCCESS."
B. "I CANNOT PROVE ANY OF THE ALTERNATIVES FROM THE FACTS I KNOW."
C. "STATEMENT i IS TRUE WHEN X_1 IS . . ."

The program first tries to answer the first elementary question, PQ_i, for a short time; it then cycles through all the elementary questions, and it spends an increasing amount of time on each question until an answer is found. In one specific simple scheme, the program spends t (say a hundredth of a second) on the first elementary question, then $2t$ on the second, then $4t$ on the third, . . ., then $2^{n-1}t$ on the nth, then $2^n t$ more on the first, etc. An alternative question may be used directly, although it is more usual for the program to obtain one by preprocessing a YES-NO for multiple-choice questions. For example, the program transforms the YES-NO question P(IS s), where s is a predicate calculus statement (containing no FINDS), into the alternative question P(ALTS s –s), where –s is the negation of the statement s. The answer to the alternative question is transformed into the answer to the YES-NO question in a straightforward manner. This involves replacing a type C answer to the alternative question by transforming STATEMENT 1 IS TRUE into YES and by transforming STATEMENT 2 IS TRUE into NO.

If the program gives an answer of type A to an elementary or alternative question, the user may ask the program the question, CONTINUE. In this case, the program continues to try to answer the preceding question with a time limit greater than T.

A factual question is preceded by S and can be any predicate calculus statement. The program stores the statement as a fact in its memory unless the statement is obviously true or false. The program first treats the statement as a YES-NO question with a very short time limit, say a tenth of a second. If it answers the question either YES or NO, it says so and does not store the statement. Otherwise, it stores the fact as one or more clauses in its memory.

After the program has given any answer of type C, the user may ask the question PROOF, which causes the program to give a proof of its last answer and to state how many clauses were generated on the proof tree before the proof was completed.

Table 10-1 gives a mythical example of the behavior of the proposed program. This example is based on a real example of the behavior of the program of Green and Raphael (1968). Their program is able to answer much more difficult questions, and so will the proposed program. In Table 10-1, the lines in capital letters are typed by the human or the program, whereas other lines are given as explanations.

Table 10-1 A mythical example of the behavior of the proposed deductive question-answering program

S (IN JOHN BOY)
OK
The statement that John is a member of the set of boys is accepted,
and the program's response is "OK."
Q (IN JOHN BOY)
The elementary question is, "Verify that John is in the set of boys"
or, equivalently, "John is in the set of boys, isn't he?"
YES
Q (EX X (IN JOHN X))
Verify that there exists an *X* such that John is in the set *X*.
YES
Q (FIND X (IN JOHN X))
Find an *X* such that John is in the set *X*.
YES WHEN X IS BOY
Q (IN MIKE BOY)
I CANNOT PROVE THE STATEMENT FROM THE FACTS I KNOW
S (NOT (IN JOHN BOY))
YOUR STATEMENT OBVIOUSLY CONFLICTS WITH PREVIOUS FACTS
S (NOT (IN MARY BOY))
OK
Q (IS (IN MARY BOY))
Is Mary in the set of boys?
NO
S (FA X (IF (IN X BOY) (IN X HUMAN)))
OK
This says that every boy is a human, or more literally, that for
all *X* if *X* is a boy then *X* is a human.
Q (FIND X (IN X HUMAN))
YES WHEN X IS JOHN
The theorem prover uses two statements, namely, "John is a boy" and
"Every boy is a human."

Table 10-1—*continued*

PROOF

The user asks for a proof of the last answer.

1 (IN JOHN BOY)	FACT
2 (NOT (IN X HUMAN))	NEG OF QSTN
3 (IF (IN X BOY) (IN X HUMAN))	FACT
4 (NOT (IN X BOY))	FROM 2, 3
5 CONTRADICTION	FROM 1, 4
6 CLAUSES GENERATED	

In the proof, each of the first five lines corresponds to one clause. Each clause comes either from a fact, from the negation of the question, or from two previous clauses by resolution. The last line is the number of clauses generated in the entire proof tree before the contradiction is generated.

S (FA X (IF (IN X HUMAN) (HP X ARM 2)))

OK

Note that (HP X ARM 2) means that *X* has as parts two elements of the set of all arms.

Q (HP JOHN ARM 2)

YES

EXERCISES

1. For a question-answering program, discuss briefly the relative advantages of keeping a domain's data in

- **a.** A list of facts.
- **b.** Tables.
- **c.** A network model.

2. Do you think that it is better to emphasize English or deduction in a question-answering program? Why?

3. Simplify the following subordinate clauses.

- **a.** WHEN X_2 IS EITHER (F D), (G A X_4), (F X_3), C BUT I DO NOT KNOW WHICH.
- **b.** WHEN X_3 IS EITHER BUT I DO NOT KNOW WHICH.
- **c.** WHEN X_4 IS EITHER (G A X_3) BUT I DO NOT KNOW WHICH.

4. In the YES-NO question P(IS s) why must the predicate calculus statement s contain no FINDS?

5. What is the difference between the elementary questions (EX X (IN JOHN X)) and (FIND X (IN JOHN X))?

6. What is the difference between the elementary question (IN JOHN BOY) and the YES-NO question (IS (IN JOHN BOY))?

7. Transform the YES-NO question (IS (IN MARY BOY)) into an alternative question.

8. At the end of Table 10-1, what should the program answer if the user asks Q (FIND X (HP JOHN ARM X))?

BIBLIOGRAPHY

Black, Fischer: "A Deductive Question-answering System," doctoral dissertation in applied mathematics, Division of Engineering and Applied Physics, Harvard University, Cambridge, Mass., June, 1964.

Bobrow, Daniel: A Question-answering System for High School Algebra Word Problems, *Proc. AFIPS Annu. Fall Joint Computer Conf.*, 1964, pp. 591–614.

Charniak, Eugene: Computer Solution of Calculus Word Problems, *Proc. Intern. Joint Conf. Artificial Intelligence*, 1969.

Cooper, William S.: Fact Retrieval and Deductive Question-answering Information Retrieval Systems, *J. ACM*, vol. 11, pp. 117–137, April, 1964.

Darlington, Jared L.: Theorem Provers as Question Answerers, *Proc. Intern. Joint Conf. Artificial Intelligence*, 1969.

Green, Bert, Alice K. Wolf, Carol Chomsky, and Kenneth Laughery: BASEBALL: An Automatic Question-answerer, *Proc. Western Joint Computer Conf.*, 1962, pp. 219–224. Reprinted in Edward Feigenbaum and Julian Feldman (eds.), "Computers and Thought," McGraw-Hill Book Company, New York, 1963.

Green, C., and Bertram Raphael: The Use of Theorem Proving Techniques in Question Answering Systems, *Proc. ACM Natl. Conf.*, 1968, pp. 169–181.

Levien, R. E., and M. E. Maron: Computer System for Inference Execution and Data Retrieval, *Commun. ACM*, vol. 10, no. 11, November, 1967.

Lindsay, Robert K.: Inferential Memory as the Basis of Machines Which Understand Natural Language, in Edward Feigenbaum and Julian Feldman (eds.), "Computers and Thought," McGraw-Hill Book Company, New York, 1963, pp. 217–233.

McCarthy, John: Programs with Common Sense, "Journal Proceedings of the Symposium on the Mechanization of Thought Processes," Her Majesty's Stationery Office, London, 1959, pp. 75–84.

———: Situations, Actions, and Causal Laws, *Stanford Artificial Intelligence Project Memo* 2, Palo Alto, Calif., July, 1963.

———, and Patrick Hayes: Some Philosophical Problems from the Standpoint of Artificial Intelligence, *Machine Intelligence*, vol. 4, 1969.

Quillian, M. Ross: "Semantic Memory," doctoral dissertation, Carnegie Institute of Technology, Pittsburgh, Pa., October, 1966. Published as "Scientific Report 5" by Bolt, Beranek & Newman, Inc., Cambridge, Mass.

Simmons, Robert S.: Answering English Questions by Computer: A Survey, *Commun. ACM*, vol. VIII, no. 1, pp. 53–70, January, 1965.

Slagle, James R.: "Experiments with a Deductive Question-answering Program," *Commun. ACM*, vol. VIII, no. 12, pp. 792–798, December, 1965.

Thompson, Fred: English for Computers, *Proc. AFIPS Annu. Fall Joint Computer Conf.*, 1966, pp. 349–356.

11
Automatically Finding Linear Functions That Make Evaluations and Recognize Patterns

Before starting our detailed treatment in Section 11.1, we shall present a brief overview of the chapter. A linear evaluation function is a function of the form $C \cdot Y$, where Y is a feature vector $(y_1, y_2, \ldots, y_n)$ and C is a coefficient (weight) vector. The author calls the following important problem the m,n-evaluation problem. Given a set $\{Y_i'$ is preferred to $Y_i\}$ of m preferences in n space, find a coefficient vector C such that, for as many preferences as possible, $C \cdot Y_i' > C \cdot Y_i$. Finding an evaluation function may be applied to utility theory, automatic extracting, game playing, international relations, purchasing and selling, and the evaluation of personnel and computer programs.

The $m,(n-1)$–pattern problem consists of finding a hyperplane in $(n-1)$ space which approximately separates m pattern samples (instances) into two pattern classes. Once found, a linear function that makes evaluations or recognizes patterns may be used for various purposes. Notably, a computer program may use the function to approximate the function used by a particular individual or consensus of experts. By finding a function which approximates the function used by an expert (or experts), the program may be said to learn. We shall define the m,n-half-space problem and prove that every m,n-evaluation problem and every $m,(n-1)$-pattern problem can be transformed into an m,n-half-space problem. Eight procedures are presented that attempt to find a good C for the m,n-half-space problem. When an error-free C exists, the relaxation procedure will find such a C. When n is 2, the gain-loss procedure is practical for finding an optimal C even when m is large.

11.1 TRANSFORMATION OF THE m,n-EVALUATION PROBLEM AND THE $m,(n-1)$-PATTERN PROBLEM INTO THE m,n-HALF-SPACE PROBLEM

The Evaluation Problem Formally, an evaluation function is defined as a real-valued function h which has $n > 0$ arguments, that is, $v = h(y_1, y_2, \ldots, y_n)$. We shall also write $v = h(Y)$, where Y is the vector (or point) $Y = (y_1, y_2, \ldots, y_n)$. In the interpretation of an evaluation function, the vector Y_1 is preferred to the vector Y_2 (denoted by $Y_1 \succ Y_2$) if and only if $h(Y_1) > h(Y_2)$. Each y_j is called a feature, and Y is called a feature vector. A very important and general problem is, "Given the form (for example, linear) of the evaluation function and given some data, find an evaluation function that "fits" the form and data." Of course if the data are simply a set of $(n+1)$-tuples $(y_1, y_2, \ldots, y_n, v)$, approximation theory furnishes many excellent procedures, for example, the least-squares procedure. However, the data given with the form of the evaluation function are often obtained from a subject (or subjects) as a set $\{Y_i' \succ Y_i\}$ of explicit or implicit preferences. The problem is important because the subject may be either unable or unwilling to divulge his evaluation function but may supply preferences, either implicitly, by his behavior, or explicitly. Once found, the evaluation function may be used for various purposes. Notably, a computer program may use the evaluation function to approximate the evaluation function used by a particular individual or consensus of experts. By finding an evaluation function which approximates the evaluation function used by an expert (or experts), the program may be said to have learned to make good evaluations.

One important kind of evaluation function is the utility function. See the article by Patrick Suppes and Karol Walsh (1959), for example. In one kind of utility experiment, an experimenter presents two choices, and the subject says which he prefers. For example, the experimenter asks, "Would you rather be given \$100.00 and 3 days of vacation or be given \$300.00 and 1 day vacation?" The subject then says which he prefers. The experimenter asks the subject many other such questions and obtains data concerning the subject's preferences. The experimenter then tries to obtain a utility function which has a certain form and which fits the data, at least approximately.

One way to do automatic extracting is to have the computer use an evaluation function to assign high values to the important sentences and low values to the unimportant sentences in a document. If an extract of a certain length is desired, the computer merely selects the most important sentences according to the evaluation function. A good evaluation function for the computer to use may be found by trying to "fit" the implicit preferences of experts as represented by the extracts they produce. Every sentence included in an extract of a document is preferred to every sentence excluded from the extract by that expert. Some features of sentences that might be useful in automatic extracting are:

y_1 = proportion of italicized words

y_2 = proportion of important words, for example, "conclusion," "important," words appearing in the title, etc.

y_3 = 1 if the sentence is the first sentence in a paragraph
0 if not the first sentence in a paragraph

y_4 = 1 if the last sentence in a paragraph
0 if not the last sentence in a paragraph

To play checkers well, a computer needs, among other things, an evaluation function to assign high values to positions that are good for the computer and low values to positions that are bad for the computer. A good evaluation function for the computer to use may be found by trying to "fit" the implicit preferences of experts as represented by their move choices in "the book." A position expected to arise if the book move is chosen is preferred to positions expected to arise if some alternative to the book move is chosen. The evaluation problem for checkers is the following. Using data obtained from the checker book, find an evaluation function which orders the set of all checker positions approximately according to goodness for black. Two of the many possible features are:

y_1 = piece advantage

y_2 = mobility advantage

Arthur Samuel (1967) was the first to program a computer to learn a good evaluation function (of 27 checker features) from many thousands of book moves. In his most successful effort, new features, which he called *signatures*, were defined in terms of the original 27 features. A discussion of how a program might learn the coefficients for a linear evaluation function in checkers is presented later in the present chapter.

In international relations, it would be desirable to learn the evaluation function used by various nations as represented implicitly by their decisions. It could be useful in itself to make the United States evaluation function explicit and might facilitate future decision making. It would be useful to learn the evaluation functions of the other nations in order to predict their decisions. Some of the features that might be used are:

y_1 = value of resources
y_2 = population
y_3 = area under control
y_4 = number of military men
y_5 = total value of weapons
y_6 = gross national product
y_7 = world opinion (somehow quantified)
y_8 = domestic opinion (somehow quantified)

There are many other applications in which it is desirable to find evaluation functions automatically, including the following. The ability to find an individual's utility function can be applied to purchasing and selling. In this case, one feature is the price; the other features are the features of the item being sold (for example, for a house, the number of rooms, floor area, lot area, etc). Other applications may be made in the evaluation of personnel and computer programs.

For the sake of simplicity, we assume that the evaluation function to be found is linear, that is, $v = c_1y_1 + c_2y_2 + \ldots + c_ny_n$; equivalently, it can be represented by the scalar product $C \cdot Y$, where each coefficient c_j is the weight of the corresponding y_j. Actually all we need to assume is that the evaluation function is linear with respect to the coefficients. For example, the "quadratic" (with respect to the features) evaluation function $c_1y_1 + c_2y_2 + c_3y_1^2 + c_4y_1y_2 + c_5y_2^2$ may be replaced by the linear evaluation function $c_1y_1 + c_2y_2 + c_3z_3 + c_4z_4 + c_5z_5$ by simply defining three new features in terms of the two old features: $z_3 = y_1^2$; $z_4 = y_1y_2$; $z_5 = y_2^2$.

A Detailed Example of Finding a Linear Evaluation Function Suppose, contrary to fact, that checkers had only two features, say piece advantage and mobility advantage. Suppose we were going to use only two book moves rather than thousands. Let the first book position (arrived at by making the first book move) have a piece advantage of 3 and a mobility advantage of 4. Hence the book position has a feature vector $Y' = (3, 4)$. The 3 might represent the fact that the player whose turn it is to move has one more king than his opponent but the same number of plain men. The 4 represents the fact that the player has four more move choices than does his opponent. Suppose that the alternative positions to the book position have feature vectors $Y_1 = (4,-5)$; $Y_2 = (2,6)$; $Y_3 = (1,3)$ (see Figure 11-1). In Figure 11-1 the dotted lines are intended to suggest that feature vectors are in practice backed up from deeper levels on the tree of possible future moves. From the implicit preferences of the experts as represented by the book move, we have obtained the explicit preferences: $Y' \succ Y_1$; $Y' \succ Y_2$; $Y' \succ Y_3$. Suppose that for the

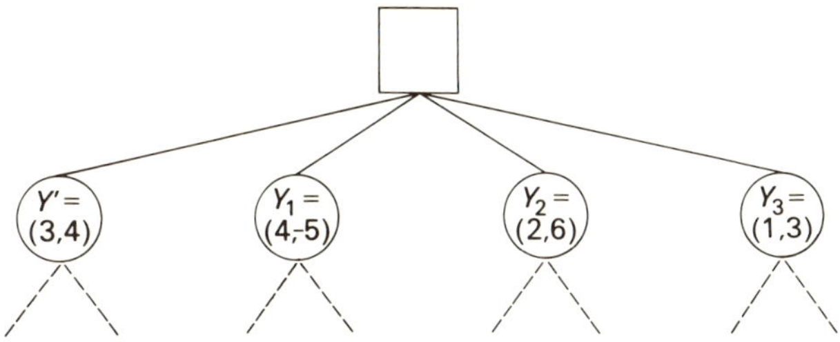

Figure 11-1 The first book move and its three alternatives.

second book move the feature vector for the book position is $Y'' = (2,5)$ and the feature vectors for its two alternatives are $Y_4 = (3,6)$; $Y_5 = (1,3)$. The explicit preferences are $Y'' \succ Y_4$; $Y'' \succ Y_5$. If we denote by Y_i' the vector of the book position that corresponds to the vector Y_i of its alternative, then all five explicit preferences may be written $Y_i' \succ Y_i$ for $i = 1, 2, 3, 4, 5$. We want to find a coefficient vector $C = (c_1, c_2)$ such that, for as many of the five points as possible,

$$C \cdot Y_i' > C \cdot Y_i \tag{1}$$

This will be called a 5,2-evaluation problem because there are five explicit preferences and two components of each feature vector. This problem can be transformed into what we shall call a 5,2–half-space problem as follows. Inequality (1) may be written $C \cdot (Y_i' - Y_i) > 0$. If $X_i = Y_i' - Y_i$, then

$$\begin{aligned}
X_1 &= (3,4) - (4,-5) = (-1,9)\\
X_2 &= (3,4) - (2,6) = (1,-2)\\
X_3 &= (3,4) - (1,3) = (2,1)\\
X_4 &= (2,5) - (3,6) = (-1,-1)\\
X_5 &= (2,5) - (1,3) = (1,2)
\end{aligned}$$

The 5,2-evaluation problem has been transformed into the following problem. Given the vectors $X_1, X_2, \ldots, X_5$, as in Figure 11-2, find a vector $C = (C_1, C_2)$ such that, for as many i as possible, $C \cdot X_i > 0$. In other words, find a line through the origin $C \cdot X = 0$ (equivalently, $c_1x_1 + c_2x_2 = 0$) dividing the space into two regions and having a normal C pointing into the "positive" region such that the positive region contains as many of the X_i as possible. On the x_1x_2 plane any set of all points lying on one side of a line through the origin $C \cdot X = 0$ is called a 2 half-space; for example, in Figure 11-2, each of the regions lying to the right and left of the line L is a 2 half-space. In this terminology, the problem is to find a 2 half-space containing as many points X_i as possible. In Figure 11-2, the 2 half-space lying to the right of the line L contains four of the five points. Inspection of Figure 11-2 shows that some other 2 half spaces

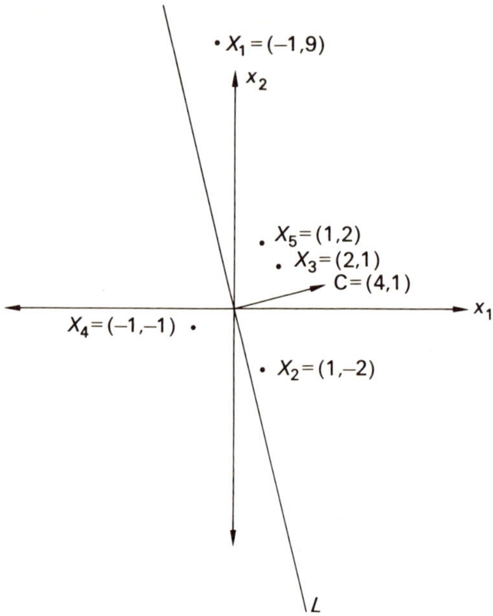

Figure 11-2 A solution to a (5,2)–half-space problem.

contain four points, but no 2 half-space contains more than four points. Let C be a vector that is normal to the line L and that points into (rather than away from) the 2 half-space, for example, $C = (4,1)$. The corresponding evaluation function is $v = (4,1) \cdot Y = 4y_1 + y_2$. As a check, we see that this evaluation function gives for the feature vector of the first book position a value of $C \cdot Y' = (4,1) \cdot (3,4) = 16$. Similarly, for the alternatives:

$$C \cdot Y_1 = (4,1) \cdot (4,-5) = 11$$
$$C \cdot Y_2 = 14$$
$$C \cdot Y_3 = 7$$

For the second book move $C \cdot Y'' = 13$; $C \cdot Y_4 = 18$; $C \cdot Y_5 = 7$. Thus for four of the five explicit preferences, we have that $C \cdot Y_i' > C \cdot Y_i$. With this motivation, we are now in a position to state the *m,n*-evaluation problem and the *m,n*–half-space problem and to show that every *m,n*-evaluation problem can be transformed into an *m,n*–half-space problem.

The *m,n*-Evaluation Problem Given a set $\{Y_i' \succ Y_i\}$ of m preferences in n space, find a coefficient vector C such that, for as many preferences as possible,

$$C \cdot Y_i' > C \cdot Y_i \tag{2}$$

The *m,n*–Half-space Problem In n space, any set of all points lying on one side of a hyperplane through the origin which is defined by the equation $c_1x_1 + c_2x_2 + \cdots + c_nx_n = 0$ is called an n half-space. An m,n–half-space problem is defined as follows. Given a set of m points X_i in n space, find an n half-space containing as many of the m points as possible.

THEOREM 1 *Every* m,n-*evaluation problem can be transformed into an* m,n–*half-space problem.*

Proof Assume that we are given an m,n-evaluation problem. Inequality (2) may be written $C\cdot(Y' - Y_i) > 0$. If we let $X_i = Y_i' - Y_i$, we have $C\cdot X_i > 0$. We have transformed the m,n-evaluation problem into the following problem. Given the vectors $X_1, X_2, \ldots, X_m$, find a vector C such that, for as many i as possible, $C\cdot X_i > 0$. In other words, find a hyperplane through the origin $C\cdot X = 0$ dividing n space into two regions and having normal C pointing into the "positive" region such that for as many i as possible the positive region contains X_i. The proof is now completed by noting that this problem can be immediately transformed into the m,n–half-space problem of finding the n half-space containing as many points X_i as possible.

The Pattern Problem Many researchers have worked on many kinds of pattern recognition problems. Some of the people who have published material relevant to the pattern recognition problem discussed in this chapter are R. O. Duda (1968), B. Efron (1964), W. H. Highleyman (1962), C. H. Mays (1964), and N. Nilsson (1965). Some other references relevant to pattern recognition in the nonseparable case are discussed briefly below. If one knows the form of the pattern distribution, statistical decision theory provides the framework for finding the minimum error-rate solution. The book by T. W. Anderson (1958) is a standard reference for the multivariate normal case where the solution is a hyperplane if the covariance matrices for the different categories are equal. N. Abramson and D. Braverman (1962) observe some nice recursive properties of this solution and interpret them as exhibiting a form of learning. An alternative approach, still in the statistical framework, was provided by R. A. Fisher (1950). He produces a hyperplane indirectly by seeking that linear function of the features that minimizes the ratio of the sum of the variances for each category to the square of the difference between the means. B. Widrow and N. E. Hoff (1960) proposed a least-mean-square algorithm for finding such a solution by iterative means. J. S. Koford and G. F. Groner (1966) discuss these matters in some detail and show that in the multivariate-normal, equal-covariance-matrix, two-category case all of these approaches yield the same solution.

The following is a specific example of what we shall later define as the $m,(n-1)$–pattern problem. Given samples (each labeled as either an

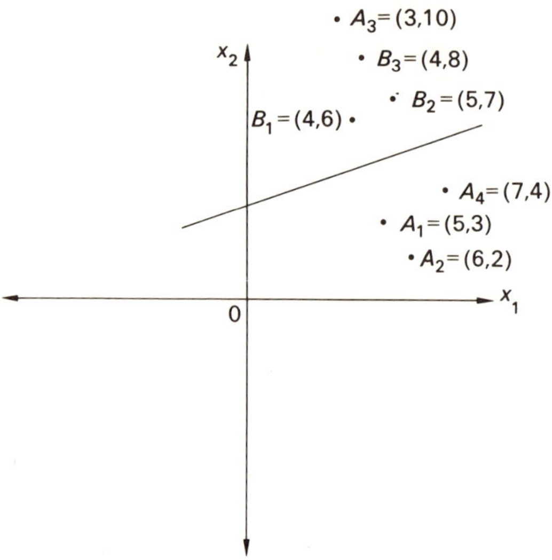

Figure 11-3 A solution to a (7,2)-pattern problem.

A sample or a B sample) and features of letters such as the number of vertices, the number of edges, find coefficients which (at least approximately) separate the A's from the B's. Suppose, for example, that the first A sample has five vertices and three edges. We say that its feature vector is $A_1 = (5,3)$. Corresponding to the other A samples, we might have $A_2 = (6,2)$; $A_3 = (3,10)$; $A_4 = (7,4)$. Similarly, corresponding to the B samples we might have $B_1 = (4,6)$; $B_2 = (5,7)$; $B_3 = (4,8)$. The problem is to find a weight vector $C = (c_1,c_2,c_3)$ such that, for as many samples as possible, $c_1x_1 + c_2x_2 + c_3$ is

a. Positive when the sample is an A sample
b. Negative when the sample is a B sample

The seven sample points (vectors) are plotted in Figure 11-3. The problem is to find a line (not necessarily through the origin) $c_1x_1 + c_2x_2 + c_3 = 0$ which divides the space into a region for A's and a region for B's. Of course in general, the pattern classes may be any two pattern classes and not just the classes of the actual letters A and B.

The *m*,(*n* – 1)–Pattern Problem Given m vectors, some of which are A samples and the rest of which are B samples, in $(n - 1)$ space, find a coefficient vector $(c_1, c_2, \ldots, c_n)$ such that, for as many of the samples as possible, $c_1x_1 + c_2x_2 + \ldots + c_{n-1}\, x_{n-1} + c_n$ is

1. Positive when the sample is an A sample
2. Negative when the sample is a B sample

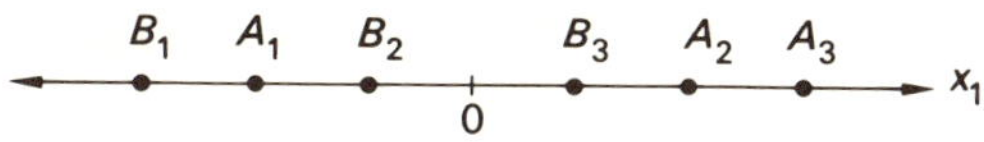

Figure 11-4 A (6,1)-pattern problem.

This is equivalent to the following problem. Find a hyperplane (not necessarily through the origin) $c_1x_1 + c_2x_2 + \dots + c_{n-1}\, x_{n-1} + c_n = 0$ which (at least approximately) divides the region for A's from the region for B's.

Theorem 2, which is proved below, is well known. (See, for example, the book by N. Nilsson, 1965). It states that any $m,(n-1)$–pattern problem can be transformed into an m,n–half-space problem. The reader will get the idea from the following example of the one-feature-pattern problem shown in Figure 11-4. The problem is to find the point $c_1x_1 + c_2 = 0$ approximately dividing the A's from the B's, that is, to find the point $x_1 = -c_2/c_1$ that approximately divides the A's from the B's. As shown in Figure 11-5, we move to two dimensions and move the samples up to the line $x_2 = 1$. Now the problem is to find a line through the origin that approximately divides the A samples from the B samples. The x_1 projection of the intersection of such a line and the line $x_2 = 1$ is a solution to the original (one-dimensional) problem. Now move each B sample to the line $x_2 = -1$ by reflecting the B sample through the origin, that is, by replacing the vector B by $-B$. The result is shown in Figure 11-6. The solution to the former (two-dimensional) problem and

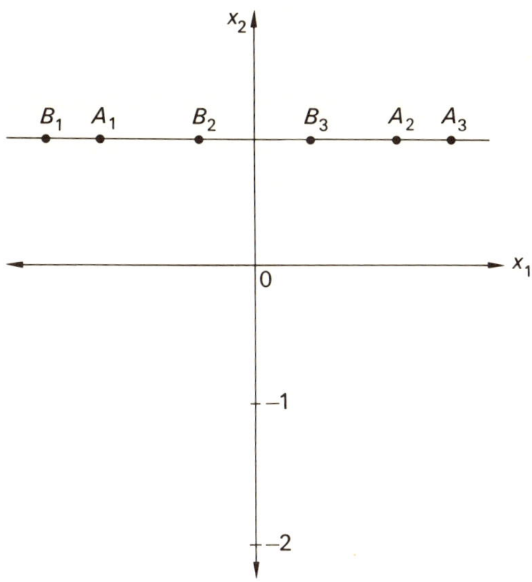

Figure 11-5 A transformation of the problem of Figure 11-4.

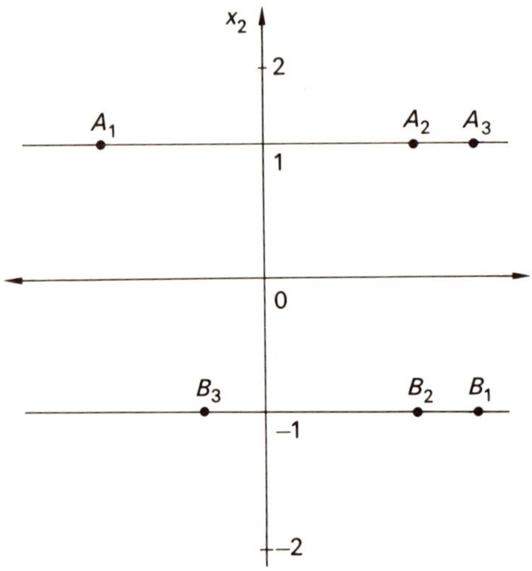

Figure 11-6 The (6,1)-pattern problem of Figure 11-4 has been transformed into a (6,2)–half-space problem.

therefore the original problem is the same as the solution to the 2–half-space problem obtained by this reflection. Hence we have transformed the original (one-dimensional) problem into a 2–half-space problem. The reader should think through the two-feature-pattern problem of Figure 11-3. The samples are first moved up to the plane $x_3 = 1$. Next the B samples are reflected by negation. This yields a 3–half-space problem.

THEOREM 2 *Any* m,(n − 1)*–pattern problem can be transformed into an* m,n*–half-space problem.*

Proof Suppose we are given an $m,(n-1)$–pattern problem. It is equivalent to the following problem. Given m vectors which have $n-1$ components, some of which are A samples and the others of which are B samples, find a hyperplane (not necessarily through the origin)

$$c_1x_1 + c_2x_2 + \ldots + c_{n-1}\,x_{n-1} + c_n = 0$$

which approximately divides the region for the A's from the region for the B's. First we embed the $(n-1)$ space in an n space and move the samples "up" to the hyperplane $x_n = 1$. Now the problem is to find a hyperplane through the origin that approximately divides the A samples from the B samples. The $x_1x_2 \ldots x_{n-1}$ projection of the intersection of such a hyperplane and the hyperplane $x_n = 1$ is a solution to the original ($n-1$–dimensional) problem.

Now each B sample is again moved, this time to the hyperplane $x_n = -1$ by reflecting the B sample through the origin, that is, by replacing each n-dimensional B vector by its negation. The solution to the former (n-dimensional) problem is the same as the solution to the m,n–half-space problem obtained by this reflection. Thus any solution to this m,n–half-space problem yields a solution to the original $m,(n-1)$–pattern problem, as was to be shown.

11.2 CRITERIA FOR PROCEDURES FOR THE m,n–HALF-SPACE PROBLEM

Since every m,n-evaluation problem and every $m,(n-1)$–pattern problem can be transformed into an m,n–half-space problem, it is extremely important to find procedures that compute good coefficients for the m,n–half-space problem. Before several such procedures are presented, four criteria are given for assessing the value of such a procedure. These criteria will help the reader in judging the value of each method and they should also be helpful to researchers who obtain other procedures. The ideas given under the third criterion are used throughout the rest of this chapter. The criteria presented are the growth of computation with increasing m and n, invariance with respect to nonsingular linear transformations, error rate, and independence of the magnitudes of the X_i.

Growth of Computation with Increasing m and n For what size m and n is it practical to compute coefficients with the given procedure? For any procedure, the amount of computation grows with increasing m and n. A procedure is good to the extent that the amount of computation grows slowly as m and n increase so that half-space problems with large m and n may be handled.

Invariance Is the half-space procedure invariant with respect to nonsingular linear transformations, including rotation and stretching? A good procedure will tend to be invariant. A procedure is called invariant with respect to a transformation if and only if for every m,n–half-space problem, the transformation of the solution obtained by the procedure is the same as the solution of the transformation of the problem. A transformation is called a stretch by the positive factor p of the jth coordinate if and only if $z_j = px_j$ and all other coordinates are unchanged.

Error Rate How good are the coefficients? By definition, the error rate of a coefficient vector C with respect to $X_1, X_2, \ldots, X_m$ is the proportion of vectors X_i such that $C \cdot X_i \leqslant 0$. The following are the corresponding definitions of error rate for the evaluation problem and the pattern problem. Given a set $\{Y_i' \succ Y_i\}$ of m preferences, the evaluation error rate of a coefficient vector C is the proportion of preferences for which $C \cdot Y_i' \leqslant C \cdot Y_i$. Given a set of m

A samples and B samples, the pattern error rate of a coefficient vector C is the proportion of samples for which $C \cdot X$ is

1. Nonpositive when X is an A sample
2. Nonnegative when X is a B sample

Of course one wishes to get a procedure which will produce a C with a low error rate. For a set of X_i, a coefficient vector C is said to be optimal if and only if no coefficient vector has a lower error rate than does C.

Independence of Magnitudes Is the C obtained by the procedure independent of the magnitudes of the half-space vectors X_i? A good procedure tends to yield a solution independent of such magnitudes. Except as explained with the relaxation procedure, each of the procedures to be presented has the independence property. For some of the procedures, this independence is obtained by replacing each X_i by a unit vector pointing in the same direction. Note that only the direction and not the magnitudes of the X_i affects the measure of error rates. Therefore, no generality is lost when a procedure for computing C requires that the vectors X_i lie on the surface of the unit hypersphere or hypercube. Incidentally, this same observation allows us to transform the m,3–half-space problem into the following problem, which is very simple to state but for which no practical procedure is known for finding an optimal solution when m is large. Given an ordinary sphere with m points on its surface, find a hemisphere which contains at least as many of the points as does any other hemisphere. Any m,2–half-space problem may be transformed into the following problem, which is very simple to state and for which the gain-loss procedure (see below) is a practical way to find an optimal solution even when m is large. Given a circle with m points on its circumference, find a semicircle which contains at least as many of the points as does any other semicircle.

11.3 SOME REPRESENTATIVE PROCEDURES FOR THE *m,n*–HALF-SPACE PROBLEM

Modifications of many of the very large number of known procedures (see N. Nilsson, 1965, for example), for the $m,(n-1)$–pattern problem are applicable to the m,n–half-space problem. This chapter gives only a few representative procedures and not a complete survey of procedures for the m,n–half-space problem. Several procedures are given because, except for two special kinds of half-space problems, no practical procedure is known which will always obtain optimal coefficients. Thus, given a practical problem, one should try several of the procedures which might be good for that problem. The procedures to be described are gain-loss in the two-dimensional case, combining coefficients obtained from projections, correlation-coefficient procedure, summing unitized normalized vectors, least-squares, relaxation, averaging relaxation, and local minimization. The relaxation procedure finds an error-free C when such a C exists. The gain-loss procedure is a practical procedure for finding an optimal C when n is 2 even if m is large. When $n > 2$ and m is large and no error-free C exists, no practical procedure is known for computing optimal coefficients. For this case, plausibility arguments are given with the procedures to show why they might compute a good (not necessarily optimal) C.

Gain-loss Procedure in the Two-dimensional Case For a two-dimensional half-space problem, an optimal C can be easily computed when, as is often the case in practice, the number of directions in which the vectors X_i can point is finite. When the number of directions in which the vectors can point is infinite, the procedure will usually compute good coefficients after direction is quantized. As was pointed out previously, no generality is lost if the points X_i are required to lie on the circumference of the unit circle. For each of the (finitely many) directions in which an X_i might point, a count is kept of the number of X_i that actually point in that direction. In Figure 11-7, for example, 8 of the 50 vectors X_i point straight up (in the 12 o'clock direction); 9 of the X_i point in the 2 o'clock direction; etc. (The clock terminology is used only as a convenience in this illustrative example in which each of the X_i points in one of six equally spaced directions.) Now choose some initial C, say pointing straight up. The number of errors can be obtained simply by adding the numbers associated with the directions away from C. Thus the number of errors for the initial C in Figure 11-7 is $7 + 3 + 11 = 21$. Rotate C (say clockwise) one "notch" and find the corresponding number of errors by adjusting the previous tally by the number of errors gained by the trailing

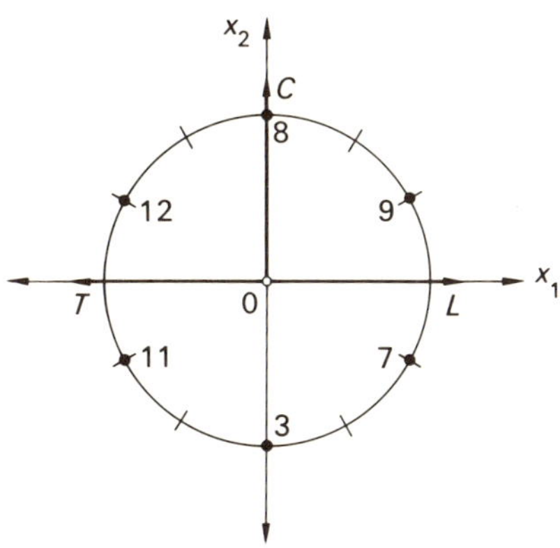

Figure 11-7 Initial position of C for the gain-loss procedure.

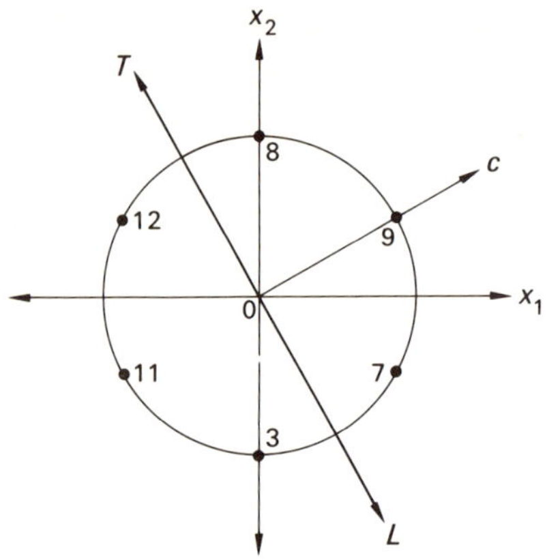

Figure 11-8 Position of C has been rotated one "notch" in the gain-loss procedure.

vector T and lost by the leading vector L. Thus in Figure 11-8 we have rotated the initial C by 2 hr. Twelve errors have been gained by the trailing vector T, and seven have been lost by the leading vector L. The adjusted tally is $21 + 12 - 7 = 26$. Choose the best C obtained during a complete rotation of the C vector. As shown in Figure 11-9, the best C points at 10 o'clock, so that an optimal solution is $C = (-\sqrt{3},1)$. This C has 19 errors and a 38 per cent error rate. Actually the above procedure can easily be made even more efficient so that C needs to be rotated only 180°.

Procedure of Combining Coefficients Obtained from Projections To illustrate this idea, suppose we wish to compute a good $C = (c_1,c_2,c_3)$. Suppose that optimal coefficients computed when all the X_i are projected into the x_1x_2 plane are $c_1 = 1$; $c_2 = 2$. This pair of coefficients would be computed by the gain-loss procedure. Similarly, suppose that optimal coefficients obtained by projecting into the x_2x_3 plane are $c_2 = 4$; $c_3 = 5$. It is plausible

C direction (o'clock)	12	2	4	6	8	10
number of errors	21	26	31	29	24	19
error rate (percent)	42	52	62	58	48	38

Figure 11-9 Results from the gain-loss procedure.

that the vector (2,4,5) is probably good for the original three-dimensional problem, since this C preserves the relative weights found for the projections. Of course such a C need not be optimal even though the coefficients obtained for the projections are optimal. A good C in the many-dimension case may sometimes be obtained by a procedure based on this idea of combining coefficients obtained from projections.

Normalizing of Features In most of the remaining procedures it is desirable for the features to be normalized. Let ξ_j be the average of the absolute value of x_{ij}, that is,

$$\xi_j = \frac{1}{m} \sum_{i=1}^{m} |x_{ij}|$$

The features would already be normalized if $\xi_1 = \xi_2 = \ldots = \xi_n$, but this is generally not the case. However, we can obtain this desirable situation by redefining our features, which is either Y in the evaluation problem case or $(x_1, x_2, \ldots, x_{n-1})$ in the pattern case. The features are redefined, so that the new half-space problem is in Z space where $z_j = x_j/\xi_j$. Now the features are normalized, since for all j we have

$$\frac{1}{m} \sum_{i=1}^{m} |z_{ij}| = 1$$

One must remember that the solution obtained to the half-space problem in Z space is $c_1z_1 + c_2z_2 + \ldots + c_nz_n = 0$. Hence the coefficient for the *original* jth feature is c_j/ξ_j.

Correlation-coefficient Procedure This procedure, due to Arthur Samuel (1967), gets its name from the fact that the value of each c_j ranges from minus 1 to plus 1 as do ordinary correlation coefficients. Let p_j be the number of times that x_{ij} is positive, and let n_j be the number of times that x_{ij} is negative, so that $p_j + n_j \leqslant m$. In this procedure, we simply set $c_j = (p_j - n_j)/(p_j + n_j)$. If all the x_{ij} are positive, then c_j reaches its maximum value of plus one. If all the x_{ij} are negative, then c_j reaches its minimum value of minus 1. If half the x_{ij} are positive and half are negative, then c_j is 0. If the original features are not normalized, suppose we normalize them as described in the previous subsection. (Arthur Samuel uses a slightly different normalization.) The coefficient for the original jth feature is c_j/ξ_j.

Unitizing the Vectors In most applications of the remaining procedures it is desirable to unitize the vectors X_i, that is, to replace X_i by a unit vector pointing in the same direction. Formally, we replace X_i by $U_i = X_i/|X_i|$. By unitizing the vectors, we may be assured of the desirable property that C does not depend on the magnitudes of the vectors X_i.

Procedure of Summing Unitized Normalized Vectors In this simple procedure, each vector X_i is normalized (normalizing the features) and then unitized into a vector U_i. We then simply set

$$C = \sum_{i=1}^{m} U_i$$

Unfortunately, the procedure does not always compute optimal coefficients. In Figure 11-10 the procedure computes the vector C pointing to the right, which is not optimal since only one scalar product is then positive.

However, there are some plausibility arguments for this procedure. First of all, it is rotationally invariant. Second, in the three-dimensional case, suppose that the vector sum of points on the unit sphere is considered to point in the direction of the north pole of the sphere. It is intuitively plausible that relatively many points will generally lie on the northern hemisphere. As a final plausibility argument, we now prove that the procedure computes the dividing hyperplane (through the origin) which maximizes the sum of the signed distances of the U_i from that hyperplane. For any hyperplane through the origin with normal C, the sum of such distances is

$$\sum_{i=1}^{m} \frac{C}{|C|} U_i = \frac{C}{|C|} \sum_{i=1}^{m} U_i$$

The claim is now simply established by noting that the right-hand side of this equation is maximized when C points in the direction of $\sum_{i=1}^{m} U_i$.

Least-squares Procedure In this procedure too, each vector X_i is normalized and then unitized into a vector U_i. We take as our coefficient vector the best

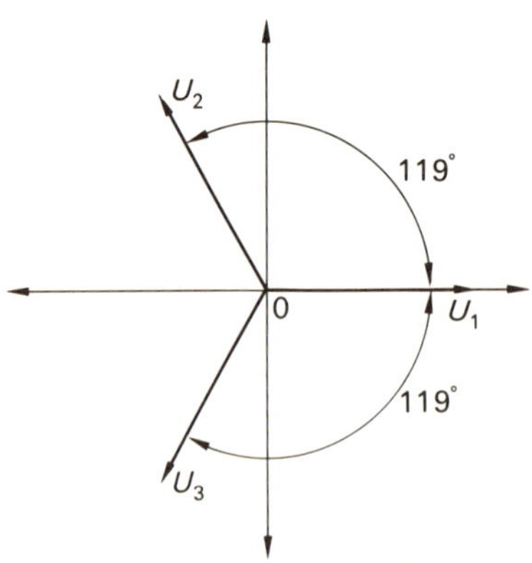

Figure 11-10 The vector sum C points to the right and is therefore not an optimal coefficient vector.

solution C in the least-squares sense of the system of m equations, $C \cdot X_i = 1$. The plausibility argument is simply that, if $C \cdot X_i$ is approximately plus 1, then $C \cdot X_i$ tends to be positive and consequently C will have a low error rate.

Relaxation Procedure This well-known procedure is described in Nilsson's book (1965) among other places. The procedure makes one or more passes through the X_i, one by one, and sometimes makes corrections to the coefficient vector C. Initially $C = (0, 0, \ldots, 0)$. In each step s, the procedure considers an X_i. If no error occurs with the current C, that is, $C \cdot X_i > 0$, then no correction is made to C. However, if an error occurs, that is, $C \cdot X_i \leqslant 0$, then a correction is made to C. The correction is an increment added to the current C. The size of the increment is $\Delta C = kX_i$, where $k > 0$. It has been found desirable to choose k to be inversely proportional to n. See the article by C. H. May (1964).

A set of X_i is said to be linearly separable if and only if there is a C that has a zero error rate. If the set of X_i is linearly separable, then there is an integer s such that the relaxation procedure in s steps yields a coefficient vector having a zero error rate. This theorem has been proved by several people, for example, Nilsson (1965). The theorem is true even if X_i is neither normalized nor unitized. The C obtained depends on the magnitudes of the X_i. However, no matter how the magnitudes of the X_i are varied, the coefficient vector obtained will always have a zero error rate.

The relaxation procedure may be used even when the set of X_i is not linearly separable. In this case each X_i should be normalized and then unitized. The procedure will not necessarily yield an optimal coefficient vector. The plausibility argument for this procedure is the following: Since it yields an error-free coefficient vector when the set of X_i is linearly separable, perhaps it will yield a good coefficient vector when the set of X_i is not linearly separable.

B. Efron (1964) analyzed this type of procedure for nonseparable situations.

Averaging Relaxation Procedure In this procedure too, each X_i should be normalized and then unitized. When the set of X_i is not linearly separable, the coefficient vector obtained by the relaxation procedure, described in the previous subsection, may fluctuate wildly in an attempt to eliminate one error and then another. In the present more plausible procedure, due to Richard Duda (1968), the coefficient vector is chosen to be the average of the C vector in the relaxation procedure.

Local Minimization Procedure The coefficients obtained by a nonoptimal procedure can generally be improved by local minimization techniques, that is, by slowly changing C in the direction of decreasing error rate until a local minimum is reached. One hopes that the local minimum thus obtained will not be too much greater than the global minimum.

Conclusions Although several procedures were presented for computing coefficients for the m,n–half-space problem, no procedure was given to compute optimal coefficients for more than two dimensions in the linearly nonseparable case. Solving the m,n–half-space problem is important because it can be applied to pattern recognition, utility theory, automatic extracting, game playing, international relations, purchasing and selling, and the evaluation of personnel and computer programs. Because of this importance, more work should be devoted to obtaining other procedures. These procedures, together with those in the present chapter, should be compared theoretically and, if necessary, experimentally.

EXERCISES

1. Prove that every m,n–half-space problem can be transformed into an m,n-evaluation problem.

2. Is the coefficient vector C obtained by the gain-loss procedure independent of the magnitudes of the half-space vectors X_i?

3. Suppose that a computer program applies the procedure of summing unitized normalized vectors to vectors that are already normalized and unitized.

a. If it takes 2 microsec to add a pair of numbers, how long does it take to find a solution to a 21,5–half-space problem?

b. If it takes time t to add a pair of numbers, how long does it take to find a solution to an m,n–half-space problem?

4. **a.** What is the error rate for C in Figure 11-2?

b. Is C optimal?

c. If the features are normalized for the 5,2-evaluation problem leading to the half-space problem given in Section 11.1 and depicted in Figure 11-2, what is the new half-space problem in Z space?

5. **a.** Find the coefficient vector yielded by the correlation coefficient procedure applied to the half-space problem in Z space obtained as the answer to Exercise 4c.

b. What is its error rate?

c. Is it optimal?

d. What is the corresponding solution to the half-space problem depicted in Figure 11-2?

e. What is the corresponding solution to the original 5,2-evaluation problem?

f. What is the evaluation error rate?

6. Unitize the half-space vectors in Z space obtained as the answer to Exercise 4c.

7. **a.** Starting with the answer to Exercise 6, find the coefficient vector yielded by the procedure of summing unitized normalized vectors.

b. What is its error rate?

c. Is it optimal?

d. What is the corresponding solution to the half-space problem depicted in Figure 11-2?

e. What is the corresponding solution to the original 5,2-evaluation problem?

f. What is its evaluation error rate?

8. **a.** Starting with the answer to Exercise 6, find the coefficient vector yielded by the relaxation procedure in two passes with $k = 0.5$.

b. What is its error rate?

c. Is it optimal?

d. What is the corresponding solution to the half-space problem depicted in Figure 11-2?

e. What is the corresponding solution to the original 5,2-evaluation problem?

f. What is the evaluation error rate?

9. **a.** What is the pattern error rate of the solution given in Figure 11-3?

b. Is the solution optimal?

c. Using the procedure given in the proof of Theorem 2, show numerically how the 7,2-pattern problem given in Section 11.1 and depicted in Figure 11-3 may be transformed into a 7,3–half-space problem.

d. If the features are then normalized, what is the new half-space problem in Z space?

10. **a.** Find the coefficient vector yielded by the correlation coefficient procedure applied to the half-space problem in Z space obtained as the answer to Exercise 9d.

b. What is the error rate?

c. What is the corresponding solution for the half-space problem before normalization, that is, for the half-space problem obtained as the answer to Exercise 9c?

d. What is the corresponding solution to the original 7,2-pattern problem?

11. Unitize the half-space vectors in Z space obtained as the answer to Exercise 9d.

12. **a.** Starting with the answer to Exercise 11, find the coefficient vector yielded by the procedure of summing unitized normalized vectors.

b. What is its error rate?

c. What is the corresponding solution for the half-space problem before normalization, that is, for the answer to Exercise 9c?

d. What is the corresponding solution to the original 7,2-pattern problem?

13. **a.** Starting with the answer to Exercise 11, find the coefficient vector yielded by the relaxation procedure in two passes with $k = 0.5$.

b. What is its error rate?

c. What is the corresponding solution for the half-space problem before normalization, that is, for the answer to Exercise 9c?

d. What is the corresponding solution to the original 7,2-pattern problem?

BIBLIOGRAPHY

Abramson, N., and Braverman, D.: Learning to Recognize Patterns in a Random Environment, *IRE Trans. Inform. Theory*, vol. IT-8, S58-S63, September, 1962.

Anderson, T. W.: "An Introduction to Multivariate Statistical Analysis," John Wiley & Sons, Inc., New York, 1958.

Duda, R. O.: Linear Machines and Markov Processes, *Proc. IEEE Workshop on Pattern Recognition*, Dorado, Puerto Rico, October, 1966.

Efron, B.: The Perceptor Correction Procedure in Nonseparable Situations, *Tech. Documentary Rept.* RADC-RDR-63-533, Information Processing Branch, Rome Air Development Center, Research and Technology Division, Air Force Systems Command, Griffiss Air Force Base, New York, February, 1964.

Feigenbaum, E., and Feldman, J. (eds.): "Computers and Thought," McGraw-Hill Book Company, New York, 1963.

Fisher, R. A.: The Use of Multiple Measurements in Taxionomic Problems, in "Contributions to Mathematical Statistics," John Wiley & Sons, Inc., New York, 1950, pp. 32.179–32.188.

Highleyman, W. H.: Linear Decision Functions with Application to Pattern Recognition, *Proc. IRE*, pp. 1501–1514, June, 1962.

Koford, J. S., and Groner, G. F.: The Use of an Adaptive Threshold Element to Design a Linear Optimal Pattern Classifier, *IEEE Trans. Inform. Theory*, vol. IT-12, pp. 42–50, January, 1966.

Mays, C. H.: Effects of Adaptation Parameters on Convergence Time and Tolerance for Adaptive Threshold Elements, *IEEE Trans. Electron. Computers*, pp. 465–468, August, 1964.

Nilsson, N. J.: "Learning Machines," McGraw-Hill Book Company, New York, 1965.

Samuel, A. L.: Some Studies in Machine Learning Using the Game of Checkers, *IBM J. Res. Develop.* vol. III, no. 3, pp. 210–229, July, 1959.

———: Some Studies in Machine Learning Using the Game of Checkers, II, Recent Progress, *IBM J. Res. Develop.*, vol. XI, no. 6, November, 1967.

Suppes, P., and Walsh, K.: A Nonlinear Model for the Experimental Measurement of Utility, *Behavioral Sci.*, July, 1959.

Widrow, B., and Hoff, M. E.: Adaptive Switching Circuits, 1960 WESCON *Conv. Record*, pt. 4, pp. 96–140.

12
The Elementary Perceiving and Memorizing Program

A program called EPAM (an abbreviation for Elementary Perceiver And Memorizer) was written by Edward Feigenbaum and Herbert Simon (1961, 1963, 1964). It embodies their theory of human associative memory and verbal learning. In this chapter we shall describe EPAM-II, which is an improved version of the original program.

EPAM acts as subject in rote learning experiments. It has been the subject in so-called *serial anticipation experiments*, but this work will not be described. Rather we shall describe how EPAM acts as subject in paired associate experiments. In this kind of experiment, the subject memorizes by rote several associated pairs. Each pair consists of a stimulus and a response. EPAM has been the subject in three kinds of these experiments. In the first, each stimulus is (an input code of) a spoken word, and each response is (a code of) pointing at an associated object. In the second, each stimulus is a printed word, and each response is a spoken word. In the third, each stimulus is a printed nonsense syllable, and each response is a nonsense syllable. A nonsense syllable is a meaningless three-letter "word" (such as XOP) consisting of a consonant, followed by a vowel, followed by a consonant.

Table 12-1 A mythical experiment using nonsense syllables

Trial number	*Presented stimulus*	*Subject's response*	*Presented response*
1	DAX	—	JIR
	PIB	JIR	JUK
2	PIB	JUK	JUK
	DAX	JUK	JIR
3	DAX	JIR	JIR
	PIB	JUK	JUK

For a paired associate experiment, the experimenter starts by choosing a set of stimulus-response pairs. Then he presents one of these stimuli to the subject. The subject tries to give the associated response. Next the experimenter presents the subject with the associated response. Then the experimenter presents another stimulus, and the subject tries to give the associated response. Next the associated response is presented. This cycle continues until all the stimuli have been presented exactly once. This completes the first trial. In the next trial, the stimuli are presented in a different (randomly selected) order. Trials continue until stopped by the experimenter. Usually trials stop when the subject gives all correct responses throughout a trial.

Two mythical miniature experiments are shown in Tables 12-1 and 12-2. How EPAM might have acted as subject in these experiments is described in a later section. In the experiment shown in Table 12-1, the experimenter chose two stimulus-response pairs, DAX-JIR and PIB-JUK. In the first trial, the first stimulus to be presented to the subject is DAX; that is, the subject sees the printed nonsense syllable DAX. The subject makes no response. The response presented to the subject is JIR; that is, the subject is shown the printed syllable JIR. The second stimulus is PIB, to which the subject

Table 12-2 A mythical "reading aloud" experiment

Trial number	*Presented stimulus*	*Subject's response*	*Presented response*
	CAR	—	kahr
1	DOG	kahr	dawg
	CAT	kahr	kat
	DOG	dawg	dawg
2	CAT	kat	kat
	CAR	kahr	kahr

responds JIR, which is incorrect. The presented response is JUK. In the second trial, the first stimulus is PIB, to which the subject correctly responds JUK; the presented response is JUK. The next stimulus is DAX, to which the subject incorrectly responds JUK; the presented response is JIR. In the third trial, the subject responds correctly in turn to both the stimuli, and the experiment is stopped. In the experiment shown in Table 12-2, the experimenter chose three stimulus-response pairs. Each stimulus is a printed word consisting of three capital letters. Each response is a spoken word. The spoken versions of the printed words CAR, CAT, and DOG are represented by kahr, kat, and dawg, respectively. In this task, we shall say that each stimulus is in the literal mode and that each response is in the phonemic mode. For obvious reasons, this kind of task will be called a "reading aloud" task or a literal-to-phonemic task. In the first trial, the first stimulus is CAR, to which the subject gives no response. The experimenter presents the response, kahr; that is, he pronounces the word CAR. The second stimulus is DOG, to which the subject incorrectly responds kahr; the presented response is dawg; etc.

12.1 THE EPAM PROGRAM

EPAM consists of an executive program, a responding program, and a learning program. The responder is a program which produces responses to stimuli. The learner is a program which learns to discriminate and associate stimuli and responses. The executive program uses the responder and the learner appropriately and takes care of details like printing responses. No further mention will be made of the executive program, since the responder and the learner are more interesting. Both of these programs will first be described in general terms and then will, with the aid of examples, be described in more detail.

The inputs to the responder are a response mode and a stimulus. For example, a spoken word is in the phonemic mode. The output is a response associated with the stimulus and in the required mode. The program consists of the following steps to be taken in order.

A. Use the discriminator program to discriminate the stimulus on the net corresponding to the mode of the stimulus. In this way, try to find an image of the stimulus.
B. If no such stimulus image is found, stop with no response.
C. Find the cue that is in the required (response) mode and stored with the stimulus image.
D. If no such cue is found, stop with no response.
E. Use the discriminator to discriminate the cue on the net corresponding to the required mode. In this way, try to find a response image.

(C--,
k--)

(kahr)

Figure 12-1 After the presentation of the first stimulus, CAR, and the first response, kahr, the learner creates this literal net and this phonemic net.

F. If no such response image is found, stop with no response.
G. Directly generate the response from the response image.

The discriminator is a program that discriminates (sorts) items on one of the discrimination nets. A discrimination net is a kind of sorting tree or decoding network. EPAM keeps one net for each (sensory) mode involved in the task. Figure 12-1 shows a pair of nets—a literal net and a phonemic net. A program, called a test, is stored at each nonterminal node of a net. Each terminal node of a net contains a (possibly empty) list, called an image list, in which symbolic information may be stored. The first item, if any, on an image list is called the *image*. An image is a partial or total copy of a stimulus or a response. The other members, if any, of the image list are called *cues*. Each cue on an image list corresponds to a different mode. A cue is a partial (or occasionally total) copy of a response in that mode. The discriminator is a program which takes an item (stimulus or cue) in a given mode, sorts that item in the net corresponding to that mode, and produces the image list associated with that item. The discriminator finds the test at the top node in the net and applies this program to the item. The resulting signal tells the discriminator whether to branch left or right to find the next test. The discriminator executes this program and so on until a terminal node is reached. The image list is produced and the discriminator terminates.

The learner consists of two programs, the discrimination learner and the association learner. At the beginning of an experiment, there are no discrimination nets. The discrimination learner builds discriminations by growing each net with tests and branches. The association learner builds associations between stimuli and responses by storing cues with stimulus images.

For purposes of illustration, we now describe how EPAM might work as subject in the mythical miniature experiments shown in Tables 12-1 and 12-2. In the reading aloud experiments of Table 12-2, the first presented stimulus in the first trial is CAR. Since EPAM does not yet have any nets, it makes no response. The presented response is kahr. The learner creates the "nets"

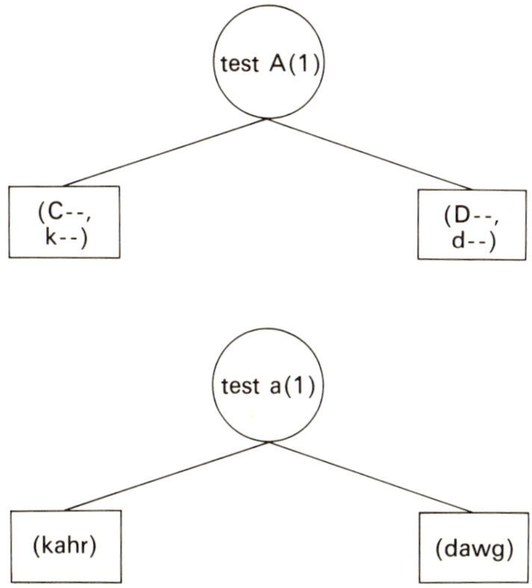

Figure 12-2 After the presentation of the second stimulus, DOG, and the second response, dawg, the learner grows these nets.

shown in Figure 1. Except for the cue, k____, the discrimination learner creates the literal net, which consists of one terminal node, and puts at this node the stimulus image, C____, a partial copy of the stimulus, CAR. The discrimination learner then creates the phonemic net, which consists of one terminal node, and puts at this node a total image of the response, kahr. This time a total image is used because, whenever a response is needed, it is needed in toto. Then the association learner stores the cue, k____, with the stimulus image, C____, in the literal net.

The second presented stimulus is DOG. The responder starts by using the discriminator on the literal net. The discriminator immediately finds the image list, (C____, k____). The responder gets the cue, k____, and then uses the discriminator on the phonemic net. The discriminator finds the image list, (kahr). The responder gets the response image, kahr. From this, the responder generates directly the response, kahr, which is wrong. The presented response is dawg.

The learner grows the nets shown in Figure 12-2 from those shown in Figure 12-1. Except for the cue d____, the discrimination learner grows the literal net. It creates the test A(1), which is a program which sorts stimuli beginning with C to the left and which sorts stimuli beginning with D to the right; stimuli beginning with other letters are sorted in either direction. The test is on the first letter because of a priority scheme called the *noticing order*. Ordinarily, the noticing order gives priority in decreasing order to the first, last, and middle parts of an item (stimulus or cue). Thus if the discrimi-

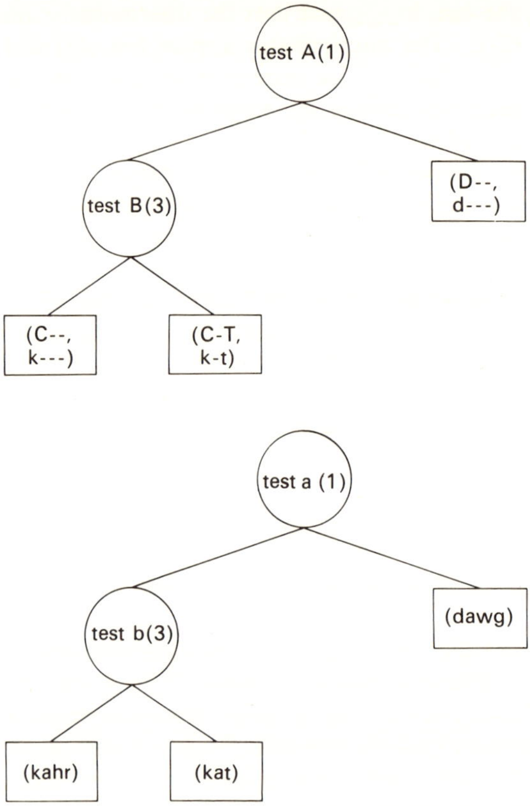

Figure 12-3 After the presentation of the third stimulus, CAT, and the third response, kat, the learner grows these nets.

nation learner had found no first-letter difference between the stimuli, it would have created instead of test A(1) the test A(3) which tests the last letter in a stimulus. For the sake of efficiency, the discrimination learner in actuality creates so-called redundant tests too. Thus, in our example, it probably would have created one redundant test, and the third terminal node so created would be empty for possible later use. We shall make no further mention of redundant tests. Now let us return to our example. The discrimination learner also generates the stimulus image, D____. Similarly, the discrimination learner then grows the phonemic net in Figure 12-2. The association learner stores the cue, d____, with the stimulus image, D____, in the literal net.

The third presented stimulus is CAT. The responder starts by using the discriminator on the literal net. The discriminator applies test A(1) to the stimulus, CAT, and branches left where it finds the image list, (C____, k___). The responder gets the cue, k___, and uses the discriminator on the phonemic net in Figure 12-2. The discriminator applies test a(1) and branches left to find the image list, (kahr). The responder gets the response image, kahr. From this, it generates directly the response kahr, which is wrong. The presented response is kat.

The learner grows the nets shown in Figure 12-3 from those shown in Figure 12-2. Except for the cue, k_t, the discrimination learner grows the literal net. Since it cannot find any difference between the first letters of the stimulus image, C___, and the stimulus, CAT, it uses the noticing order and creates the test B(3) which sorts words ending with T to the right and which sorts some of the words to the left. The discrimination learner stores the stimulus image C_t, rather than merely C___, in order to try to avoid future confusion with the old stimulus image, C___, which is a partial copy of the old stimulus, CAR. Similarly, the discrimination learner then grows the phonemic net shown in Figure 12-3. The test b(3) sorts items ending with the sound r to the left and items ending with t to the right. The association learner stores the cue, k_t, with the stimulus image, C_T. This completes the first trial.

The first stimulus in the second trial is DOG. The responder uses the discriminator on the literal net in Figure 12-3. The discriminator branches to the right at test A(1), since the first letter is D. The discriminator obtains the image list, (D___, d___). The responder gets the cue, d___, and uses the discriminator on the phonemic net in Figure 12-3. The discriminator branches to the right at test a(1) because the first sound is d and obtains the image list, (dawg). From the image, dawg, the responder directly generates the correct response, dawg. Since the presented response is dawg, no learning is performed.

The second stimulus in the second trial is CAT. The responder starts by using the discriminator on the literal net in Figure 12-3. The discriminator applies test A(1) and branches to the left since the first letter is C. It then applies test B(3) and branches to the right since the third letter is T. It then finds the terminal node containing the image list, (C_T, k_t). The responder gets the cue, k_t, and uses the discriminator on the phonemic net in Figure 12-3. The discriminator applies test a(1) and branches to the left since the first sound is k. It then applies test b(3) and branches to the right since the final sound is t. It finds the terminal node containing the image list, (kat). From the image, kat, the responder directly generates the correct response, kat. The presented response is kat, and no learning is performed.

The third stimulus in the second trial is CAR. The responder uses the discriminator on the literal net in Figure 12-3. The discriminator applies test A(1) and branches to the left since the first letter is C. It then applies test B(3) to the stimulus, CAR. Since test B(3) was created to insure that a stimulus ending in T would be sorted to the right, the stimulus, CAR, may be

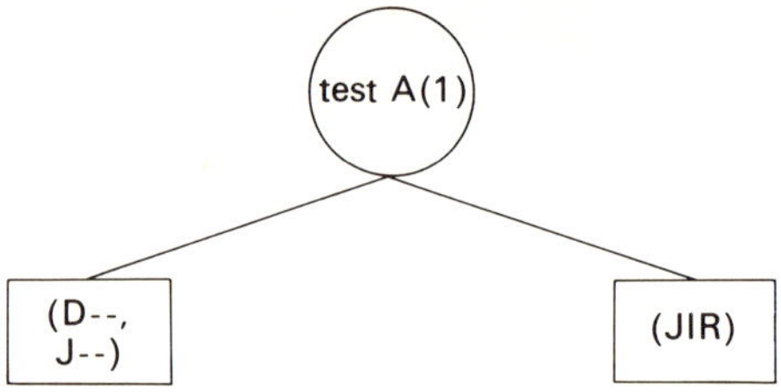

Figure 12-4 After the presentation of the first stimulus, DAX, and the first response, JIR, the learner creates this literal net.

sorted either left or right. Sorting CAR to the right leads to the incorrect response, kat, and the learner takes appropriate action. If instead CAR is sorted to the left, the responder finds the cue, k____, and uses the discriminator on the phonemic net in Figure 12-3. The discriminator applies the test a(1) and branches to the left, since the first sound is k. The discriminator then applies test b(3) to the final sound in the cue, k____. Since the final sound in the cue is unknown, test b(3) branches left or right with equal probability. If it branches to the right, the responder gives the incorrect response, kat, and the learner takes appropriate action. If it branches to the right, the responder gives the correct response, kahr, and no learning is performed. In this last eventuality, EPAM would have given only correct responses throughout the entire second trial. Thinking that EPAM had completely learned the associations, the experimenter would ordinarily stop the experiment. However, EPAM was "guessing" at the response to CAR, and there is an even chance that it would make the incorrect response, kat, in the next trial.

As a second example, we shall trace how EPAM might perform as the subject in the experiment described in Table 12-1. Since both the stimulus and the response are nonsense syllables, the only net used is the literal net. The first stimulus in the first trial is DAX. Since no net has been created yet, the responder gives no response. The presented response is JIR. The learner creates the net shown in Figure 12-4. Except for the cue, J____, the discrimination learner creates the entire net. Test A(1) branches left if the first letter is D and branches right if the first letter is J. The association learner stores the cue, J____, with the stimulus image, D____.

The second stimulus is PIB. The responder uses the discriminator on the net in Figure 12-4. If test A(1) sorts PIB to the right, the discriminator would produce the image list, (JIR); since there is no cue, the responder would give no response. However, in this example we shall assume that test A(1) sorts PIB to the left. The discriminator finds the image list, (D____, J____). The responder gets the cue, J____. It uses the discriminator on the *same* net. The discriminator finds the image list, (JIR). From the image, JIR, the responder directly generates the response, JIR, which is incorrect. The

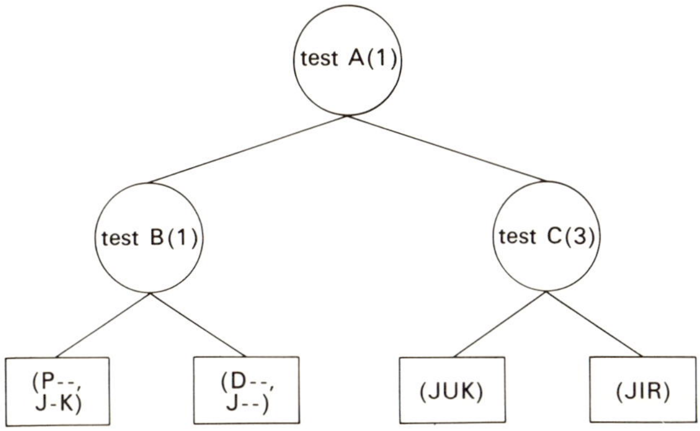

Figure 12-5 After the presentation of the second stimulus, PIB, and the second response, JUK, the learner grows this net.

presented response is JUK. The learner grows the net in Figure 12-5 from the net in Figure 12-4.

In the second trial, the first stimulus is PIB. The responder gives the correct response, JUK, and so no learning is performed. The second stimulus is DAX. The responder uses the discriminator on the net in Figure 12-5. The discriminator finds the image list, (D____, J____). The responder gets the cue, J____, and uses the discriminator on the same net. Since the third letter of the cue, J____, is unknown, test C(3) branches at random. If it branches to the right, the responder would "guess" the correct response, JIR. However, in this example, it is assumed that the test branches to the left and that consequently the responder responds JUK, which is incorrect. The presented response is JIR. The learner takes appropriate action; namely, the association learner replaces the cue J____ with the cue J__R. Now the associations are completely learned. EPAM gives only correct responses in the third trial so the experiment is stopped.

12.2 EXPERIMENTS AND CONCLUSIONS WITH EPAM

In experiments, EPAM has learned to perform many paired associate tasks involving nonsense syllables and has learned to "read." EPAM has been given nonsense syllable tasks similar to those given to human subjects. There are about 12 pairs of nonsense syllables in a typical task. The behavior of EPAM has been compared qualitatively and quantitatively to that of human subjects.

EPAM has learned to "read." When it "sees one of four printed words," it "points to the corresponding object." For example, it "points to the object dog" when it "sees the printed word DOG." To do this, it uses three nets—a literal net, a phonemic net, and an object net. The reading task

Table 12-3 EPAM learns to perform a phonemic-to-object task

Trial number	*Presented stimulus (phonemic)*	*Subject's response (object)*	*Presented response (object)*
1	kahr	—	car
	dawg	car	dog
	kat	car	cat
	bawl	car	ball
2	kahr	car	car
	dawg	ball	dog
	kat	—	cat
	bawl	ball	ball
3	bawl	ball	ball
	kahr	car	car
	kat	cat	cat
	dawg	—	dog
4	bawl	ball	ball
	kahr	car	car
	dawg	dog	dog
	kat	cat	cat

may also be called a literal-to-object task. As standard paired associate tasks, EPAM first learns a phonemic-to-object task and then a literal-to-phonemic task. In the phonemic-to-object task, EPAM learns to "point at an object" when it "hears its name." For example, when it "hears kahr," it "points to the object car." For this task, it grows a phonemic net and an object net. The actual experiment is described in Table 12-3. After an error-free trial, EPAM performs a literal-to-phonemic task similar to the "reading aloud" task discussed in the previous section. The actual experiment in which EPAM learned to perform this literal-to-phonemic task is described in Table 12-4. While learning to perform this task, EPAM further grows the phonemic net obtained at the end of the learning of the phonemic-to-object task. After EPAM has an error-free trial in the literal-to-phonemic task, it tries the reading task. The reader is a program similar to the responder, except that the reader uses the discriminator three times instead of twice. The reader sorts a literal stimulus in the literal net and finds a phonemic cue. It sorts the phonemic cue in the phonemic set and finds an object cue. It sorts the object cue in the object net and then generates an object response. After EPAM learns to perform both the phonemic-to-object task and the literal-to-phonemic task it correctly performs the reading task in the very first trial.

As for conclusions, the paired associate and "reading" experiments

Table 12-4 EPAM learns to perform a literal-to-phonemic task

Trial number	*Presented stimulus (literal)*	*Subject's response (phonemic)*	*Presented response (phonemic)*
1	CAR	—	kahr
	DOG	kahr	dawg
	CAT	kahr	kat
	BALL	—	bawl
2	DOG	—	dawg
	BALL	bawl	bawl
	CAT	bawl	kat
	CAR	kahr	kahr
3	DOG	dawg	dawg
	BALL	bawl	bawl
	CAT	—	kat
	CAR	kahr	kahr
4	DOG	dawg	dawg
	CAT	kat	kat
	BALL	bawl	bawl
	CAR	kahr	kahr

with EPAM have contributed to an understanding of human rote learning and verbal behavior and have indicated that EPAM (or some extension) may be a useful tool to help computers solve difficult problems. EPAM may be a useful tool in automatic information retrieval for example. In this application, it would be a dynamically growing index of entry points to a large number of stored items. What entry points are present depends on what items have been looked for in the past. Feigenbaum and Simon are primarily interested in the conclusions relevant to psychology. EPAM's behavior qualitatively and to some extent quantitatively agrees with many aspects of human behavior in the same experiments. EPAM and human subjects exhibit forgetting, oscillating, retroactive inhibition, interference, and stimulus and response generalization. As a consequence of later learning EPAM sometimes forgets seemingly well-learned responses. In oscillation, the subject alternately can and cannot remember a response to some stimulus. In retroactive inhibition, the subject first learns a set of stimulus-response pairs and then learns another set; the more similar the items in the second set are to the items in the first set, the more of the first set does the subject tend to forget. Interference occurs in the paired associate learning of nonsense syllables; learning is hampered to the extent that stimuli are similar to responses. If s and s' are similar stimuli and r is the correct response to the presentation of s and if r is given in response to the presentation of s', this is called *stimulus generalization.* If r and r' are similar responses and r' is given in response to the presentation of s, this is called *response generalization.*

EXERCISES

1. What is meant by "subject's response" and "presented response" in Table 12-1?

2. Describe briefly a situation in which an image list has

- **a.** No cues.
- **b.** One cue.
- **c.** Two cues.

3. After an incorrect response, why must the discrimination learner be executed before the association learner?

4. Describe how the discrimination learner grows the phonemic net shown in Figure 12-3 from the phonemic net shown in Figure 12-2.

5. Explain the fact that if test B(3) in Figure 12-3 sorts the stimulus, CAR, to the right, the responder gives the incorrect response, kat.

6. In Figure 12-5 explain why the responder gives the correct response, JUK, to the stimulus, PIB.

7. Does the fact that EPAM had error-free trials on the phonemic-to-object task and the literal-to-phonemic task necessarily imply that it would correctly perform the reading task on the first trial? Explain your answer.

BIBLIOGRAPHY

Feigenbaum, Edward: The Simulation of Verbal Learning Behavior, *Proc. Western Joint Computer Conf.*, pp. 121–132, May, 1961.

———, and Herbert Simon: Performance of a Reading Task by an Elementary Perceiving and Memorizing Program, *Behavioral Sci.*, vol. VIII, no. 3, pp. 72–87, January, 1963.

Simon, Herbert A., and Edward Feigenbaum: An Information-processing Theory of Some Effects of Similarity, Familiarization, and Meaningfulness in Verbal Learning, *J. Verbal Learning, Verbal Behavior*, vol. III, no. 5, pp. 385–396, October, 1964.

13
Concluding Remarks

In previous chapters, we have described many heuristic programs. We are now in a position to discuss heuristic programming more abstractly. Into what categories or aspects can the problem of heuristic programming be divided? What advice can be given to the potential heuristic programmer? What problems should he work on? How should he go about actually writing a heuristic program? What are the future applications of heuristic programming? Will there really be robots? What are the philosophical and social implications of the advent of intelligent machines?

13.1 ASPECTS OF THE HEURISTIC PROGRAMMING PROBLEM

The problem of heuristic programming may be divided into six categories: (1) generality, (2) searching, (3) functions that make evaluations and recognize patterns, (4) matching data structures to determine appropriate substitutions for variables, (5) learning, and (6) planning.

Generality A heuristic program is said to be multipurpose (general or broad) if it can solve a wide variety of problems or answer a wide variety of questions

(Newell and Ernst, 1965). Since the intelligence of a human is multipurpose, there is a definite trend toward getting heuristic programs to be multipurpose, even if this means sacrificing the solution of some problems that are difficult. The hope is that once multipurpose programs can be written to solve simple problems, the programs can be extended to solve more difficult problems. Multipurpose programs may some day solve some of their own problems such as how to learn, search, make evaluations, recognize patterns, plan, write broader programs, etc. Some starts in the direction of multipurpose programs are MULTIPLE, General Problem Solver, the general probabilistic procedure (Section 9.1), and the deductive question-answering programs.

Searching When a certain problem cannot be solved directly, it is often possible to write a program to search for a solution (Slagle, 1970). If the number of possibilities to be searched in order to find a solution is sufficiently small, the problem is trivial, since the program can consider all possibilities. For an intellectually difficult problem, the number of possibilities to be searched is sufficiently large (sometimes infinite) so that for all practical purposes there is no exhaustive procedure. In most kinds of theorem proving, including predicate calculus, the number of possibilities to be searched is potentially infinite. In order to guarantee a perfect first move in checkers, the program would have to search through about 10^{40} possible games. In chess the number is about 10^{120}. Even tremendous improvements in hardware would hardly dent tasks requiring the search of so many possibilities. It is much better to consider alternative ways of defining the search and modifying the search. For example, in theorem proving, the geometry program and the Logic Theorist might have worked forward from the axioms and hypotheses to the conclusion. Searching in this forward direction would have been far less efficient than searching backwards as in the actual programs. In predicate calculus, the search using the resolution principle is far more efficient (smaller) than the search using the Herbrand expansion. The geometry program of Gelernter uses a model (geometric diagram) to narrow the search, and the author has described how a resolution program can use a model to narrow the search in predicate calculus. Often it is desirable (even necessary) to replace a search procedure guaranteed to work in principle by an unguaranteed search procedure which is good in practice. This happens, for example, when the procedure uses forward pruning or searches only the top few levels of a game tree rather than the complete game tree and when a breadth-first procedure in problem solving and theorem proving is replaced by certain other procedures. After being modified in this way, a search can sometimes be replaced by a more efficient equivalent search. Thus a depth-first minimax search may be replaced by an alpha-beta search. In all cases, one strives to obtain a search procedure with a large measure of success for the least expenditure of resources such as computer time and memory space. It is usually desirable to search the most promising possibilities first. In games, this allows alpha-beta cutoffs to occur. Similarly, the search may be terminated as soon as a solution is found in problem-solving programs such as MULTIPLE or in the resolution-principle programs. Of course there are many other tricks for improving search, but they shall not be repeated here. One can often find an optimal (in a sense) procedure for searching a disjunctive goal tree such as the tree that occurs in the Logic Theorist. For the very important case of the disjunctive-conjunctive tree, one would like to improve further on the MULTIPLE search procedure.

Functions That Make Evaluations and Recognize Patterns The intimate connection between making evaluations and recognizing patterns and the importance of such functions were explained in Chapter 11. Two important problems concerning such functions for heuristic programming are the generation of new useful features and the useful combination of features to obtain good functions. An intelligent program must be able to make evaluations in order to know that one situation is preferable to another. A good example is the evaluation function in the checker program. If a heuristic program can classify a problem into a particular pattern class, it can then try the appropriate transformations. Thus in GPS, the differences between two objects are the features which suggest one or more operators to reduce the most difficult difference. The program that plans, finds lemmas, and learns written by Larry Travis (Section 6.3) uses a simple scheme of classifying problems to obtain associated transformations. The integration program, SAINT, recognizes whether an integrand is an instance of a certain pattern class and if so applies appropriate transformations.

Matching Data Structures to Determine Appropriate Substitutions for Variables Matching data structures to determine appropriate substitutions for variables occurs in the Logic Theorist, the geometry program, the integration program, GPS, the resolution programs, and the deductive question-answering programs. It is far more efficient to match two expressions than to substitute blindly for the variables and then to see whether the expressions have become identical. So far the amount of data has been relatively small, and a rather straightforward implementation of matching has been adequate. When the amount of data becomes very large, as surely it will, the program will need to be much more clever in how it goes about matching.

Learning A heuristic program is said to learn when it uses experience to improve its performance. Although all agree that it is very desirable for heuristic programs to learn, only limited progress has been made to date. The checker program learns by rote; it also does some generalization learning, that is, learns how to combine features into a good evaluation function.

The program of Travis learns by rote and abstraction of the solution of a problem in order to try using that solution to help similar future problems. In the computer experiments reported by Friedberg et al. (Section 9.3) learned behavior was actually inferior to random behavior. These experiments should be interpreted as meaning that the learning mechanisms used, although plausible and somewhat complicated, are inadequate. One approach that holds promise for the future is to get a heuristic program to write a nontrivial program. Such a program could improve itself by improving one of its own programs and then using the improved program. The Heuristic Compiler of Simon (Section 9.2) is a start in this direction. In the author's opinion, the most promising approach to the learning problem is to write a multipurpose heuristic program (possibly a deductive question-answering program). This program would solve many different kinds of problems, including the problem of doing its own learning. Newell has made a start by proposing that GPS might learn new differences (features) in a newly presented problem domain. It would be desirable for a program to learn in the sense of inventing its own models.

Planning By definition, a plan is a rough outline of a possible solution. In one kind of plan, some of the details in the problem or in the transformations are omitted. In another, certain steps in the possible solution are omitted with the hope that they can be filled in later. Travis' program has both kinds of planning. It solves abstractions of the given problem by leaving out the order in which the transformations are performed. It does the second kind of planning by finding and using lemmas, that is, possible intermediate steps along a solution path. When a program can find plans which are even occasionally correct, its problem-solving ability is much improved, since it is far easier for the program to solve the several resulting small problems than the original large problem.

13.2 ADVICE TO THE POTENTIAL HEURISTIC PROGRAMMER

The best way to start to work in the field of heuristic programming is to attend one of the good universities that teach and do research in the field or to work with one of the other existing research groups in the field. Although the best way to learn how to write a heuristic program is to write one, a few pointers can be given.

The first problem that confronts the potential heuristic programmer is what problem to work on. Opportunities and challenges abound. The previous section mentions many promising problems and projects. In my opinion, some of the most promising problems to work on are learning, generality, and planning. Some of the most promising heuristic programs to write are programs that deduce answers to questions from given facts and that write nontrivial programs.

The best way, especially for the beginner, to keep up with the field of heuristic programming is to work with a research group in the field. One should also be a member of the Association for Computing Machinery, the professional society for computer scientists. Its address is 1133 Avenue of the Americas, New York, New York 10036. The ACM has four publications, all of excellent reputation: the *Communications of the ACM*, *Journal of the ACM*, *Computing Reviews*, and *Computing Surveys*. They often contain good information about the heuristic programming approach to Artificial Intelligence. (See for example, section 3.6 of *Computing Reviews*, which contains reviews of articles and books about Artificial Intelligence.) The ACM is a member of the American Federation of Information Processing Societies (AFIPS). The *Proceedings of the AFIPS Annual Spring Joint Computer Conference* and the *Proceedings of the AFIPS Annual Fall Joint Computer Conference* often contain good articles about heuristic programming. By writing to the ACM, you can find out how to join its Special Interest Group on Artificial Intelligence. This group issues a newsletter, which contains many interesting and useful items concerning heuristic programming. Other publications occasionally contain good articles in the field, but the reader should be wary of articles in the press—both popular and technical. Many articles appear which exaggerate both pros and cons of heuristic programming. Since good articles appear in many different journals, the serious researcher (or at least his group) must take the trouble to keep an up-to-date heuristic programming library.

If one wishes to work on some particular problem in the field, he should find out what has already been done on that problem. The best way is to ask someone who knows, that is, a full-time researcher in the field. The next best thing is to do a literature search. This would include searching the ACM journals described above, as well as the *Proceedings of the AFIPS Annual Spring Joint Computer Conference* and the *Proceedings of the AFIPS Annual Fall Joint Computer Conference.* Starting with the most recent issue of *Computing Reviews*, one should search back through the reviews, which will lead one to the most recent works in the field.

How to Write a Heuristic Program After familiarizing himself with the background for the chosen task to be performed, how should the potential heuristic programmer actually go about writing the program to perform the task? Although the steps are given in sequence, the steps actually interact, so that the decision concerning one step depends on decisions concerning other steps. The first step is to specify the task fairly precisely. It is desirable if one can obtain several good ways to specify the task. This step includes the preliminary specification of the representation to be used, about which more will be said later.

The second step is to specify a procedure to perform the task. Again it is desirable if more than one good procedure can be specified. An important part of this step is for the programmer to find various good heuristics for performing the task. He should use as many ways to find heuristics as is feasible. He should consider the heuristics that other programmers have used on similar tasks. He should ask the experts and be familiar with the literature concerning the task. He should use introspection and observe experts performing the task, probably with the aid of thinking aloud and tape recorders. He should analyze the task itself to see what heuristics are "natural." He should analyze correct solutions to see how an intelligent program might have thought of each solution. He should then retain only the best heuristics. A heuristic is good to the extent that it is general and cheap to use and to the extent that it produces solutions and fails to produce too many incorrect lines of attack.

The third step is to find one or more good representations for the data and the task. To illustrate the considerations involved in such a decision, suppose we wish to write a deductive question-answering program. Two possible external (to the computer) representations are English and predicate calculus. Two possible internal representations are a model (see Chapter 10) and a predicate calculus description. The upshot of the following considerations might be a decision to use predicate calculus as external input, a mixture of predicate calculus and a model as internal representation, and predicate calculus or English as external output.

Let us first consider the external representation. English is more familiar to humans and more flexible than is predicate calculus. It is not difficult to translate from a formal representation, such as predicate calculus, into English, as external output. As external input however, unrestricted English cannot yet be automatically translated into a representation (such as predicate calculus or a model) formal enough to be handled easily by a computer. It is possible to translate sufficiently restricted English into a formal representation, but then some of the advantages of English are lost. The advantages of predicate calculus as an external representation are (1) it requires no translation if predicate calculus is used as the internal representation as well, (2) it is familiar to some humans, and (3) it is reasonably flexible, yet formal enough to be automatically translated into a model.

As an internal representation, either a predicate calculus description or a model is easily handled by a computer. The advantages of predicate calculus over a model are that it requires no translation if predicate calculus is used as an external representation as well, it is more flexible, and it is more easily translated into English output. However, it is often faster for the computer to find a relevant part of a model than a relevant predicate calculus expression.

Another aspect of the representation step is the decision of what kind of data structures to use. For example, should one use list structures or character strings? The prospective heuristic programmer must make an educated guess as to which kind of data structure is more appropriate. This decision is not always obvious. Wos et al. (see Chapter 5) decided to use character strings as the data in his resolution program and he has had excellent results, even though list structures would seem more "natural" for expressing clauses.

The fourth step in writing a heuristic program is to choose a programming language. Since a heuristic program is usually large and subject to change, the dominant consideration usually should be that the language is convenient for the programmer. Of course, the language should be appropriate for the types of data structures and procedures to be used. Thus for numerical work, languages like FORTRAN and ALGOL are good. If the procedures are recursive and if the data structures are list structures, then LISP and IPL are good. The programmer must also consider what languages are easily available to him. Other considerations are computer time and memory space. Often a good strategy is to write the entire program in a convenient source language. After the program is in "final" form, if the programmer rewrites the inner loops in assembly or machine language, then the program will run almost as fast as if it were written in machine language. Of course he should also retain a version in the higher-level language, since, for example, he may want to run the program on a diffierent kind of computer.

The fifth step is to write and debug the program and to familiarize oneself with its inner workings. The principles of good programming practice apply. In addition, the large size and complexity of a heuristic program have some implications to this step. It is even more important than usual to prepare good documentation including flow diagrams. This is essential to the programmer himself and to others who might want to understand the program. A good source language with good mnemonics lightens this burden to some extent. Tracing the activity of a program as it is executed is extremely helpful in debugging and familiarization. Some source languages have very convenient tracing facilities, but the programmer should provide for tracing even if this is fairly inconvenient. The heuristic programmer must take some pains to get familiar with his program because the complexity of a heuristic program often makes its behavior difficult to predict, even by the programmer.

The sixth step is to evaluate the program and to publish the results. In order to evaluate the program, the programmer should very carefully devise a sequence of experiments designed to disprove or confirm the most important hypotheses. Note that it might be important to find that a certain plausible heuristic is of little or no value. The experiments might take the form of comparing the performance of one version of the program with another, or the performance of the program with that of an expert, "average" man, or another program. Usually the quantities of interest are the number of problems solved and the times necessary to solve them. The results of the experiments, together with the description of the program, should be published in a professional journal or at least as a report.

13.3 FUTURE APPLICATIONS OF HEURISTIC PROGRAMMING

Heuristic programming will become increasingly important as time goes by. There is already a trend away from game playing and the solution of toy problems toward the solution of problems of real economic and social value. Many better multipurpose and program-writing heuristic programs will emerge. Heuristic programs will direct robots and aid in natural language communication. They will aid in the analysis, teaching, and influencing of complex systems such as competitive industries, corporations, households, and the armed forces, as well as many of the systems which occur in economics, mathematics, law, international relations, sociology, and medicine. In the past, relatively few researchers were able to devote their full time to heuristic programming. Now the field is growing rapidly because its great importance and promise are being widely realized. Although the applications discussed below are either not yet being made at all or being made on an extremely small scale, they will certainly be widely researched in the future, and I have no doubt that they will eventually become a reality.

The growth of computation provides the framework for the applications of heuristic programming in the future. Computation is becoming widely available. Its cost is decreasing, and it is being made increasingly available through time sharing. Further, total computing capacity approximately doubles every year in the United States. This is a result of the fact that the number of computers is increasing and that the newer computers are even faster than their predecessors. With increased time sharing, computing power will become available as a utility, and some day it will be as easy to obtain as electric power is today. It will be available to the housewife as well as to the business man. Almost everyone will be able to afford to use a large computer in real time. In particular, they will be able to use heuristic programs, as explained later. Persons in widely scattered locations can, by means of telephone lines say, use the same computer essentially simultaneously. At present, the user generally communicates with the computer via a teletype, although research is being performed on automatic speech recognition, so that in the future the human will be able to "talk" to the computer.

Robots In the future, heuristic programs will be directing robots. There will be machines with wheels and mechanical hands and eyes. Some work has already been done on such machines, and some vigorous research is in progress. Some of the first applications will be in remote and hostile environments such as radioactive locations, the earth's polar regions, other planets, and underwater. They will also be used as automatic "maids" and "assemblers." They will be able to carry out complex activities from instructions similar to those given to humans. Heinrich Ernst (1962) connected a computer at the Massachusetts Institute of Technology to a mechanical manipulator (hand) fitted with "sense elements." He programmed the computer so that the hand builds small structures from blocks or puts blocks into boxes. One of the two "hand-eye" projects now in progress is being directed by Prof. John McCarthy at Stanford University (Feldman et al., 1969). The other is being directed by Prof. Marvin Minsky at M.I.T. The computer is connected to a mechanical hand and mechanical eye, basically in the form of a television camera. Thus the computer can "see" what it is handling.

Research has been performed on mobile robots as well. Such a robot does not need to be connected to a computer by a cable. A computer can control a robot by radio; or, since computers are getting very much smaller, a future computer could be mounted in the robot. Nils Nilsson (1969), Bertram Raphael, and others at the Stanford Research Institute have written heuristic programs to direct a robot on wheels. One "talks" to the robot by typing restricted English (Coles, 1969). Professor McCarthy and others at Stanford University are doing research on a self-guided cart. The goal is for the cart to travel unaided over existing roads. This research might serve as the basis for an automatically chauffeured automobile. A car under the control of a machine could be safer and would be more convenient than one under human control. It could find itself a place to park and take itself to the shop for maintenance. It would be extremely helpful to those who cannot drive, for example, children and the visually handicapped.

A. George Carlton, John G. Chubbuck, and others at the Applied Physics Laboratory of Johns Hopkins University built a very interesting machine called The Beast. Actually they built two such machines, but only the later and improved one will be described. It is a battery-operated cylinder on wheels that is 18 in. in diameter. It is equipped with hardware logic and steering, and it has tactile, sonar, and optical apparatus. The sonarlike apparatus permits The Beast to find its way down the center of the hall. When its battery becomes sufficiently run-down, The Beast "looks" for (optically locates) an electric outlet and plugs itself in to recharge its battery. It can optically locate an outlet. The Beast was often let loose to roam in the halls and offices at the Applied Physics Laboratory in order to see, among other things, how long it could survive without "starving." Once it survived 40.6 hr. Many a new and unsuspecting secretary has been startled when The Beast entered her office, plugged itself into an electric outlet, and then departed. When it feels a step down, it knows enough to turn around, so that it does not fall downstairs. This logic however sometimes causes it to starve when it encounters a raised threshold. After getting on the threshold, it thinks it is about to fall, and so it turns around. After turning around it again thinks it is going to fall, and so it turns back and forth until it starves. It also starved when some workmen changed all the outlets from the flush to the projecting type. To cope with the new situation, the researchers changed some of the hardware logic. A command and telemetering unit can be used at distances up to 400 ft. The author believes that it would be a good idea to replace most of the hardware logic by a programmed computer, which would direct The Beast by means of the command and telemetering unit.

Communication in Natural Languages In another future application, intelligent heuristic programs will act as automatic translators and interpreters of natural languages such as English and Russian. It will become much less expensive, and therefore much more widespread, to have simultaneous interpreter systems such as the one that the United Nations now has. The speaker will speak in his own language, and an intelligent heuristic program will interpret what is said so that each listener will hear his own language in his earphones. Similarly, two people could converse via telephone in their own languages. By promoting communications among nations, such heuristic programs could help in bringing peace and unity to the earth.

The Analysis, Teaching, and Influencing of Complex Systems Other applications of intelligent heuristic programs will be made with complex systems. The analyst should embody in a heuristic program his theory on how the system works. As we saw before, embodying a model in a computer program has two important advantages. The model is completely specified, and consequences of the model may be obtained by simply running the program on a computer. The idea is to make these computer models far more realistic and sophisticated than models produced heretofore. War, a law trial, international relations, and industrial competition may be considered as *n*-player games. Each nation, competing corporation, etc., is a player and can take various actions; it evaluates situations and tries to maximize the value from its own point of view. The game theory evolving from heuristic programming is far more relevant to these models than is the game theory based on the game matrix. The second stage in analysis of the "games" is to simulate the behavior of the other "players." This simulation is based on past experience with the actions and the reactions of the other players. Running the armed forces, a corporation, or a family household is a problem-solving task roughly analogous to what occurs in the geometry, calculus, and checkmate programs. The problem solver has various possible actions which will lead to situations in which (possibly) different actions are possible, etc. Possible future situations can be roughly evaluated. The problem is to perform an action which leads to the greatest possible expected value.

There are several ways in which heuristic programming will help in teaching about complex systems. Once the analyst has produced a fairly realistic computer model, the student can participate in the model as player or problem solver. The student can be taught the content of the model so that he will have a deep understanding of the complex system under study. As a teaching machine, the computer can use the computer model to teach the student the content of the model and how to solve problems arising in the complex system.

Four of the ways in which heuristic programming will help in the influencing of a complex system are listed below in order of increasing sophistication.

1. By retrieving documents and facts quickly and accurately, a heuristic program will greatly aid the person who is influencing the complex system.
2. An intelligent heuristic program will deduce answers to questions from the given facts. Such a program will be a descendant of the programs discussed in Chapter 10.
3. Once an analyst has produced a fairly realistic computer model, the decision maker can try out his ideas in the model before trying them out in reality. The model tells him what other "players" will and might do. In this way, he can make very intelligent decisions.
4. In the even more distant future, a heuristic program will make its own very intelligent decisions, perhaps beyond the capability of any human.

13.4 IMPLICATIONS OF INTELLIGENT MACHINES

The future presence of obviously intelligent machines will have tremendous philosophical and social implications. In philosophy, the presence of such machines will shed light on Mechanism, the perennial "mind-body problem," and the role of man in the universe. In itself, the existence of intelligent machines would bolster the claims of Mechanism that man is nothing but a machine and that the answer to the mind-body problem is that there is only a body and no thing that can be called "mind." However, in the process of obtaining intelligent machines, certain intrinsic differences between man and machines may or may not become apparent, and this will constitute evidence for or against Mechanism. What about those who claim that such differences are already apparent? They argue, for example, that a computer can do only what it is told to do, and that people can do more. A Mechanist would counter this argument by saying that people can do only what they are told to do in the same sense as machines can do only what they are told to do. That is, man's heredity "tells" him what to do, including how to learn from his environment; a program tells a machine what to do, including how to learn from its environment. Arguments that "show" that a machine cannot in principle be as intelligent as a man are equally spurious. The question is awaiting final proof or disproof. The presence of intelligent machines will show man that he is not the only intelligent creature. The effect of this on man's image of himself will be even greater than the effect of man's realization that he inhabits a minor planet revolving around a minor star revolving in a minor galaxy, or the realization that he evolved from lower forms of life. One of his more cherished, if not his most cherised, claims to uniqueness, that is, his intelligence, will be matched by a "mere" machine.

What are the social implications of intelligent machines? Will the computer be our slave, brother, or master? Will even our most skilled workers be displaced by the new automation? What will be the impact of intelligent machines on the right to privacy? What does the author believe lies in the distant future?

The computer will be our slave and in a sense our brother in the near future, and will continue to be so in the far future, if we take proper precautions. If we do not take the proper precautions, there is some danger that intelligent machines will eventually "take over." It is one of the great lessons of history that human slaves sooner or later become free, often by revolution. However, nature builds into each human a set of primary wants or goals. Hence we must be careful that the "top goal" given to a highly intelligent machine be the welfare of humanity and not some private goal of the machine. Similarly, we must be sure that no private individual (or group) can get the machine to work for his purpose to the great detriment of society as a whole. Finally, we must be careful in stating society's goal and the means to be employed in reaching it. Otherwise the goal may not be stated correctly or the goal may be achieved by the machine by means that are obviously unacceptable to humans but are nowhere proscribed for the machine. It will be relatively easy to take these precautions if enlightened people of the future learn the capabilities and limitations of highly intelligent machines. The computer will be our brother in the sense that the human and the machine will work together to solve problems.

As for right to privacy, even present-day computers can be given information about individuals from business, medical, political, income tax, draft, school, and bank files, as well as information derived from psychological tests, job applications, etc. Invasion of privacy would be far easier if all this information were available to a single computer, since obtaining it would not involve a time-consuming and expensive manual search. The danger will be increased with the advent of intelligent machines, which would be able to summarize and otherwise combine heretofore unrelated information in order to deduce "new" facts from old ones. This danger, once recognized, can be readily met by taking precautions similar to those already mentioned.

As is usual with technological change, the development of intelligent machines will lead to some benefits and some temporary dislocations. So far, automation has taken away jobs at the unskilled and semiskilled levels and caused particular problems for many nonwhite workers and teenagers. With the development of very intelligent machines, even highly skilled workers will be displaced. There will be a need to replace the "Protestant Ethic" that hard work, and the long working day, is good in itself. Many people will be able to transfer to social service work. Leisure activities will need to be greatly enlarged.

Of course, neither I nor anyone else knows what the future will bring. I will, however, make the following predictions. Before the end of this century, computer solution of intellectually difficult problems will play a dominant role in bringing enormous material prosperity to the world. In less than a century, computers will be making substantial progress on the social problems, including the overriding problem of war and peace. Then, at last, the world may be able to live in peace and prosperity.

EXERCISES

1. Describe briefly the matching of data structures which occurs in

- **a.** The Logic Theorist.
- **b.** The geometry program.
- **c.** SAINT.
- **d.** The General Problem Solver.
- **e.** The resolution programs.

2. Which of the following programs do you think is the most promising start in obtaining a truly multipurpose program—MULTIPLE, GPS, the assembly line balancing program (the general probabilistic procedure), or the deductive question-answering programs? Which do you think is the least promising? Give reasons for your answer.

3. Name two complex systems which occur in each of the following fields and to which future heuristic programs might be applied.

- **a.** Economics.
- **b.** Mathematics.
- **c.** Law.
- **d.** International relations.
- **e.** Sociology.
- **f.** Medicine.

4. Do you believe that a heuristic program will some day make very intelligent decisions, beyond the capability of any human? Give reasons (not proofs) for your belief.

5. Write a 200- to 400-word essay on each of the following topics.

- **a.** The most important future applications of heuristic programming.
- **b.** Robots of the future.
- **c.** Problems with the heuristic programming approach to artificial intelligence.

d. Philosophical implications of intelligent machines.

e. Social implications of intelligent machines.

6. Carry out each of the following steps and, for each step, explain briefly why you did what you did. (These steps may be used as a checklist for many heuristic programming projects.)

a. Choose a heuristic program that you think would be good to write.

b. Find out what work has already been done on the problem.

c. Obtain one or more good ways to specify the task to be performed by the program.

d. Specify one or more good procedures to perform the task.

e. Find one or more good representations for the data and the task.

f. Choose a programming language.

g. Write and debug the program and familiarize yourself with its inner workings.

h. Evaluate the program and publish the results.

BIBLIOGRAPHY

Coles, Stephen L.: Talking with a Robot in English, *Proc. Intern. Joint Conf. Artificial Intelligence*, 1969.

Ernst, Henrich: MH-1, A Computer-operated Mechanical Hand, *Proc. AFIPS Annu. Spring Joint Computer Conf.*, 1962, pp. 39–51.

Feigenbaum, Edward A.: Artificial Intelligence: Themes in the Second Decade. *Proc. IFIP Congr.*, 1968.

Feldman, J. A., G. M. Feldman, G. Falk, G. Grape, J. Pearlman, I.Sobel, and J. M. Tenenbaum: The Stanford Hand-Eye Project, *Proc. Intern. Joint Conf. Artificial Intelligence*, 1969.

Minsky, Marvin L.: Steps Toward Artificial Intelligence, *Proc. IRE*, January, 1961. Reprinted in Edward Feigenbaum and Julian Feldman (eds.), "Computers and Thought," McGraw-Hill Book Company, New York, 1963.

Newell, Allen: Some Problems of Basic Organization in Problem Solving Programs, in Yovits et al. (eds.), "Self Organizing Systems, 1962," Spartan Books, Washington, D.C., 1962, p. 393.

———, and George Ernst: The Search for Generality, *Proc. IFIP Congr.*, vol. I, Spartan Books, Washington, D.C., 1965, pp. 17–24.

Nilsson, Nils J.: A Mobile Automaton: An Application of Artificial Intelligence Techniques, *Proc. Intern. Joint Conf. Artificial Intelligence*, 1969.

Slagle, James R.: Artificial Intelligence and International Relations, in Davis Bobrow and Judah L. Schwartz (eds.), "Computers and the Policy-making Community," Prentice-Hall, Inc., Englewood Cliffs, N.J., 1968, pp. 246–252.

———: Heuristic Search Programs, in Mihajlo D. Mesarovic and Ranan B. Bannerji (eds.), "Theoretical Approaches to Non-numerical Problem Solving," Springer-Verlag, Berlin, 1970, pp. 246–273.

Index

9781032206202